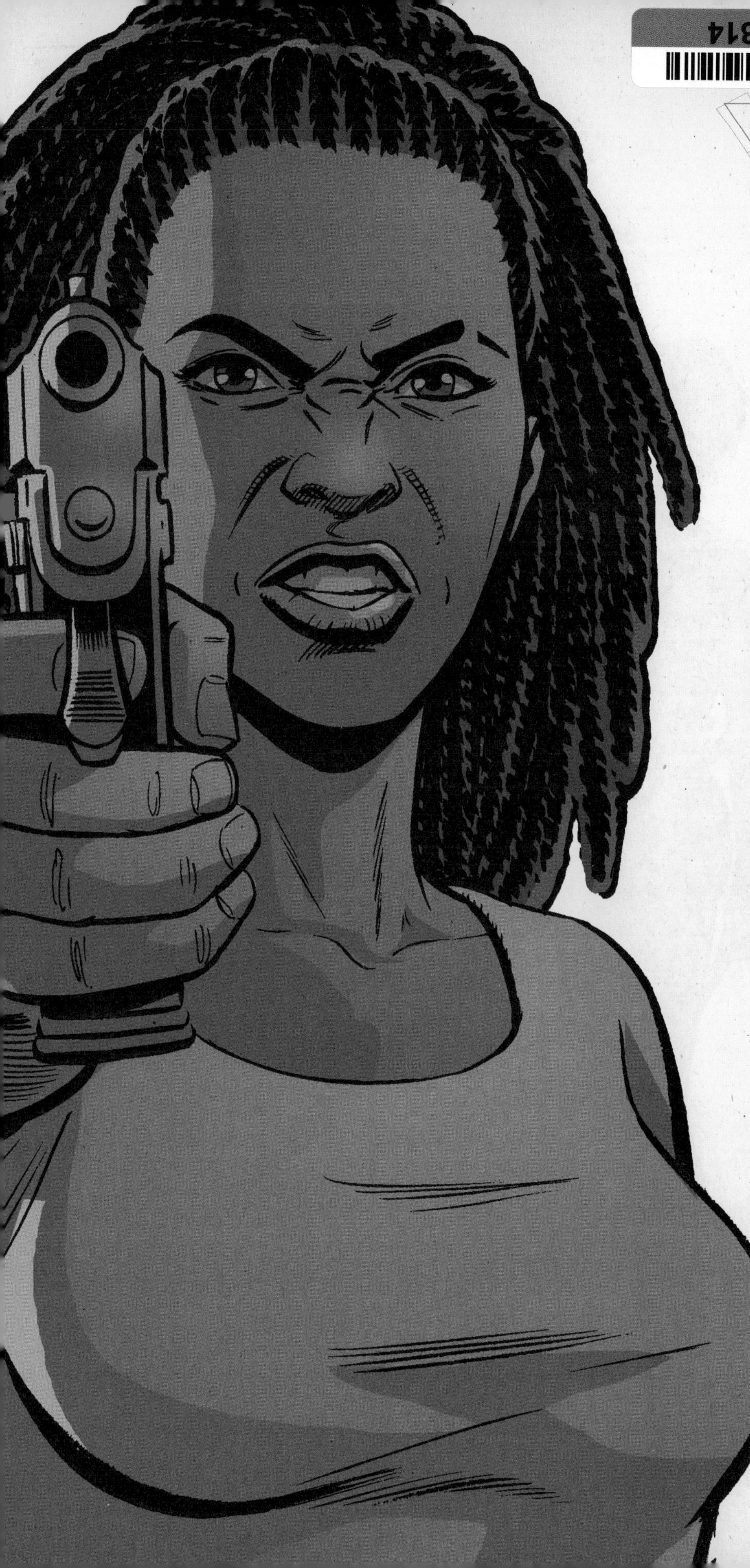

Y: THE LAST MAN — MOTHERLAND

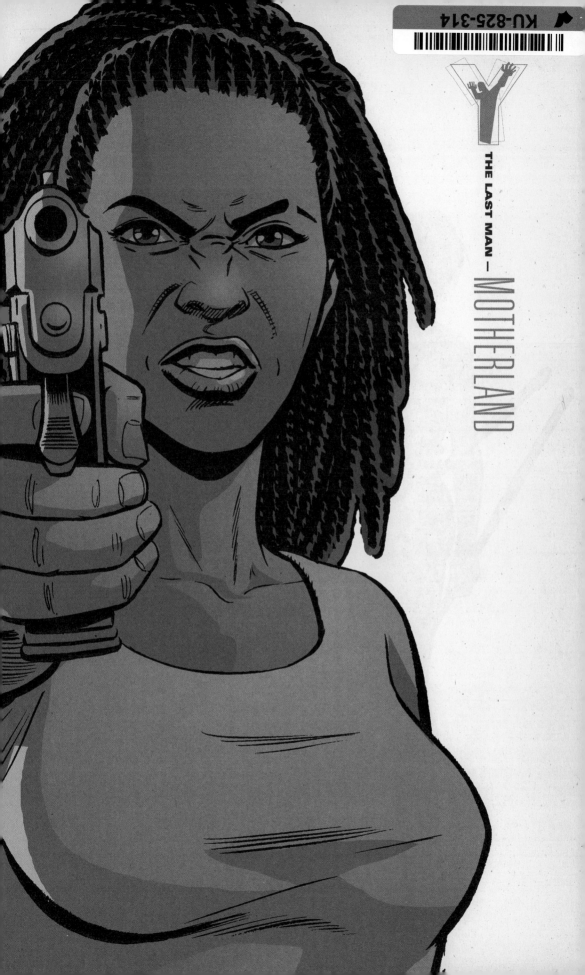

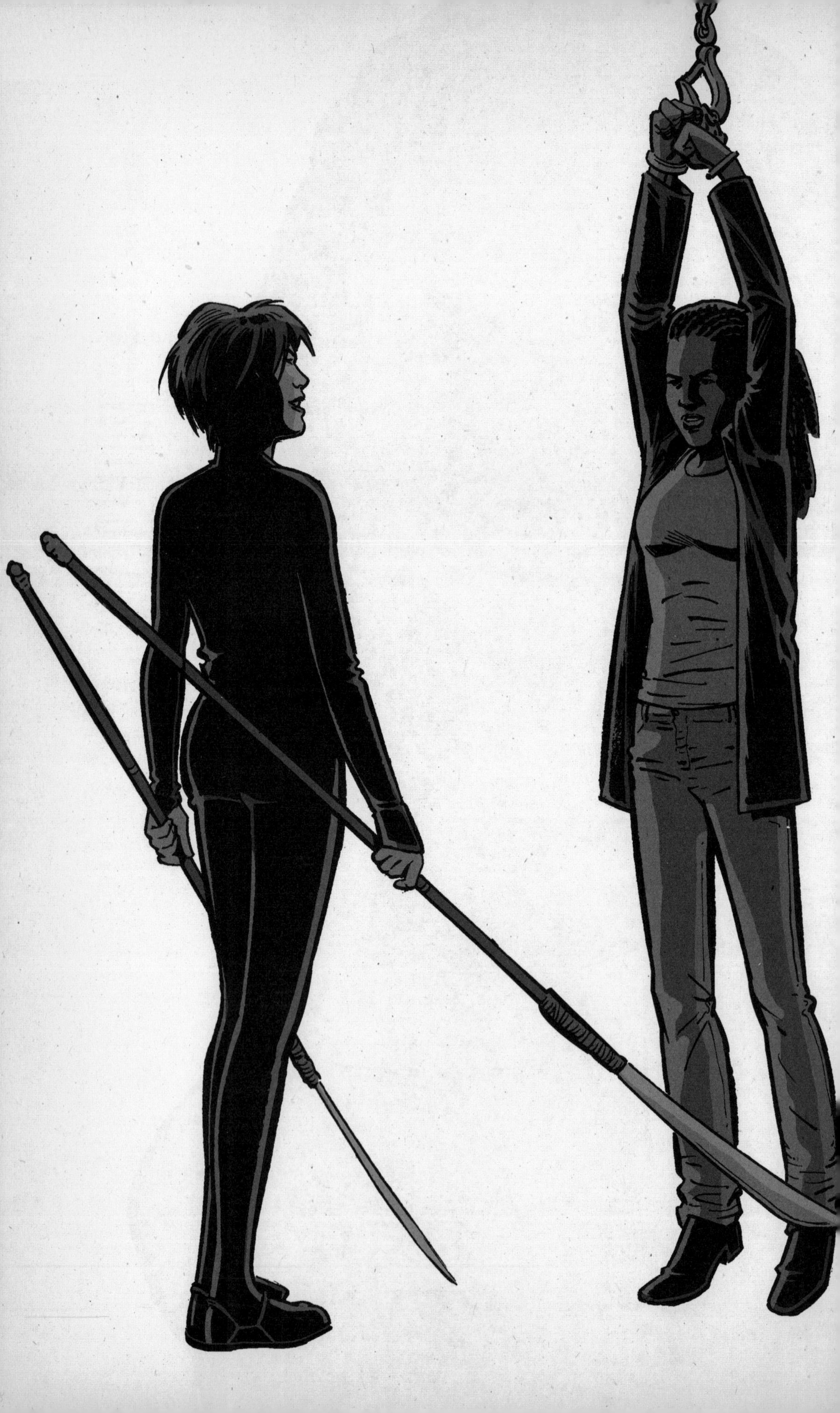

AN —

AND

aughan
Writer

Guerra
ɓudžuka
encillers

rzán, Jr.
ɓudžuka
Inkers

Zylonol
Colorist

Robins
Letterer

rnevale
s covers

reated by
ia Guerra

Will Dennis
Editor – Original Series

Casey Seijas
Assistant Editor – Original Series

Scott Nybakken
Editor

Robbin Brosterman
Design Director – Books

Louis Prandi
Publication Design

Shelly Bond
Executive Editor – Vertigo

Hank Kanalz
Senior VP – Vertigo & Integrated Publishing

Diane Nelson
President

Dan DiDio and **Jim Lee**
Co-Publishers

Geoff Johns
Chief Creative Officer

John Rood
Executive VP – Sales, Marketing &
Business Development

Amy Genkins
Senior VP – Business & Legal Affairs

Nairi Gardiner
Senior VP – Finance

Jeff Boison
VP – Publishing Planning

Mark Chiarello
VP – Art Direction & Design

John Cunningham
VP – Marketing

Terri Cunningham
VP – Editorial Administration

Alison Gill
Senior VP – Manufacturing & Operations

Jay Kogan
VP – Business & Legal Affairs, Publishing

Jack Mahan
VP – Business Affairs, Talent

Nick Napolitano
VP – Manufacturing Administration

Sue Pohja
VP – Book Sales

Courtney Simmons
Senior VP – Publicity

Bob Wayne
Senior VP – Sales

Cover illustrations by Massimo Carnevale.
Logo designs by Terry Marks.

Y: THE-LAST MAN — MOTHERLAND

Published by DC Comics. Cover and compilation Copyright © 2007 DC Comics.
All Rights Reserved.

Originally published in single magazine form as Y: THE LAST MAN 49-54. Copyright ©
2006, 2007 Brian K. Vaughan and Pia Guerra. All characters, their
distinctive likenesses and related elements featured in this publication are trademarks
of Brian K. Vaughan and Pia Guerra. VERTIGO is a trademark of DC Comics. The stories,
characters and incidents featured in this publication are entirely fictional. DC Comics
does not read or accept unsolicited submissions of ideas, stories or artwork.

DC Comics, 1700 Broadway, New York, NY 10019
A Warner Bros. Entertainment Company.
Printed in the USA. Fifth Printing.
ISBN: 978-1-4012-1351-0

Library of Congress Cataloging-in-Publication Data

Vaughan, Brian K.
    Y, the last man. Vol. 9, Motherland / winner of the Eisner Award for Best Writer Brian
K. Vaughan, Pia Guerra, Goran Sudzuka, José Marzán, Jr.
        p. cm.
    "Originally published in single magazine form as Y: The Last Man 49-54."
    ISBN 978-1-4012-1351-0 (alk. paper)
    1. Graphic novels. I. Guerra, Pia. II. Sudzuka, Goran. III. Marzán, José. IV. Title. V. Title:
Motherland.
    PN6728.Y2V39 2012
    741.5'973–dc23
                                                        2012024701

THE LAST MAN — Contents

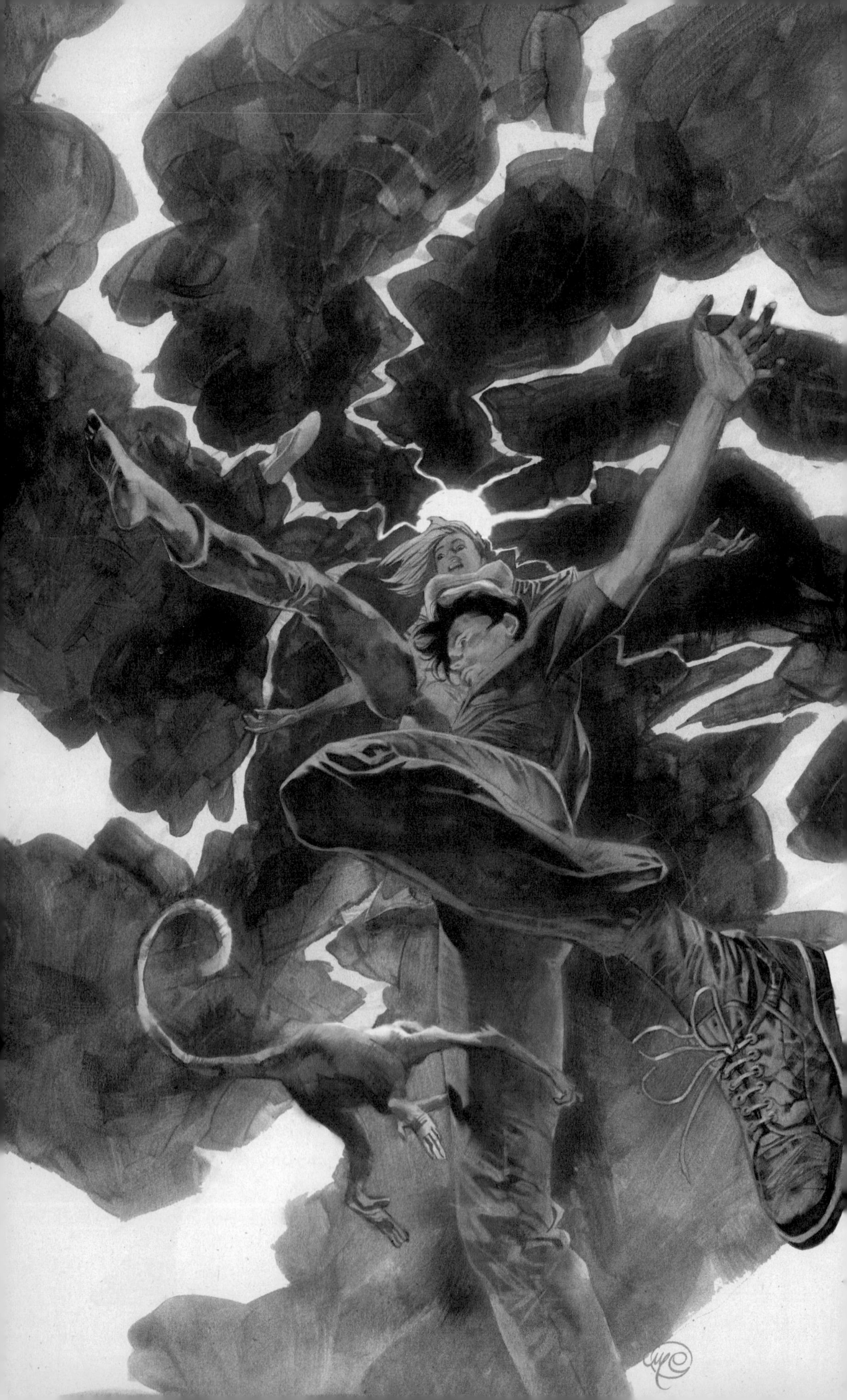

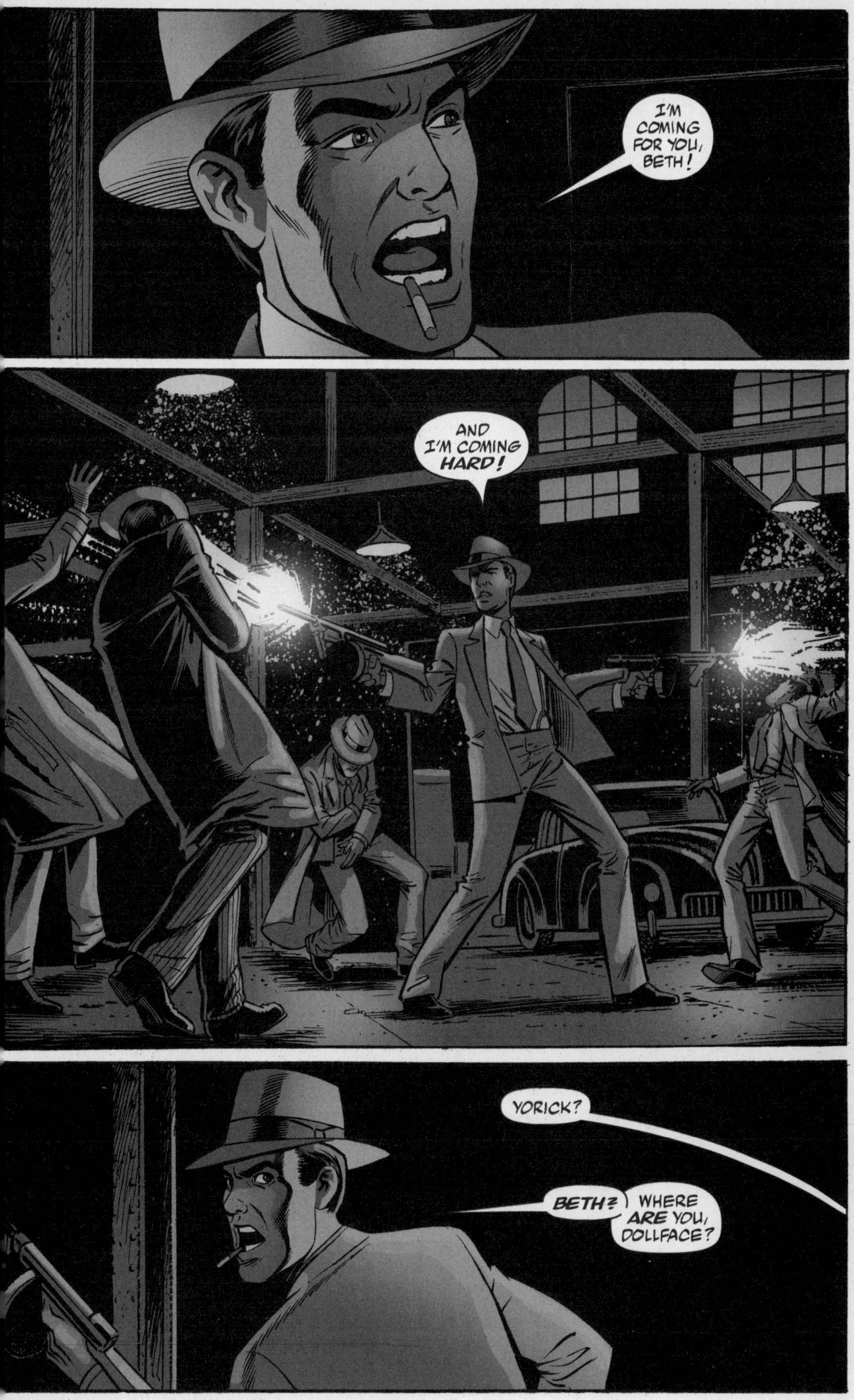
I'M COMING FOR YOU, BETH!
AND I'M COMING HARD!
YORICK?
BETH? WHERE ARE YOU, DOLLFACE?

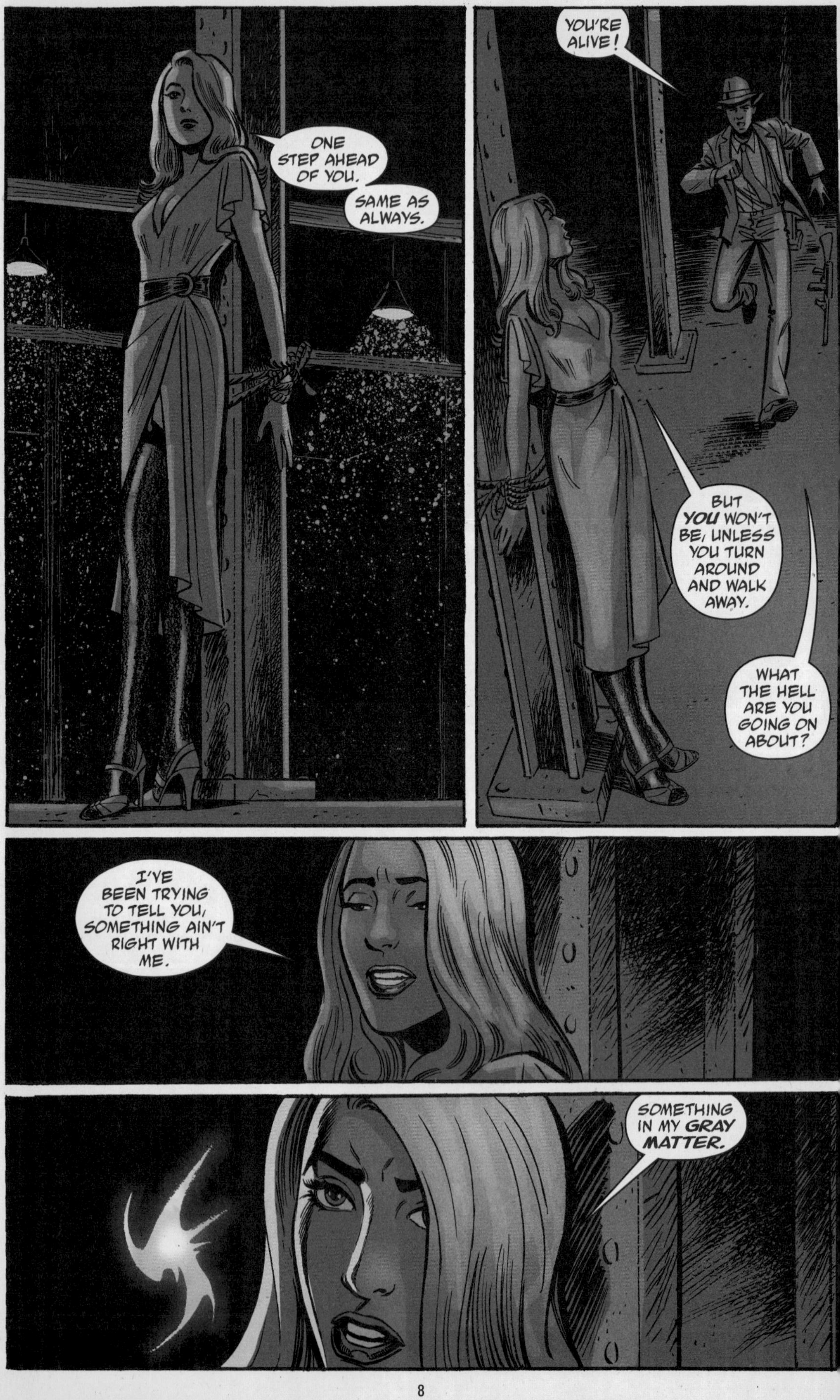
ONE STEP AHEAD OF YOU.
SAME AS ALWAYS.
YOU'RE ALIVE!
BUT YOU WON'T BE, UNLESS YOU TURN AROUND AND WALK AWAY.
WHAT THE HELL ARE YOU GOING ON ABOUT?
I'VE BEEN TRYING TO TELL YOU, SOMETHING AIN'T RIGHT WITH ME.
SOMETHING IN MY GRAY MATTER.

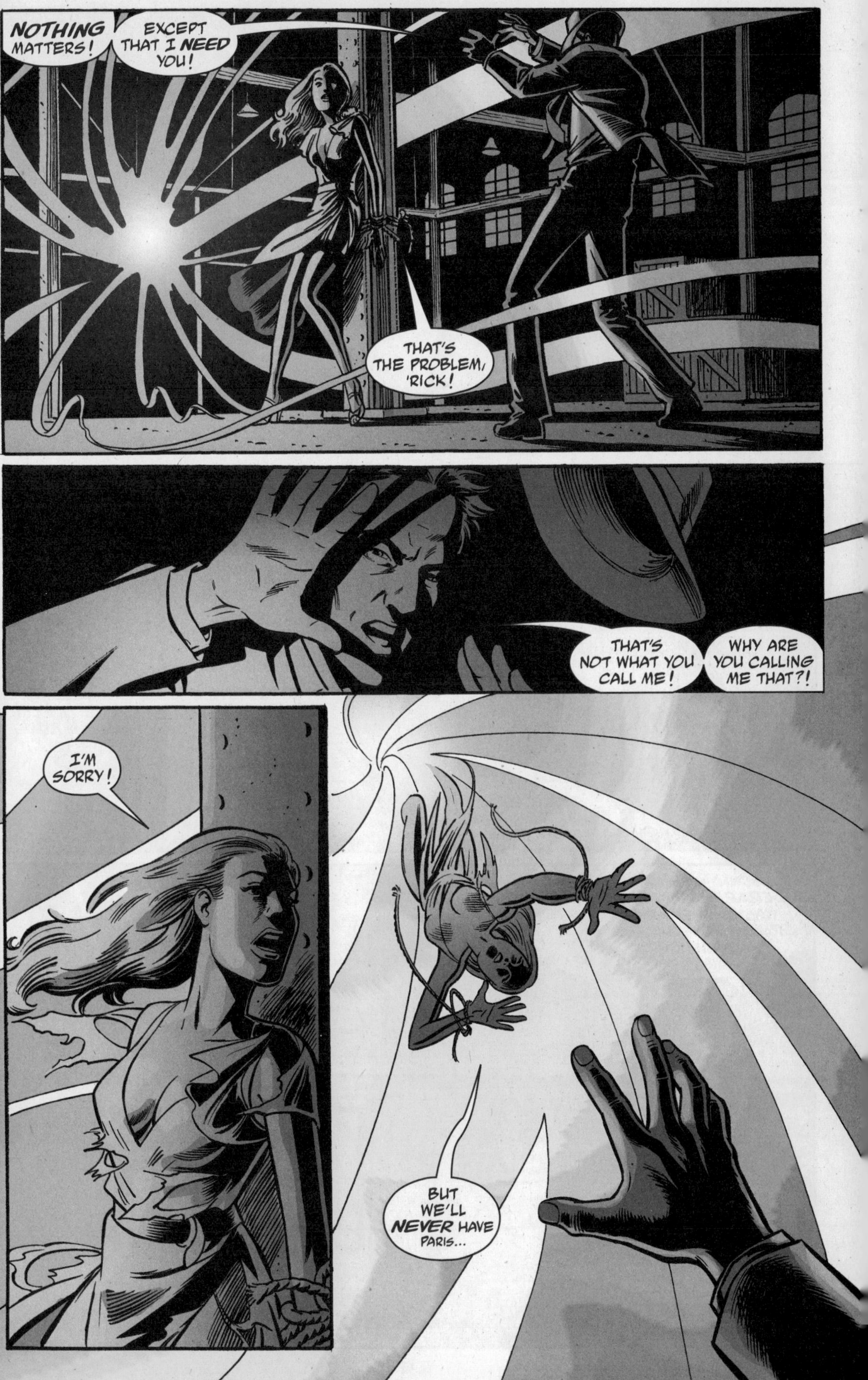
NOTHING MATTERS!
EXCEPT THAT I NEED YOU!
THAT'S THE PROBLEM, 'RICK!
THAT'S NOT WHAT YOU CALL ME!
WHY ARE YOU CALLING ME THAT?!
I'M SORRY!
BUT WE'LL NEVER HAVE PARIS...

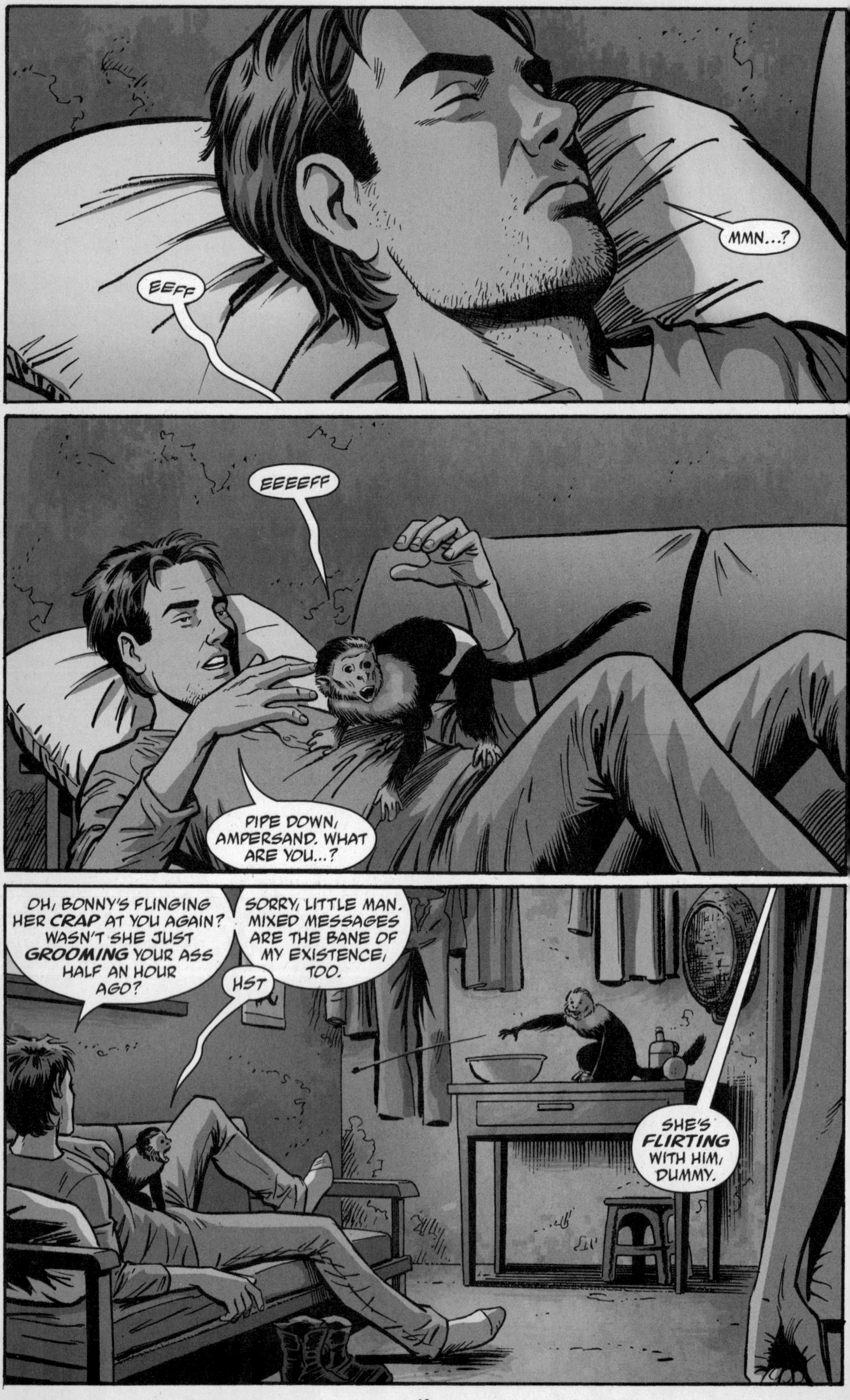
MMN...?
EEFF
EEEEFF
PIPE DOWN, AMPERSAND. WHAT ARE YOU...?
OH, BONNY'S FLINGING HER CRAP AT YOU AGAIN? WASN'T SHE JUST GROOMING YOUR ASS HALF AN HOUR AGO?
HST
SORRY, LITTLE MAN. MIXED MESSAGES ARE THE BANE OF MY EXISTENCE, TOO.
SHE'S FLIRTING WITH HIM, DUMMY.

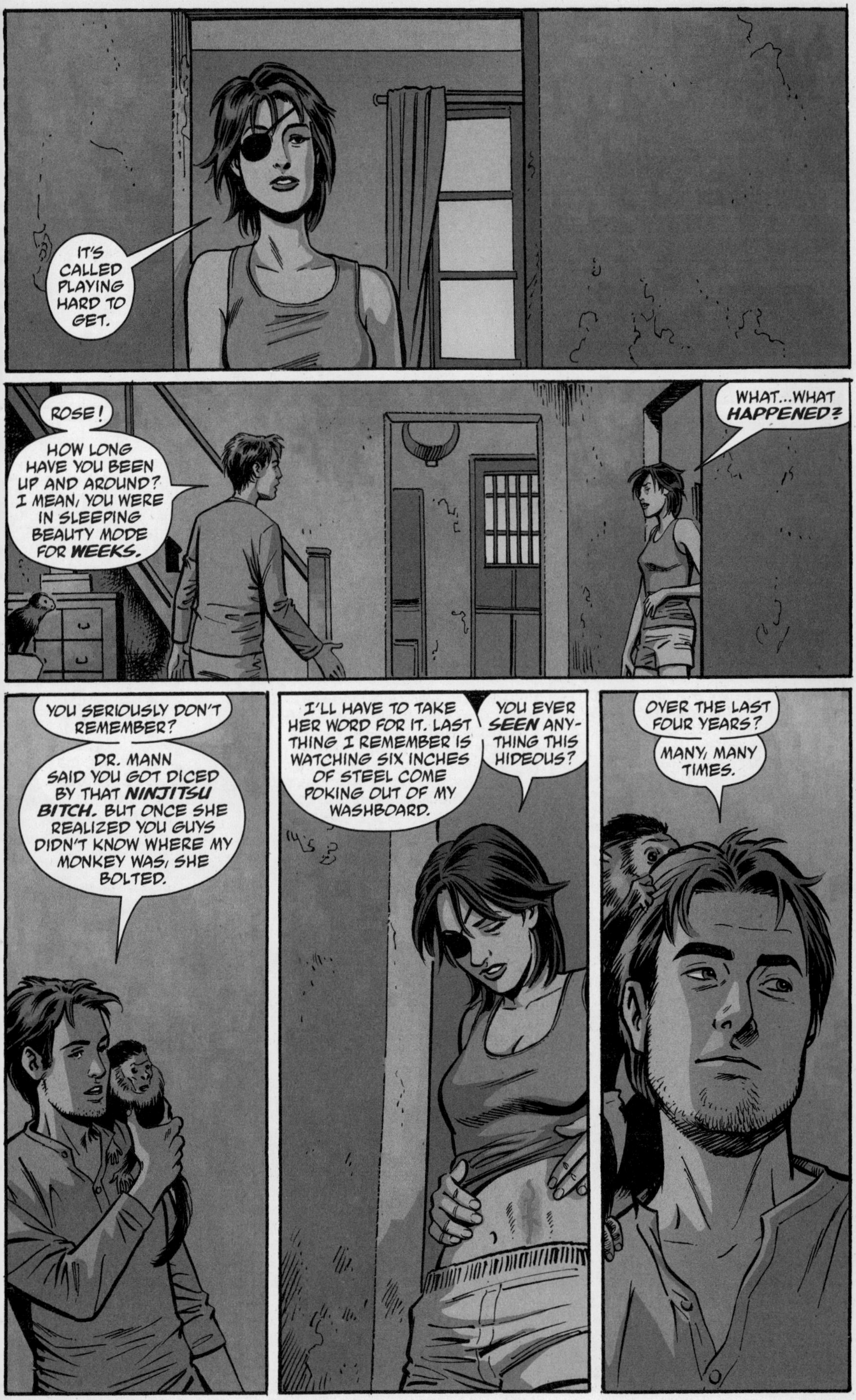

IT'S CALLED PLAYING HARD TO GET.
ROSE!
HOW LONG HAVE YOU BEEN UP AND AROUND? I MEAN, YOU WERE IN SLEEPING BEAUTY MODE FOR WEEKS.
WHAT...WHAT HAPPENED?
YOU SERIOUSLY DON'T REMEMBER?
DR. MANN SAID YOU GOT DICED BY THAT NINJITSU BITCH. BUT ONCE SHE REALIZED YOU GUYS DIDN'T KNOW WHERE MY MONKEY WAS, SHE BOLTED.
I'LL HAVE TO TAKE HER WORD FOR IT. LAST THING I REMEMBER IS WATCHING SIX INCHES OF STEEL COME POKING OUT OF MY WASHBOARD.
YOU EVER SEEN ANYTHING THIS HIDEOUS?
OVER THE LAST FOUR YEARS?
MANY, MANY TIMES.

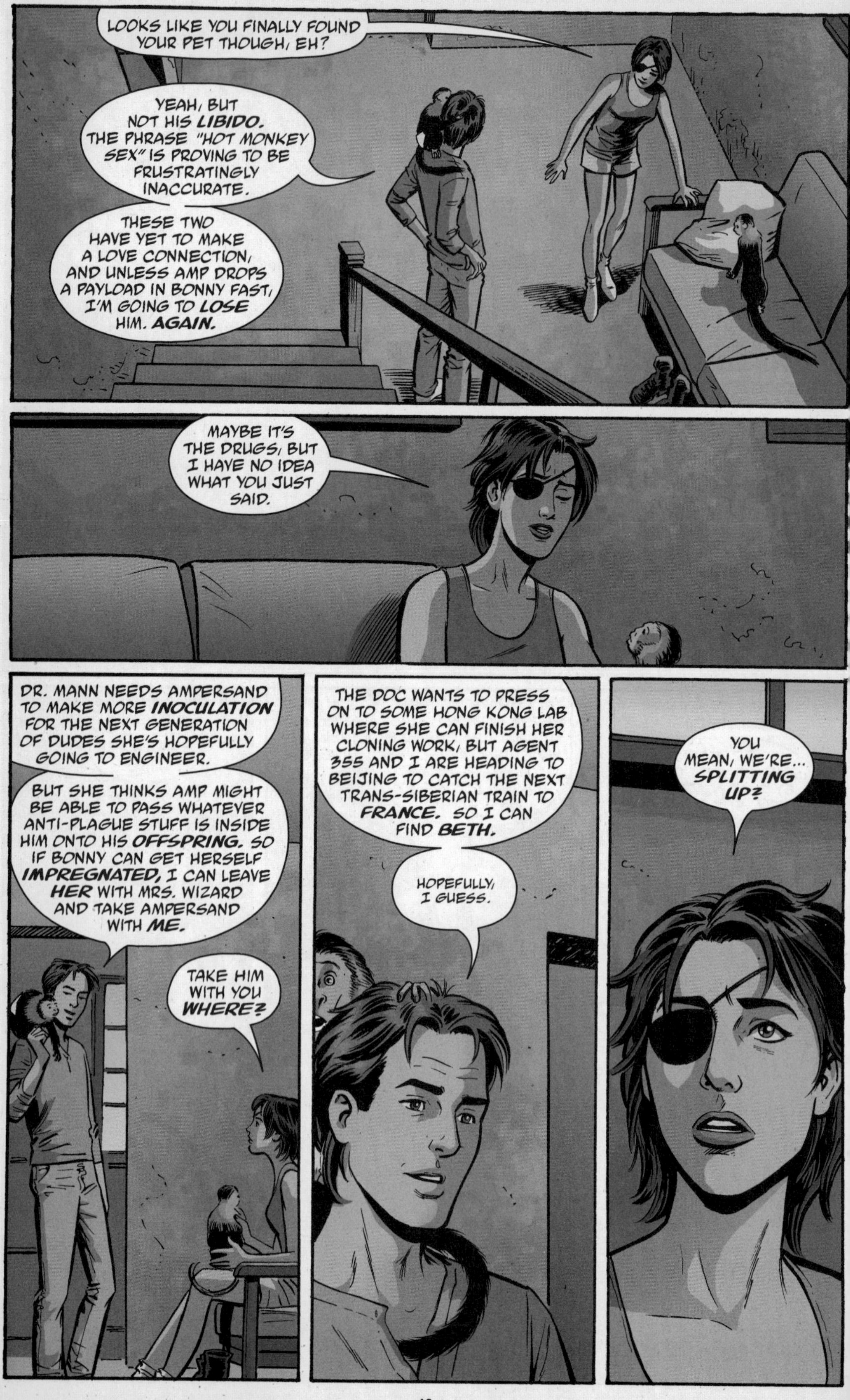
LOOKS LIKE YOU FINALLY FOUND YOUR PET THOUGH, EH?
YEAH, BUT NOT HIS LIBIDO. THE PHRASE "HOT MONKEY SEX" IS PROVING TO BE FRUSTRATINGLY INACCURATE.
THESE TWO HAVE YET TO MAKE A LOVE CONNECTION, AND UNLESS AMP DROPS A PAYLOAD IN BONNY FAST, I'M GOING TO LOSE HIM. AGAIN.
MAYBE IT'S THE DRUGS, BUT I HAVE NO IDEA WHAT YOU JUST SAID.
DR. MANN NEEDS AMPERSAND TO MAKE MORE INOCULATION FOR THE NEXT GENERATION OF DUDES SHE'S HOPEFULLY GOING TO ENGINEER.
BUT SHE THINKS AMP MIGHT BE ABLE TO PASS WHATEVER ANTI-PLAGUE STUFF IS INSIDE HIM ONTO HIS OFFSPRING. SO IF BONNY CAN GET HERSELF IMPREGNATED, I CAN LEAVE HER WITH MRS. WIZARD AND TAKE AMPERSAND WITH ME.
TAKE HIM WITH YOU WHERE?
THE DOC WANTS TO PRESS ON TO SOME HONG KONG LAB WHERE SHE CAN FINISH HER CLONING WORK, BUT AGENT 355 AND I ARE HEADING TO BEIJING TO CATCH THE NEXT TRANS-SIBERIAN TRAIN TO FRANCE. SO I CAN FIND BETH.
HOPEFULLY, I GUESS.
YOU MEAN, WE'RE... SPLITTING UP?

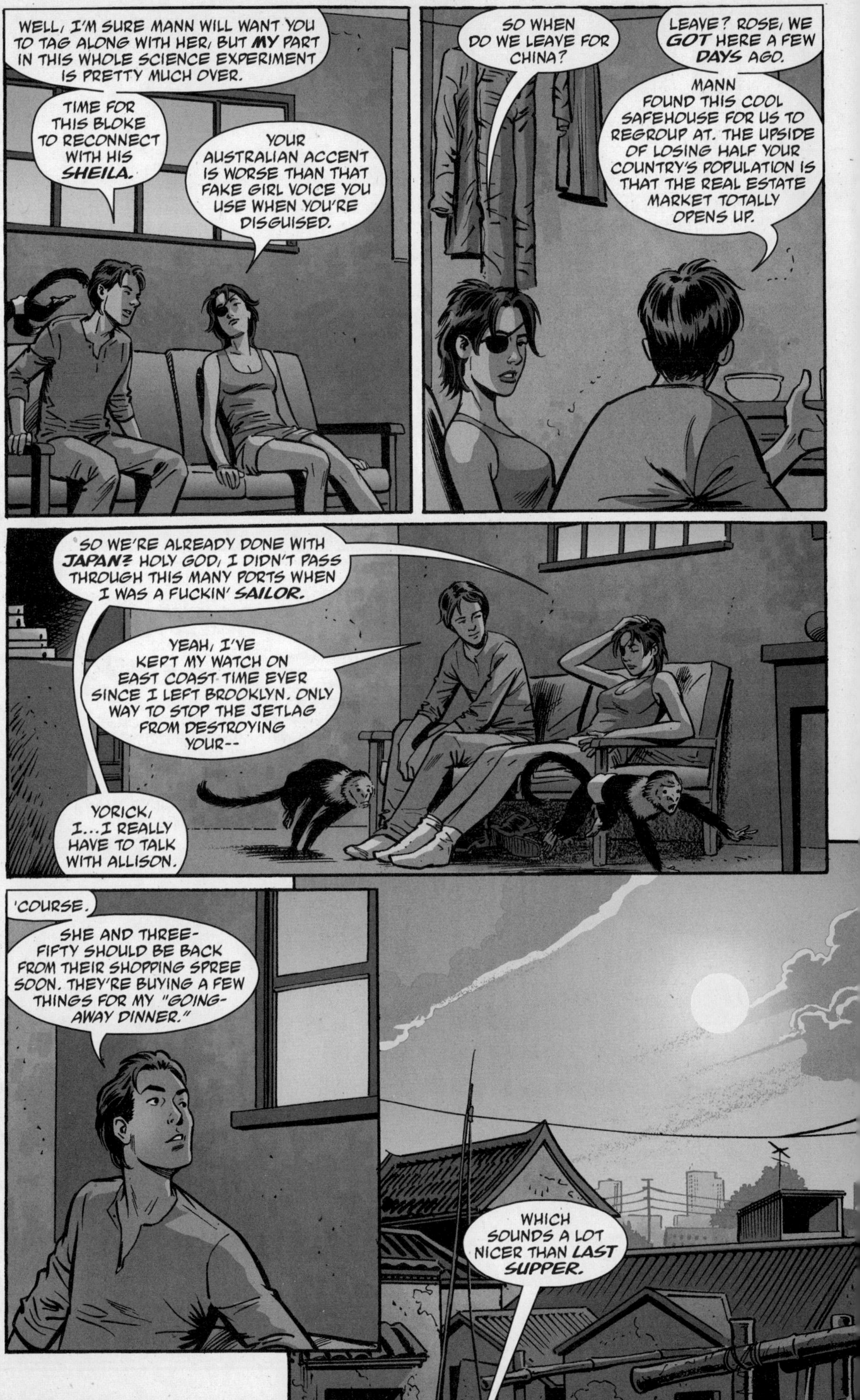
WELL, I'M SURE MANN WILL WANT YOU TO TAG ALONG WITH HER, BUT MY PART IN THIS WHOLE SCIENCE EXPERIMENT IS PRETTY MUCH OVER.
TIME FOR THIS BLOKE TO RECONNECT WITH HIS SHEILA.
YOUR AUSTRALIAN ACCENT IS WORSE THAN THAT FAKE GIRL VOICE YOU USE WHEN YOU'RE DISGUISED.
SO WHEN DO WE LEAVE FOR CHINA?
LEAVE? ROSE, WE GOT HERE A FEW DAYS AGO.
MANN FOUND THIS COOL SAFEHOUSE FOR US TO REGROUP AT. THE UPSIDE OF LOSING HALF YOUR COUNTRY'S POPULATION IS THAT THE REAL ESTATE MARKET TOTALLY OPENS UP.
SO WE'RE ALREADY DONE WITH JAPAN? HOLY GOD, I DIDN'T PASS THROUGH THIS MANY PORTS WHEN I WAS A FUCKIN' SAILOR.
YEAH, I'VE KEPT MY WATCH ON EAST COAST TIME EVER SINCE I LEFT BROOKLYN. ONLY WAY TO STOP THE JETLAG FROM DESTROYING YOUR--
YORICK, I...I REALLY HAVE TO TALK WITH ALLISON.
'COURSE.
SHE AND THREE-FIFTY SHOULD BE BACK FROM THEIR SHOPPING SPREE SOON. THEY'RE BUYING A FEW THINGS FOR MY "GOING-AWAY DINNER."
WHICH SOUNDS A LOT NICER THAN LAST SUPPER.

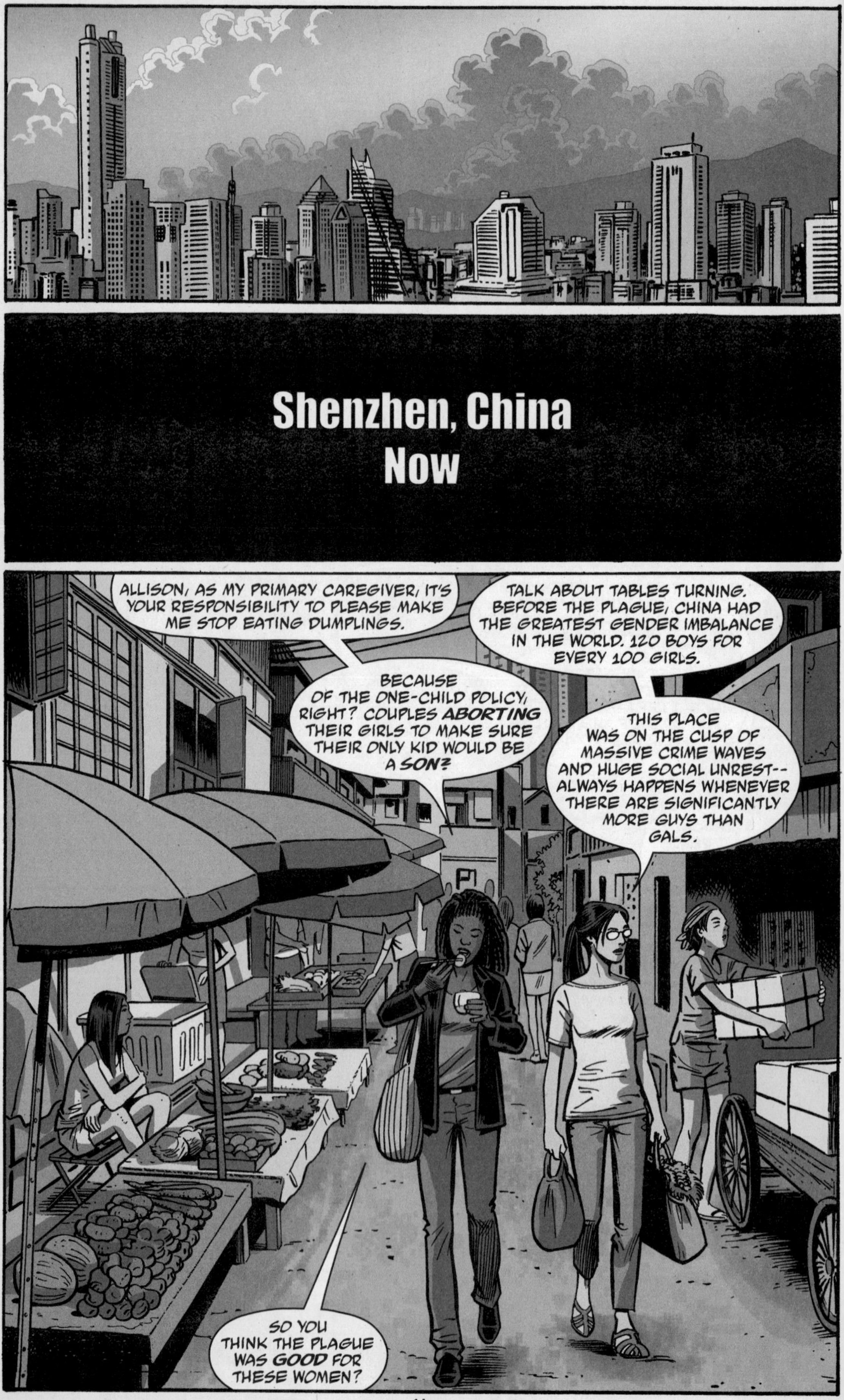
Shenzhen, China
Now
ALLISON, AS MY PRIMARY CAREGIVER, IT'S YOUR RESPONSIBILITY TO PLEASE MAKE ME STOP EATING DUMPLINGS.
TALK ABOUT TABLES TURNING. BEFORE THE PLAGUE, CHINA HAD THE GREATEST GENDER IMBALANCE IN THE WORLD. 120 BOYS FOR EVERY 100 GIRLS.
BECAUSE OF THE ONE-CHILD POLICY, RIGHT? COUPLES ABORTING THEIR GIRLS TO MAKE SURE THEIR ONLY KID WOULD BE A SON?
THIS PLACE WAS ON THE CUSP OF MASSIVE CRIME WAVES AND HUGE SOCIAL UNREST-- ALWAYS HAPPENS WHENEVER THERE ARE SIGNIFICANTLY MORE GUYS THAN GALS.
SO YOU THINK THE PLAGUE WAS GOOD FOR THESE WOMEN?

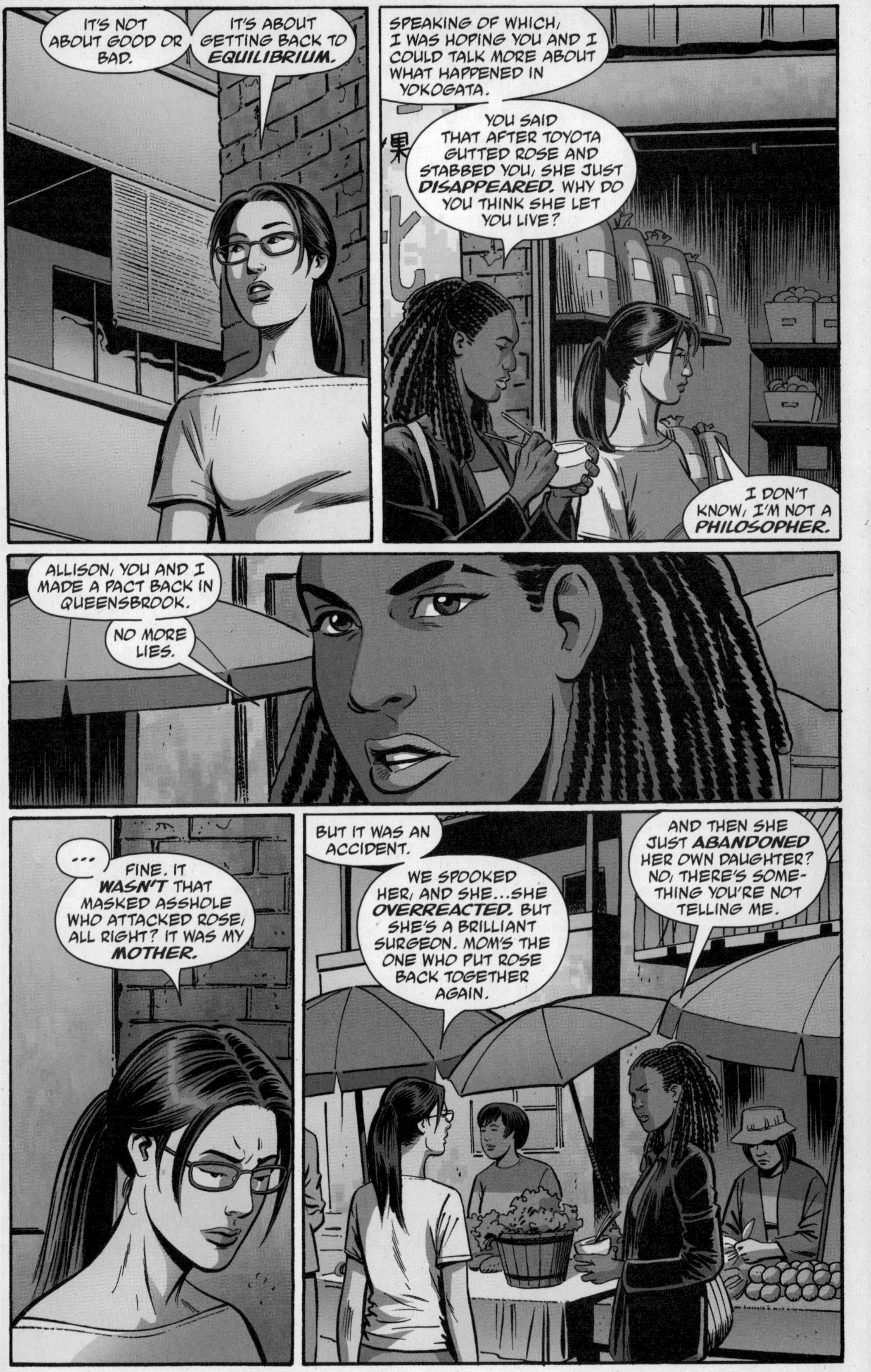
IT'S NOT ABOUT GOOD OR BAD.
IT'S ABOUT GETTING BACK TO EQUILIBRIUM.
SPEAKING OF WHICH, I WAS HOPING YOU AND I COULD TALK MORE ABOUT WHAT HAPPENED IN YOKOGATA.
YOU SAID THAT AFTER TOYOTA GUTTED ROSE AND STABBED YOU, SHE JUST DISAPPEARED. WHY DO YOU THINK SHE LET YOU LIVE?
I DON'T KNOW, I'M NOT A PHILOSOPHER.
ALLISON, YOU AND I MADE A PACT BACK IN QUEENSBROOK.
NO MORE LIES.
...
FINE. IT WASN'T THAT MASKED ASSHOLE WHO ATTACKED ROSE, ALL RIGHT? IT WAS MY MOTHER.
BUT IT WAS AN ACCIDENT.
WE SPOOKED HER, AND SHE...SHE OVERREACTED. BUT SHE'S A BRILLIANT SURGEON. MOM'S THE ONE WHO PUT ROSE BACK TOGETHER AGAIN.
AND THEN SHE JUST ABANDONED HER OWN DAUGHTER? NO, THERE'S SOMETHING YOU'RE NOT TELLING ME.

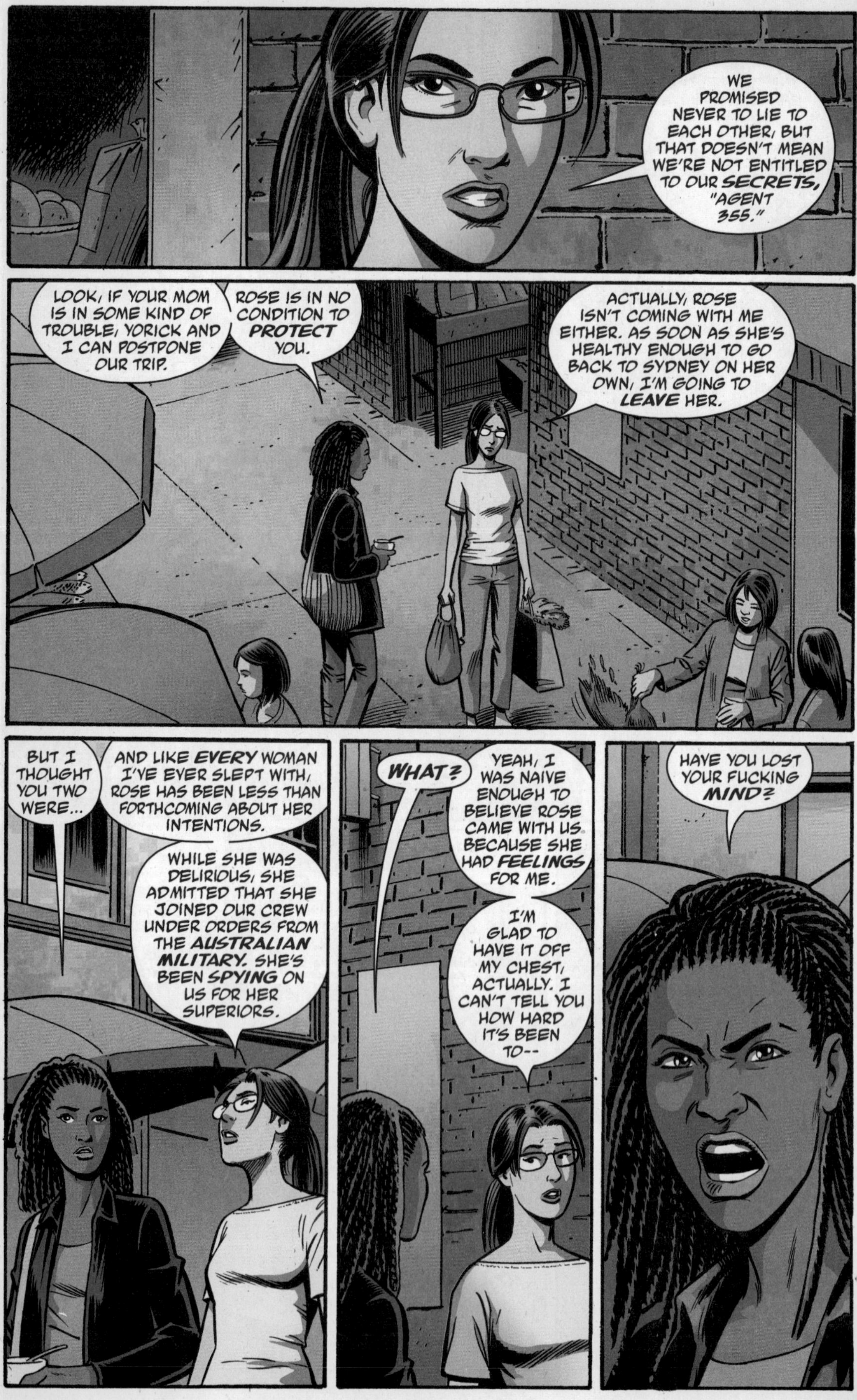
WE PROMISED NEVER TO LIE TO EACH OTHER, BUT THAT DOESN'T MEAN WE'RE NOT ENTITLED TO OUR SECRETS, "AGENT 355."
LOOK, IF YOUR MOM IS IN SOME KIND OF TROUBLE, YORICK AND I CAN POSTPONE OUR TRIP.
ROSE IS IN NO CONDITION TO PROTECT YOU.
ACTUALLY, ROSE ISN'T COMING WITH ME EITHER. AS SOON AS SHE'S HEALTHY ENOUGH TO GO BACK TO SYDNEY ON HER OWN, I'M GOING TO LEAVE HER.
BUT I THOUGHT YOU TWO WERE...
AND LIKE EVERY WOMAN I'VE EVER SLEPT WITH, ROSE HAS BEEN LESS THAN FORTHCOMING ABOUT HER INTENTIONS.
WHILE SHE WAS DELIRIOUS, SHE ADMITTED THAT SHE JOINED OUR CREW UNDER ORDERS FROM THE AUSTRALIAN MILITARY. SHE'S BEEN SPYING ON US FOR HER SUPERIORS.
WHAT?
YEAH, I WAS NAIVE ENOUGH TO BELIEVE ROSE CAME WITH US BECAUSE SHE HAD FEELINGS FOR ME.
I'M GLAD TO HAVE IT OFF MY CHEST, ACTUALLY. I CAN'T TELL YOU HOW HARD IT'S BEEN TO--
HAVE YOU LOST YOUR FUCKING MIND?

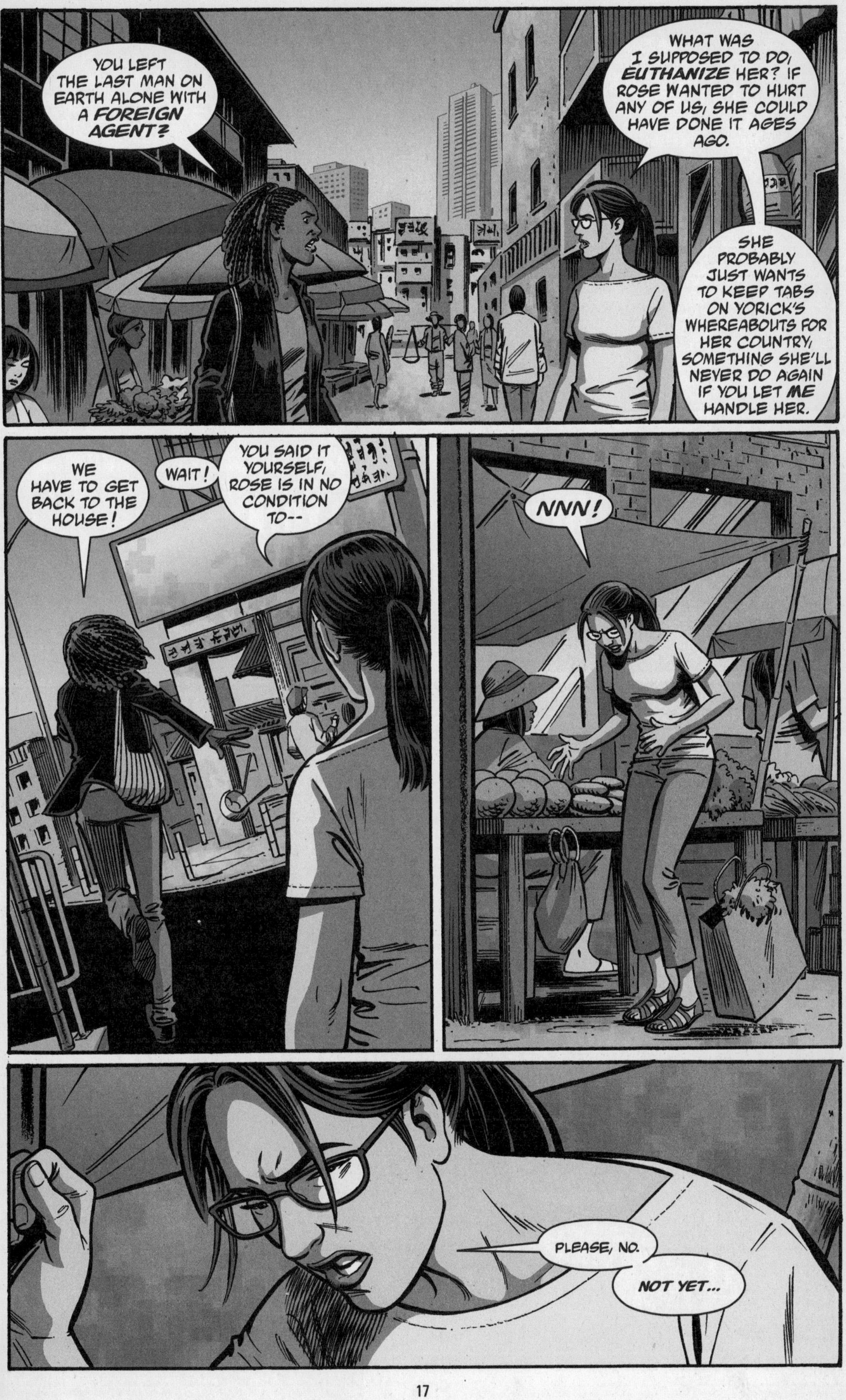

YOU LEFT THE LAST MAN ON EARTH ALONE WITH A FOREIGN AGENT?
WHAT WAS I SUPPOSED TO DO, EUTHANIZE HER? IF ROSE WANTED TO HURT ANY OF US, SHE COULD HAVE DONE IT AGES AGO.
SHE PROBABLY JUST WANTS TO KEEP TABS ON YORICK'S WHEREABOUTS FOR HER COUNTRY, SOMETHING SHE'LL NEVER DO AGAIN IF YOU LET ME HANDLE HER.
WE HAVE TO GET BACK TO THE HOUSE!
WAIT!
YOU SAID IT YOURSELF, ROSE IS IN NO CONDITION TO--
NNN!
PLEASE, NO.
NOT YET...

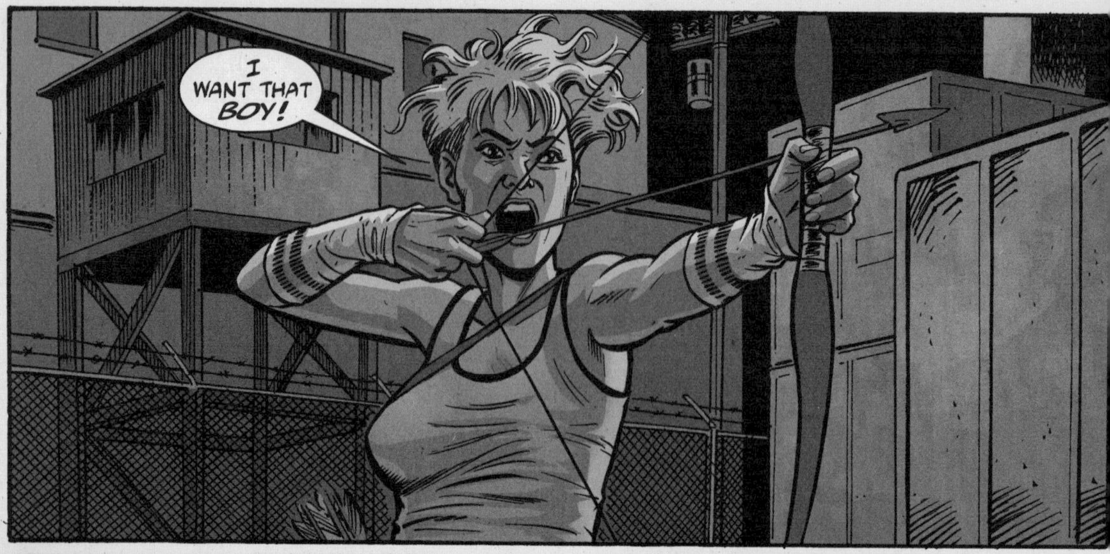
I WANT THAT BOY!

New York, New York
Now

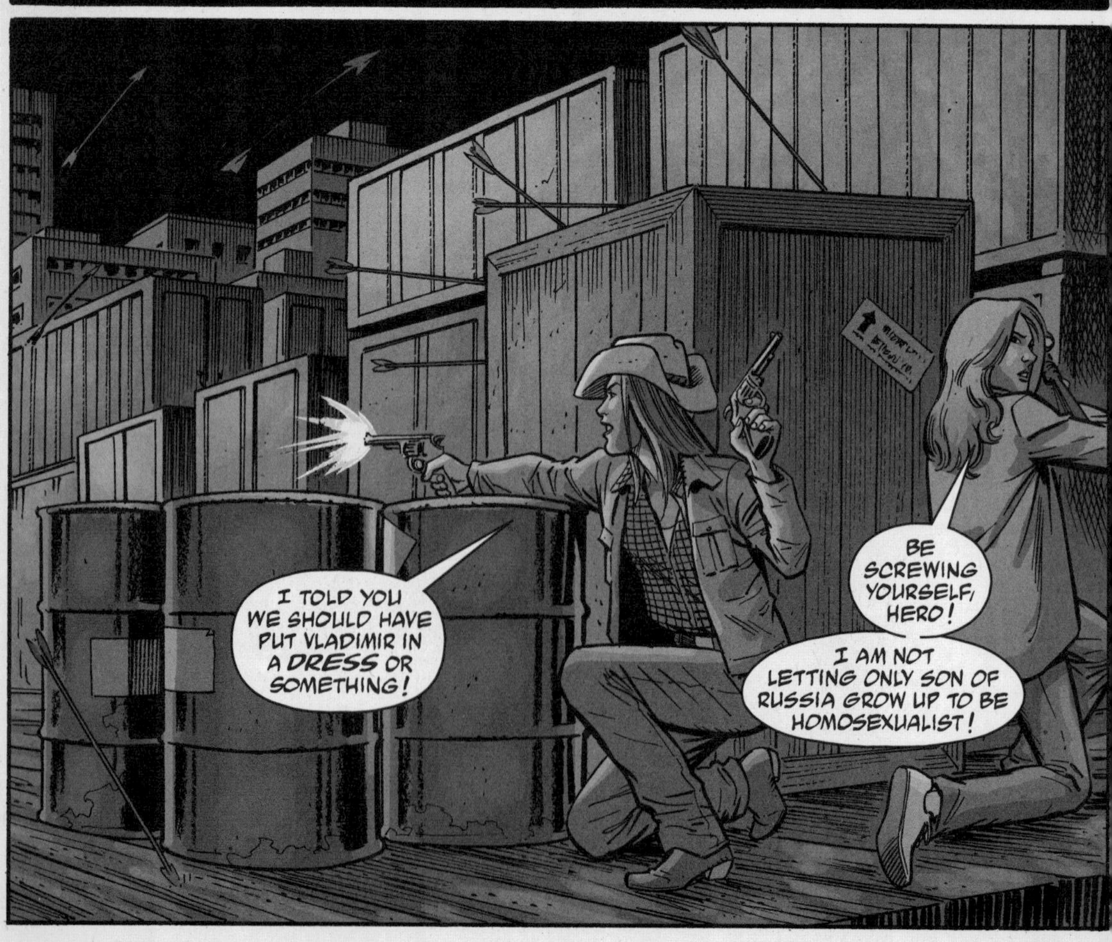
I TOLD YOU WE SHOULD HAVE PUT VLADIMIR IN A DRESS OR SOMETHING!
BE SCREWING YOURSELF, HERO!
I AM NOT LETTING ONLY SON OF RUSSIA GROW UP TO BE HOMOSEXUALIST!

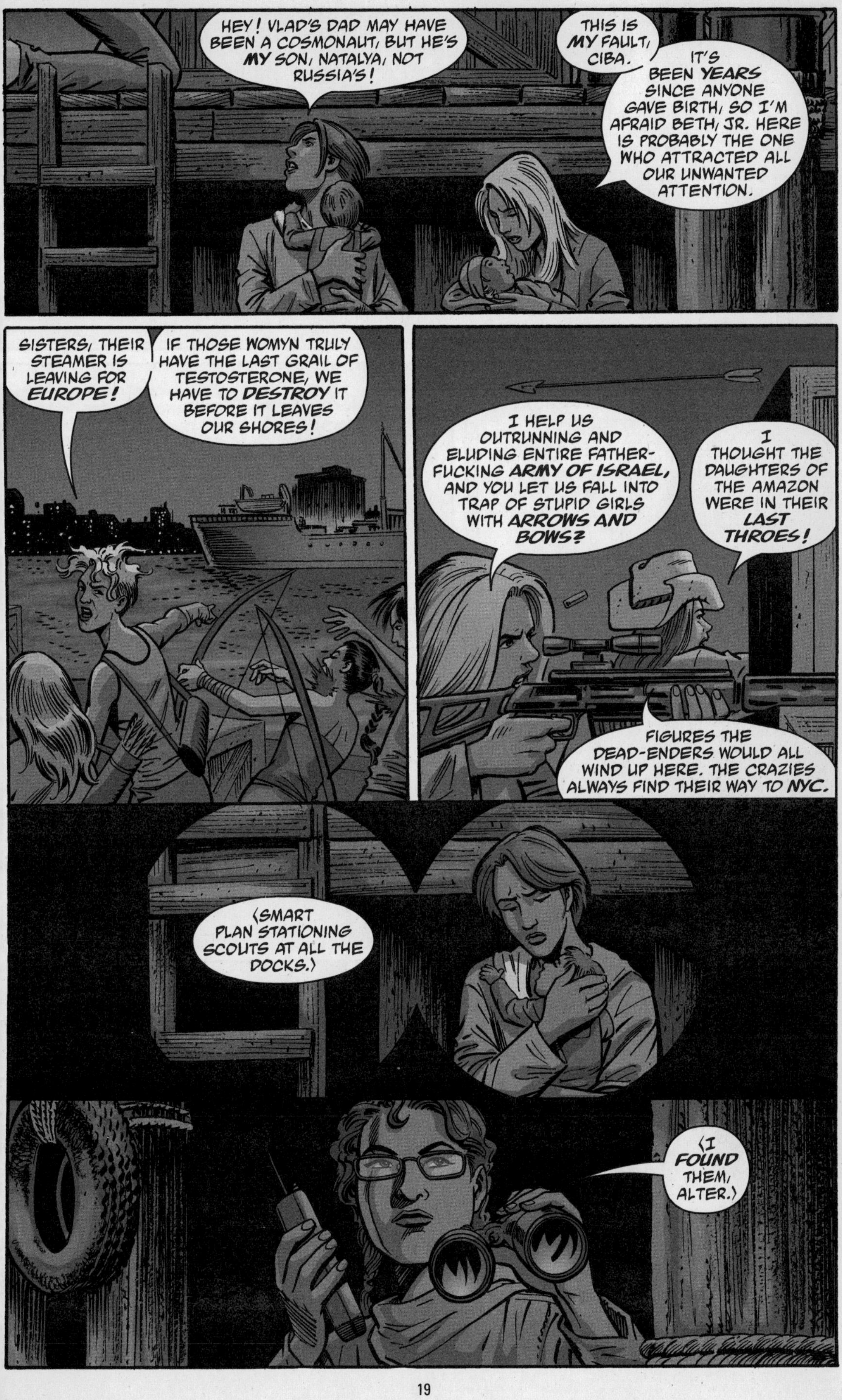
HEY! VLAD'S DAD MAY HAVE BEEN A COSMONAUT, BUT HE'S MY SON, NATALYA, NOT RUSSIA'S!
THIS IS MY FAULT, CIBA.
IT'S BEEN YEARS SINCE ANYONE GAVE BIRTH, SO I'M AFRAID BETH, JR. HERE IS PROBABLY THE ONE WHO ATTRACTED ALL OUR UNWANTED ATTENTION.
SISTERS, THEIR STEAMER IS LEAVING FOR EUROPE!
IF THOSE WOMYN TRULY HAVE THE LAST GRAIL OF TESTOSTERONE, WE HAVE TO DESTROY IT BEFORE IT LEAVES OUR SHORES!
I HELP US OUTRUNNING AND ELUDING ENTIRE FATHER-FUCKING ARMY OF ISRAEL, AND YOU LET US FALL INTO TRAP OF STUPID GIRLS WITH ARROWS AND BOWS?
I THOUGHT THE DAUGHTERS OF THE AMAZON WERE IN THEIR LAST THROES!
FIGURES THE DEAD-ENDERS WOULD ALL WIND UP HERE. THE CRAZIES ALWAYS FIND THEIR WAY TO NYC.
(SMART PLAN STATIONING SCOUTS AT ALL THE DOCKS.)
(I FOUND THEM, ALTER.)

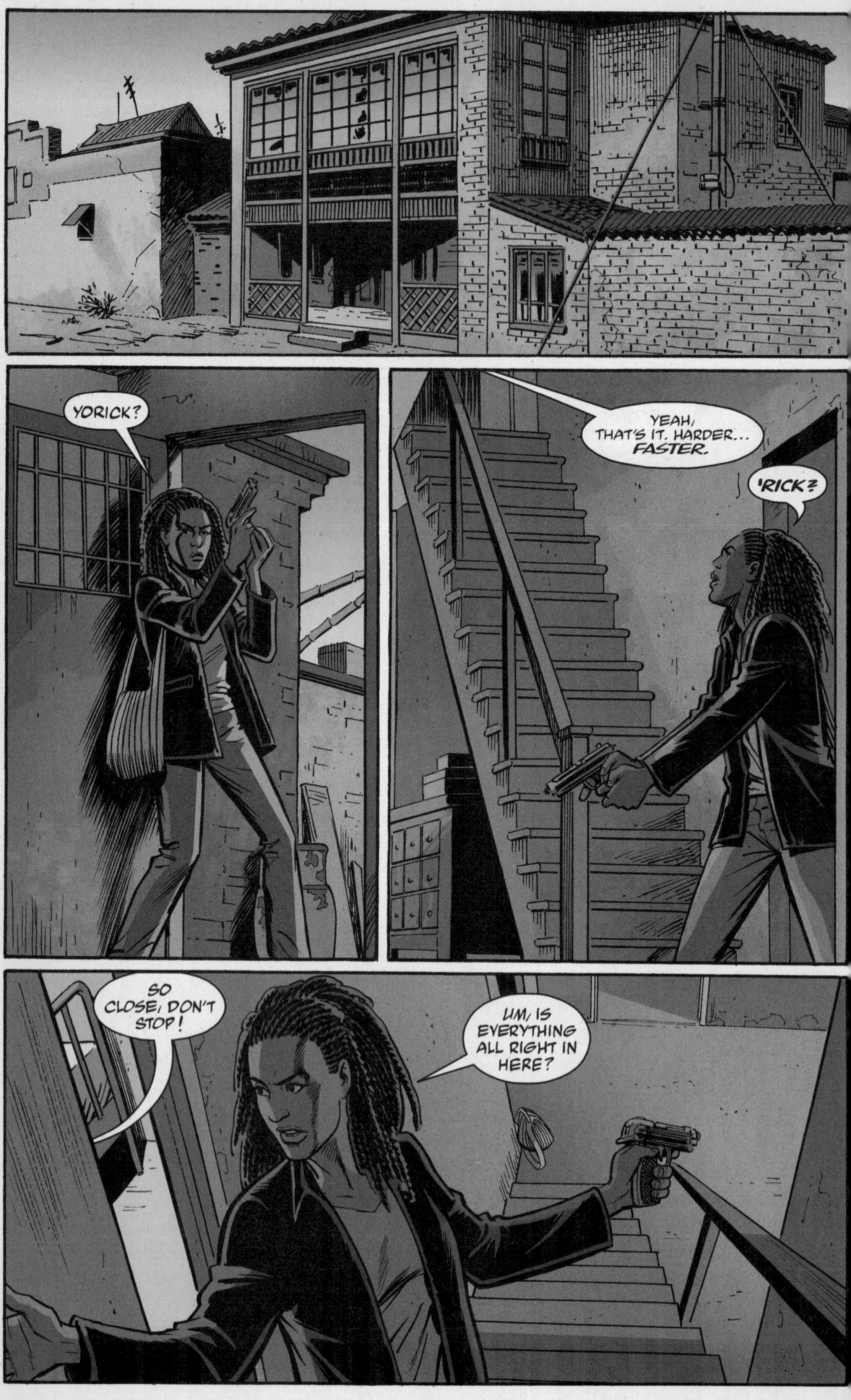
YORICK?
YEAH, THAT'S IT. HARDER... FASTER.
'RICK?
SO CLOSE, DON'T STOP!
UM, IS EVERYTHING ALL RIGHT IN HERE?

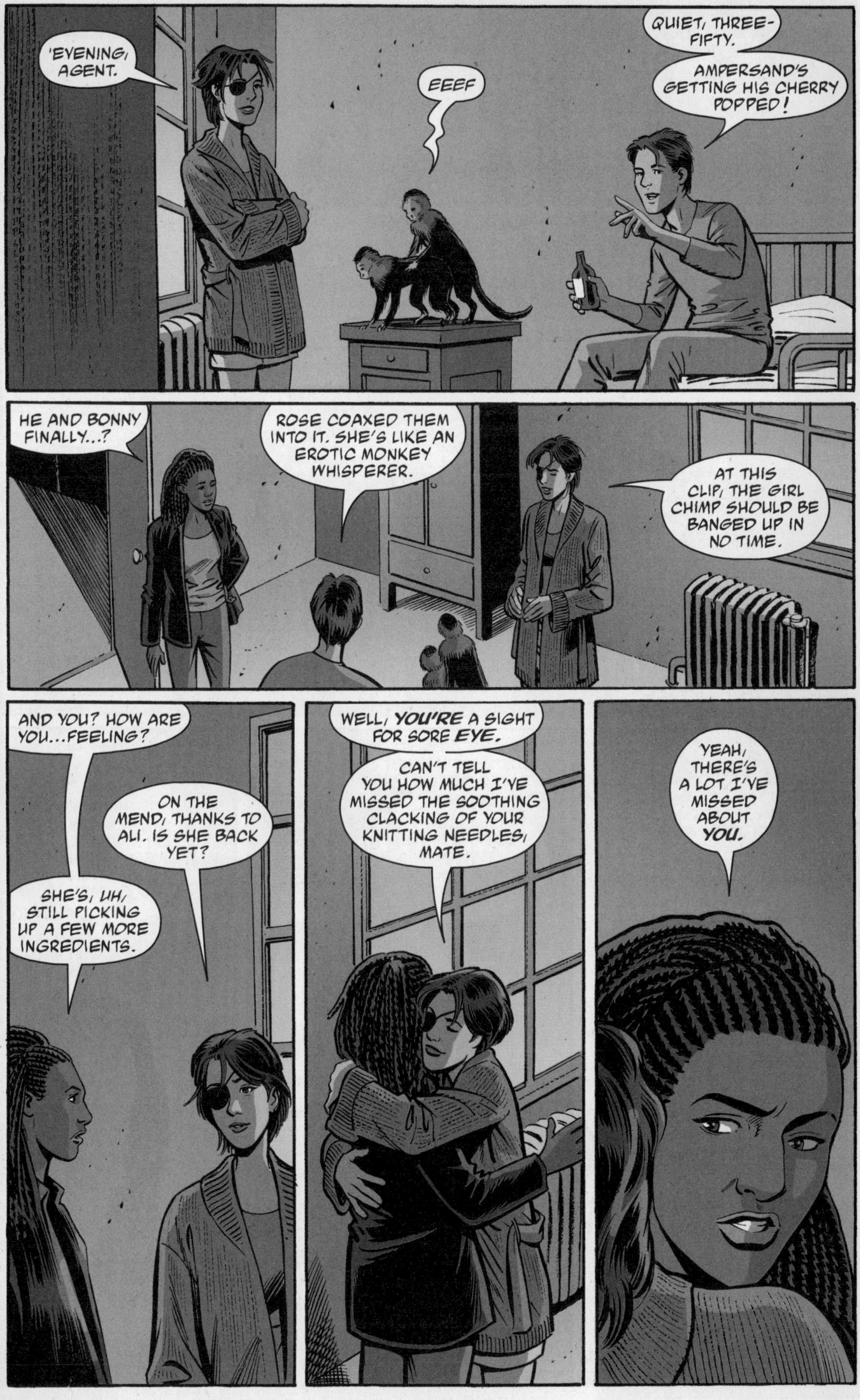
'EVENING, AGENT.
EEEF
QUIET, THREE-FIFTY.
AMPERSAND'S GETTING HIS CHERRY POPPED!
HE AND BONNY FINALLY...?
ROSE COAXED THEM INTO IT. SHE'S LIKE AN EROTIC MONKEY WHISPERER.
AT THIS CLIP, THE GIRL CHIMP SHOULD BE BANGED UP IN NO TIME.
AND YOU? HOW ARE YOU...FEELING?
ON THE MEND, THANKS TO ALI. IS SHE BACK YET?
SHE'S, UH, STILL PICKING UP A FEW MORE INGREDIENTS.
WELL, YOU'RE A SIGHT FOR SORE EYE.
CAN'T TELL YOU HOW MUCH I'VE MISSED THE SOOTHING CLACKING OF YOUR KNITTING NEEDLES, MATE.
YEAH, THERE'S A LOT I'VE MISSED ABOUT YOU.

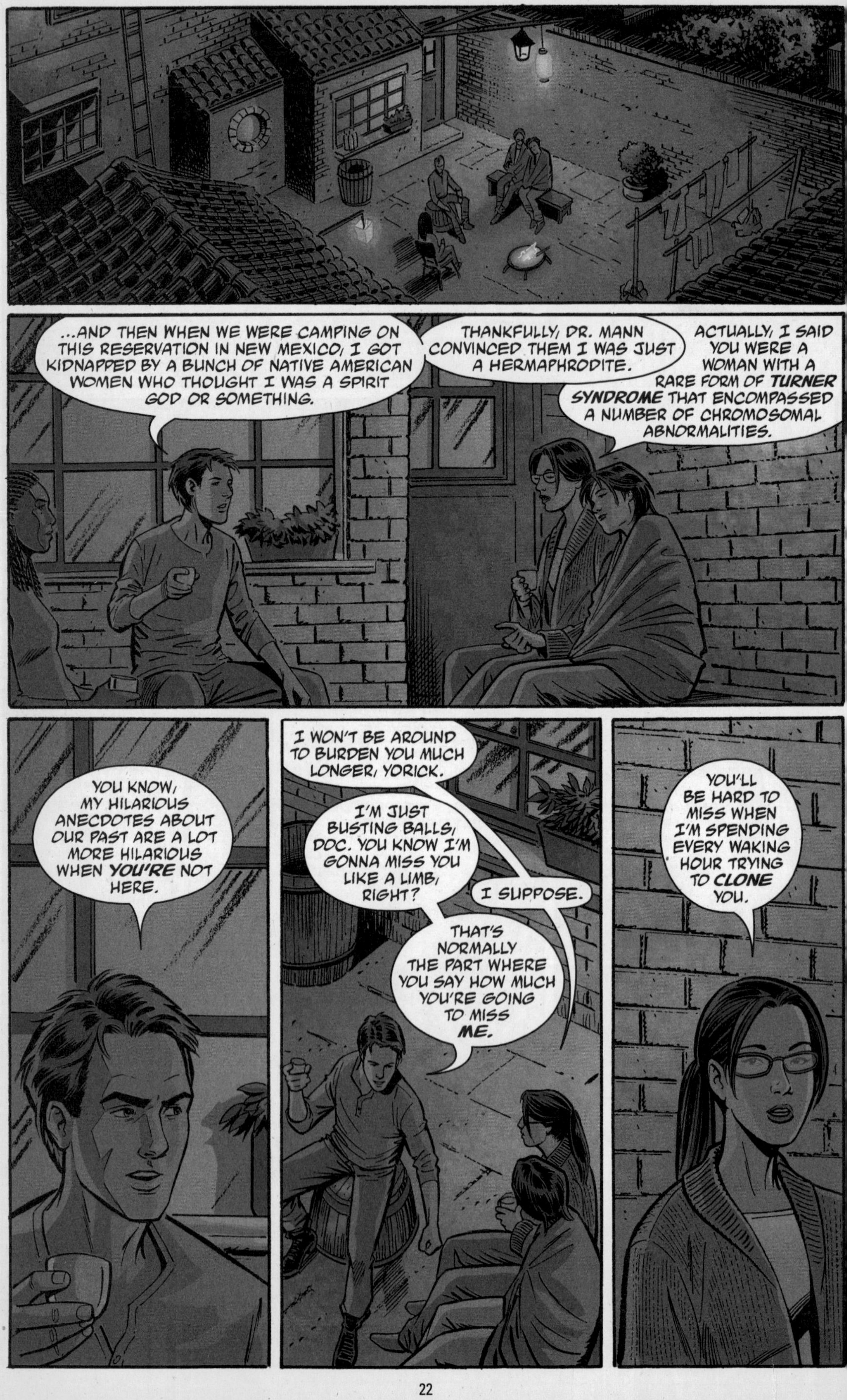
...AND THEN WHEN WE WERE CAMPING ON THIS RESERVATION IN NEW MEXICO, I GOT KIDNAPPED BY A BUNCH OF NATIVE AMERICAN WOMEN WHO THOUGHT I WAS A SPIRIT GOD OR SOMETHING.
THANKFULLY, DR. MANN CONVINCED THEM I WAS JUST A HERMAPHRODITE.
ACTUALLY, I SAID YOU WERE A WOMAN WITH A RARE FORM OF **TURNER SYNDROME** THAT ENCOMPASSED A NUMBER OF CHROMOSOMAL ABNORMALITIES.
YOU KNOW, MY HILARIOUS ANECDOTES ABOUT OUR PAST ARE A LOT MORE HILARIOUS WHEN **YOU'RE** NOT HERE.
I WON'T BE AROUND TO BURDEN YOU MUCH LONGER, YORICK.
I'M JUST BUSTING BALLS, DOC. YOU KNOW I'M GONNA MISS YOU LIKE A LIMB, RIGHT?
I SUPPOSE.
THAT'S NORMALLY THE PART WHERE YOU SAY HOW MUCH YOU'RE GOING TO MISS **ME.**
YOU'LL BE HARD TO MISS WHEN I'M SPENDING EVERY WAKING HOUR TRYING TO **CLONE** YOU.

UM, CAN YOU SAY THAT **AFTER** I HAVE A DRINK? SO I HAVE TIME FOR AN APPROPRIATE SPIT-TAKE?

ALLISON, PERHAPS WE SHOULD WAIT TO DISCUSS SENSITIVE PLANS LIKE THIS UNTIL--

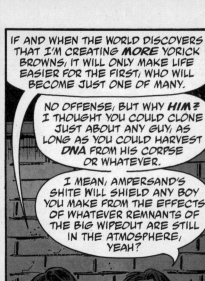

IF AND WHEN THE WORLD DISCOVERS THAT I'M CREATING **MORE** YORICK BROWNS, IT WILL ONLY MAKE LIFE EASIER FOR THE FIRST, WHO WILL BECOME JUST ONE OF MANY.

NO OFFENSE, BUT WHY **HIM**? I THOUGHT YOU COULD CLONE JUST ABOUT ANY GUY, AS LONG AS YOU COULD HARVEST **DNA** FROM HIS CORPSE OR WHATEVER.

I MEAN, AMPERSAND'S SHITE WILL SHIELD ANY BOY YOU MAKE FROM THE EFFECTS OF WHATEVER REMNANTS OF THE BIG WIPEOUT ARE STILL IN THE ATMOSPHERE, YEAH?

THEORETICALLY, BUT I HAVE NO PROOF THAT THE MONKEY'S FECES WILL WORK ON **EVERY** MALE.

YORICK MAY HAVE A UNIQUE GENETIC MAKEUP THAT REACTS TO AMPERSAND'S ANTIBODIES IN A PARTICULAR WAY.

SO IN THE FUTURE, MANKIND IS GOING TO BE MADE UP ENTIRELY OF **ME'S**?

IT'S AN ABOMINATION OF SCIENCE! OF **GRAMMAR**!

I'M ONLY **STARTING** WITH YOU. IF AND WHEN YOUR LINE OF DUPLICATES IS SUCCESSFUL, **THEN** I'LL GET TO WORK RESURRECTING AL GORE AND JOHNNY DEPP.

HOW MANY DIFFERENT...**MODELS** WILL YOU NEED TO BRING BACK BEFORE HUMANS CAN START REPOPULATING **WITHOUT** YOUR HELP?

GENETIC BOTTLENECK ISN'T MY AREA OF EXPERTISE, BUT I IMAGINE WE'LL NEED AT LEAST TWO HUNDRED SUBJECTS TO CREATE ENOUGH DIVERSITY TO LIMIT INBREEDING AND FORM AN EFFECTIVE FOUNDER POPULATION.

SO THAT MEANS I'LL EVENTUALLY BE THE GRANDFATHER OF, LIKE, POINT-FIVE-PERCENT OF EVERY MALE ON THE *PLANET?*

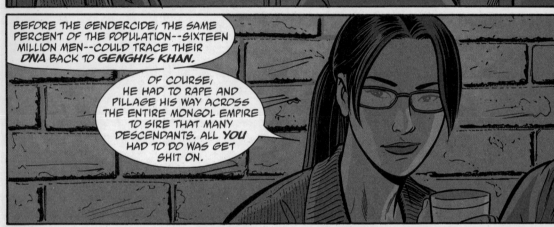

BEFORE THE GENDERCIDE, THE SAME PERCENT OF THE POPULATION--SIXTEEN MILLION MEN--COULD TRACE THEIR *DNA* BACK TO *GENGHIS KHAN.*

OF COURSE, HE HAD TO RAPE AND PILLAGE HIS WAY ACROSS THE ENTIRE MONGOL EMPIRE TO SIRE THAT MANY DESCENDANTS. ALL *YOU* HAD TO DO WAS GET SHIT ON.

AND ON THAT NOTE, I SHOULD PROBABLY RETIRE TO MY SICKBED FOR A FEW MORE HOURS.

PROMISE TO WAKE ME BEFORE YOU GO-GO, LAST MATE?

AYE-AYE, SKIP.

CARE TO JOIN ME, LOVE?

AH, IN A FEW, ROSE.

THE OLD TRIO STILL HAS A FEW LOOSE ENDS TO WRAP UP.

NO HURRY...BUT WE HAVE A LOT OF CATCHING UP TO DO.

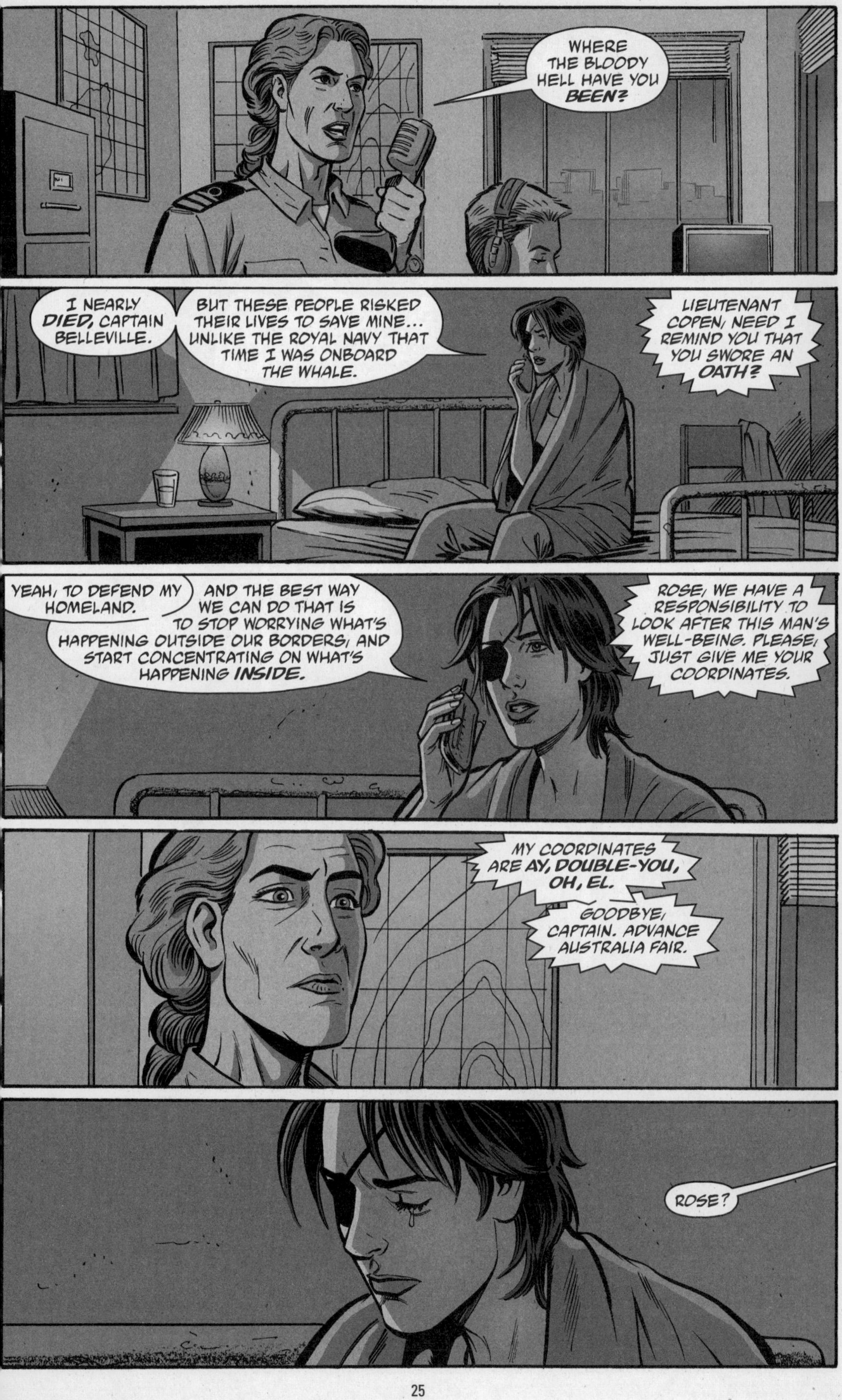
WHERE THE BLOODY HELL HAVE YOU BEEN?
I NEARLY DIED, CAPTAIN BELLEVILLE.
BUT THESE PEOPLE RISKED THEIR LIVES TO SAVE MINE... UNLIKE THE ROYAL NAVY THAT TIME I WAS ONBOARD THE WHALE.
LIEUTENANT COPEN, NEED I REMIND YOU THAT YOU SWORE AN OATH?
YEAH, TO DEFEND MY HOMELAND.
AND THE BEST WAY WE CAN DO THAT IS TO STOP WORRYING WHAT'S HAPPENING OUTSIDE OUR BORDERS, AND START CONCENTRATING ON WHAT'S HAPPENING INSIDE.
ROSE, WE HAVE A RESPONSIBILITY TO LOOK AFTER THIS MAN'S WELL-BEING. PLEASE, JUST GIVE ME YOUR COORDINATES.
MY COORDINATES ARE AY, DOUBLE-YOU, OH, EL.
GOODBYE, CAPTAIN. ADVANCE AUSTRALIA FAIR.
ROSE?

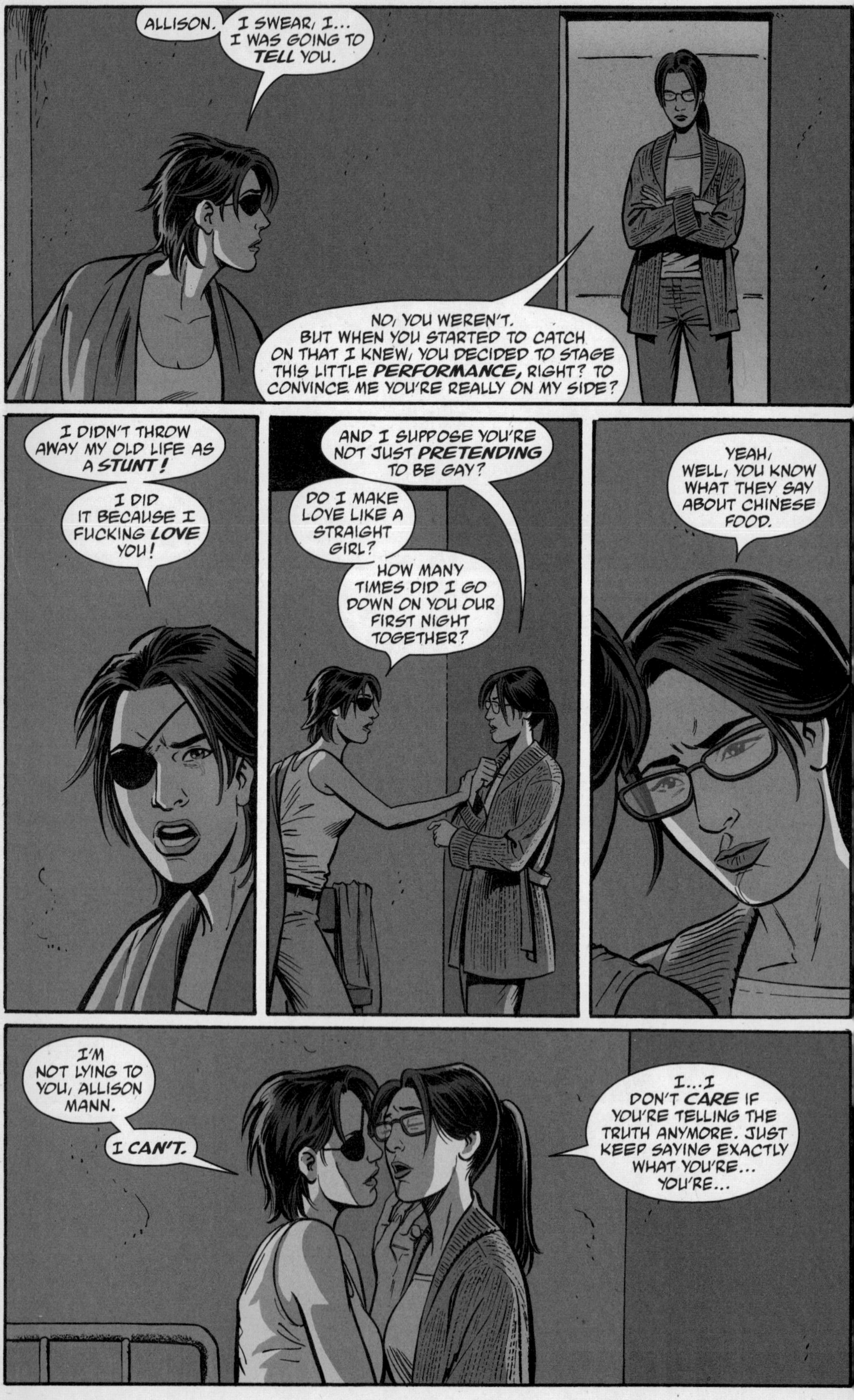
ALLISON.
I SWEAR, I... I WAS GOING TO TELL YOU.
NO, YOU WEREN'T. BUT WHEN YOU STARTED TO CATCH ON THAT I KNEW, YOU DECIDED TO STAGE THIS LITTLE PERFORMANCE, RIGHT? TO CONVINCE ME YOU'RE REALLY ON MY SIDE?
I DIDN'T THROW AWAY MY OLD LIFE AS A STUNT!
I DID IT BECAUSE I FUCKING LOVE YOU!
AND I SUPPOSE YOU'RE NOT JUST PRETENDING TO BE GAY?
DO I MAKE LOVE LIKE A STRAIGHT GIRL?
HOW MANY TIMES DID I GO DOWN ON YOU OUR FIRST NIGHT TOGETHER?
YEAH, WELL, YOU KNOW WHAT THEY SAY ABOUT CHINESE FOOD.
I'M NOT LYING TO YOU, ALLISON MANN.
I CAN'T.
I...I DON'T CARE IF YOU'RE TELLING THE TRUTH ANYMORE. JUST KEEP SAYING EXACTLY WHAT YOU'RE... YOU'RE...

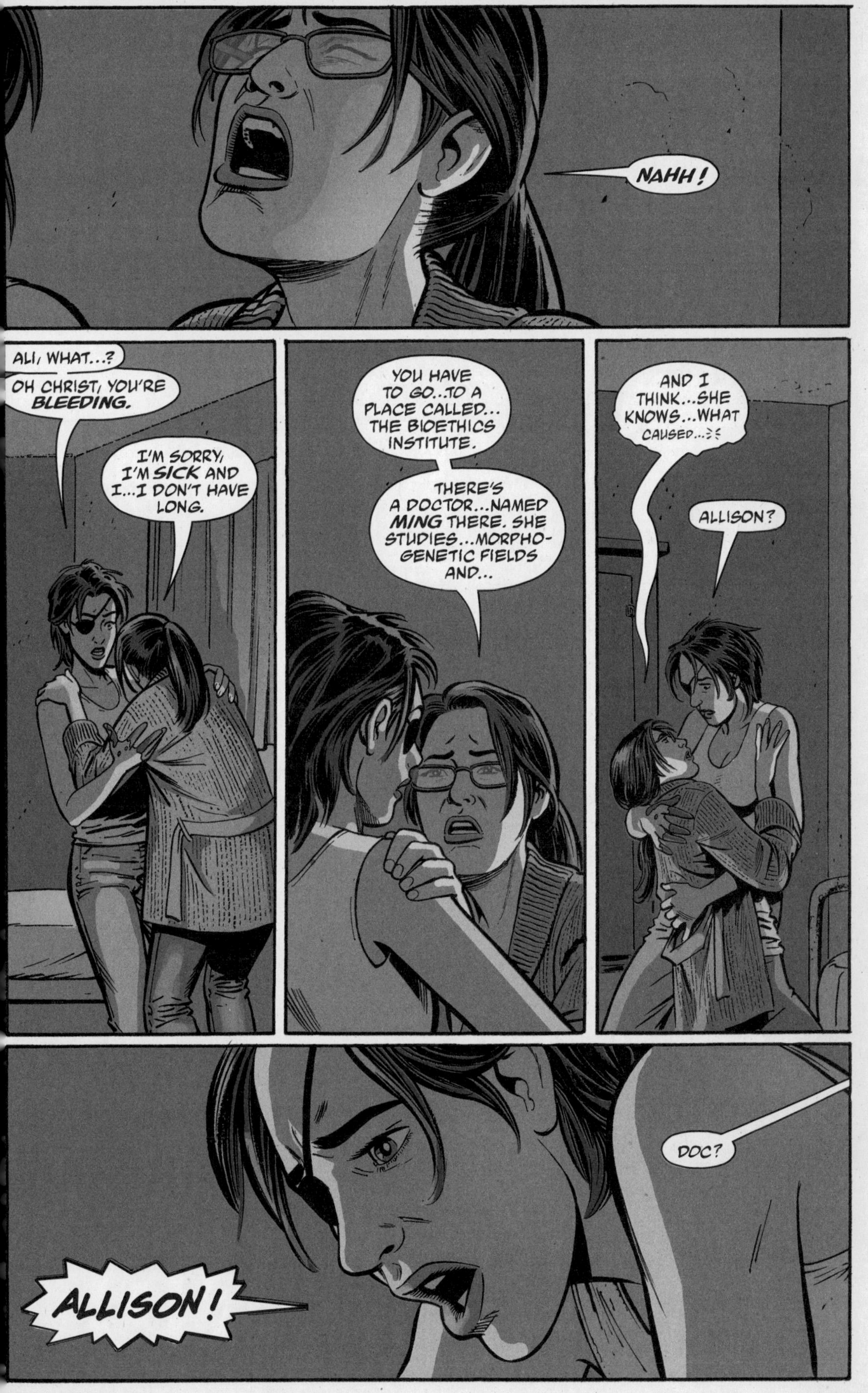
NAHH!
ALI, WHAT...?
OH CHRIST, YOU'RE BLEEDING.
I'M SORRY, I'M SICK AND I...I DON'T HAVE LONG.
YOU HAVE TO GO...TO A PLACE CALLED... THE BIOETHICS INSTITUTE.
THERE'S A DOCTOR...NAMED MING THERE. SHE STUDIES...MORPHOGENETIC FIELDS AND...
AND I THINK...SHE KNOWS...WHAT CAUSED...
ALLISON?
DOC?
ALLISON!

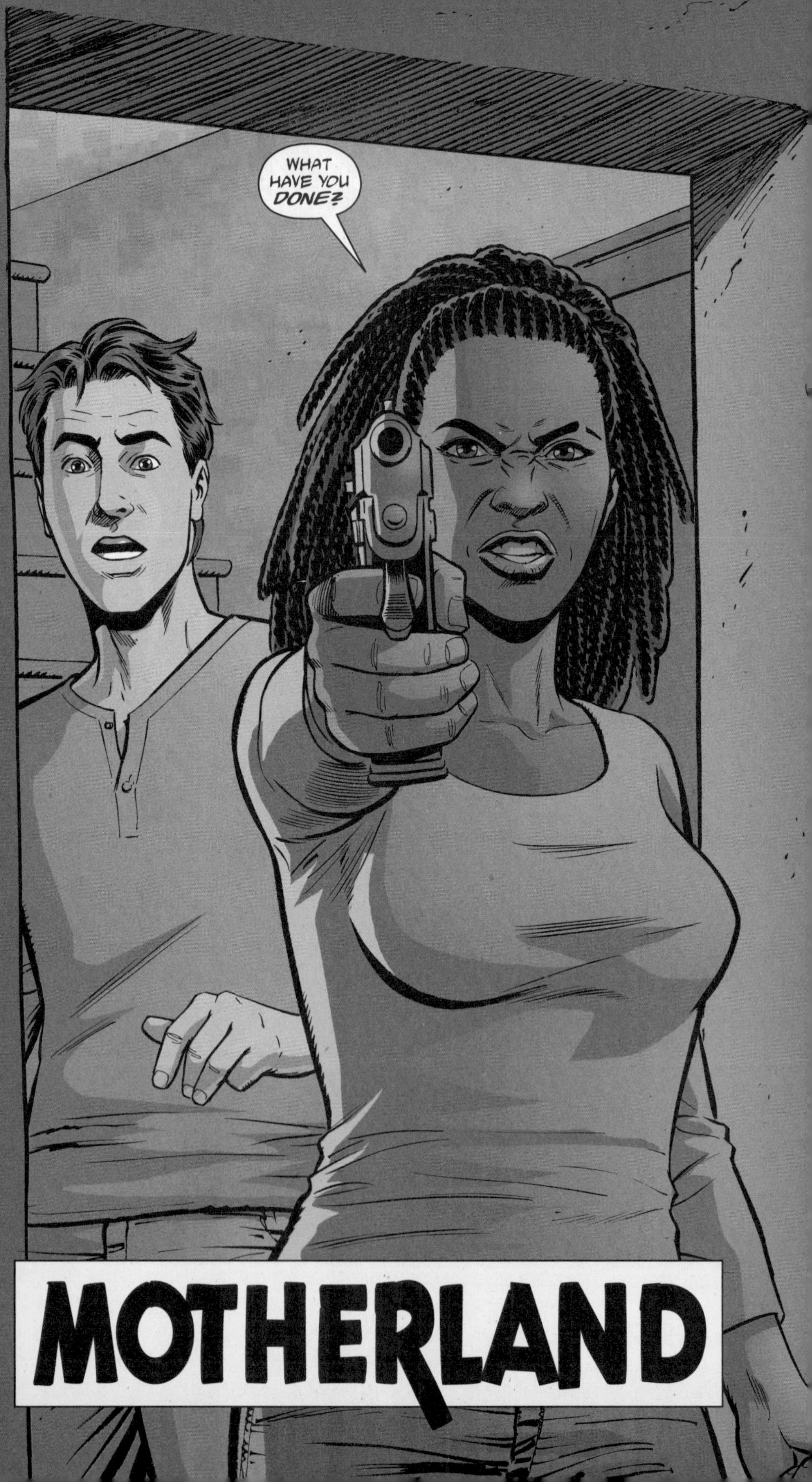
WHAT HAVE YOU DONE?
MOTHERLAND

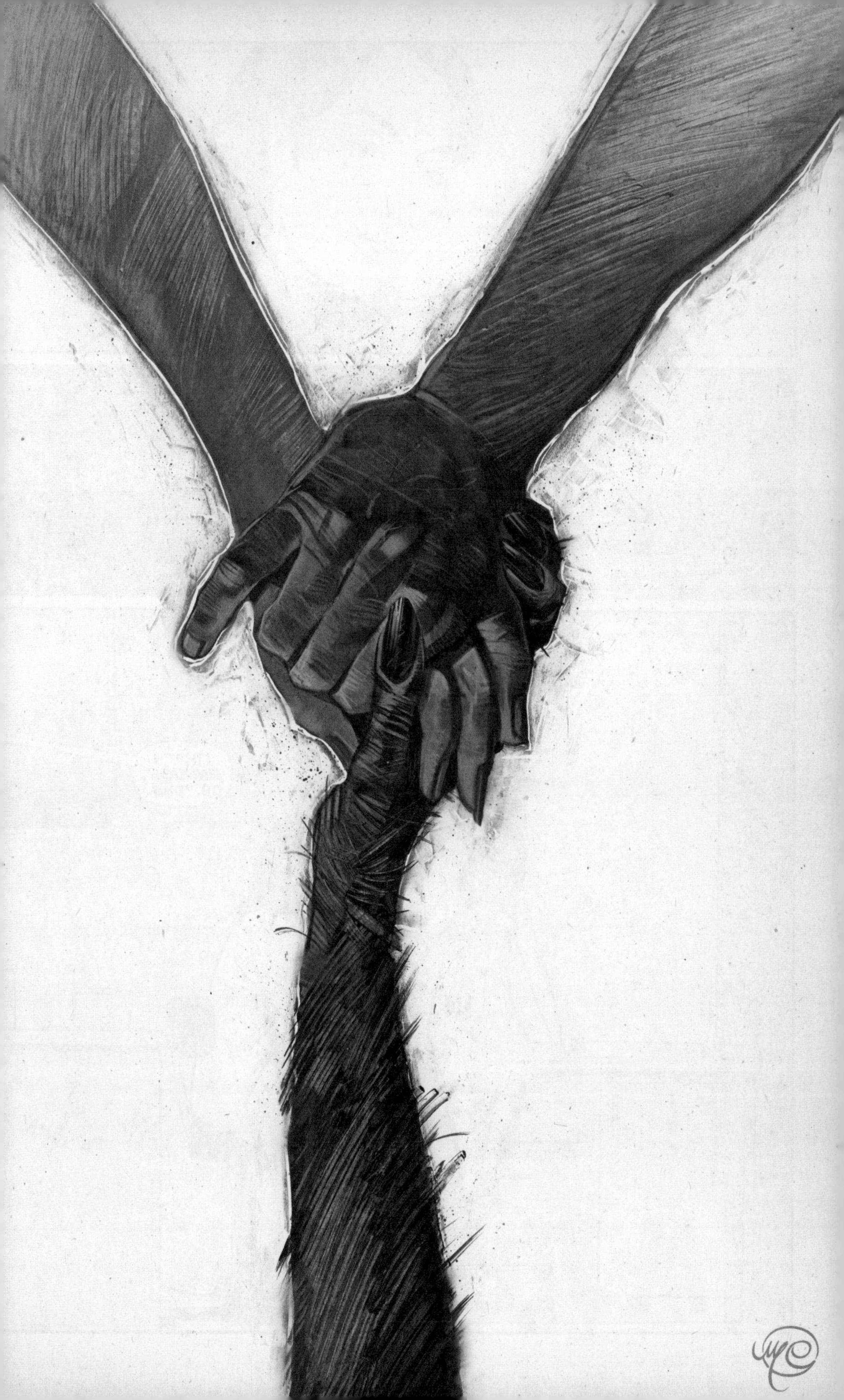

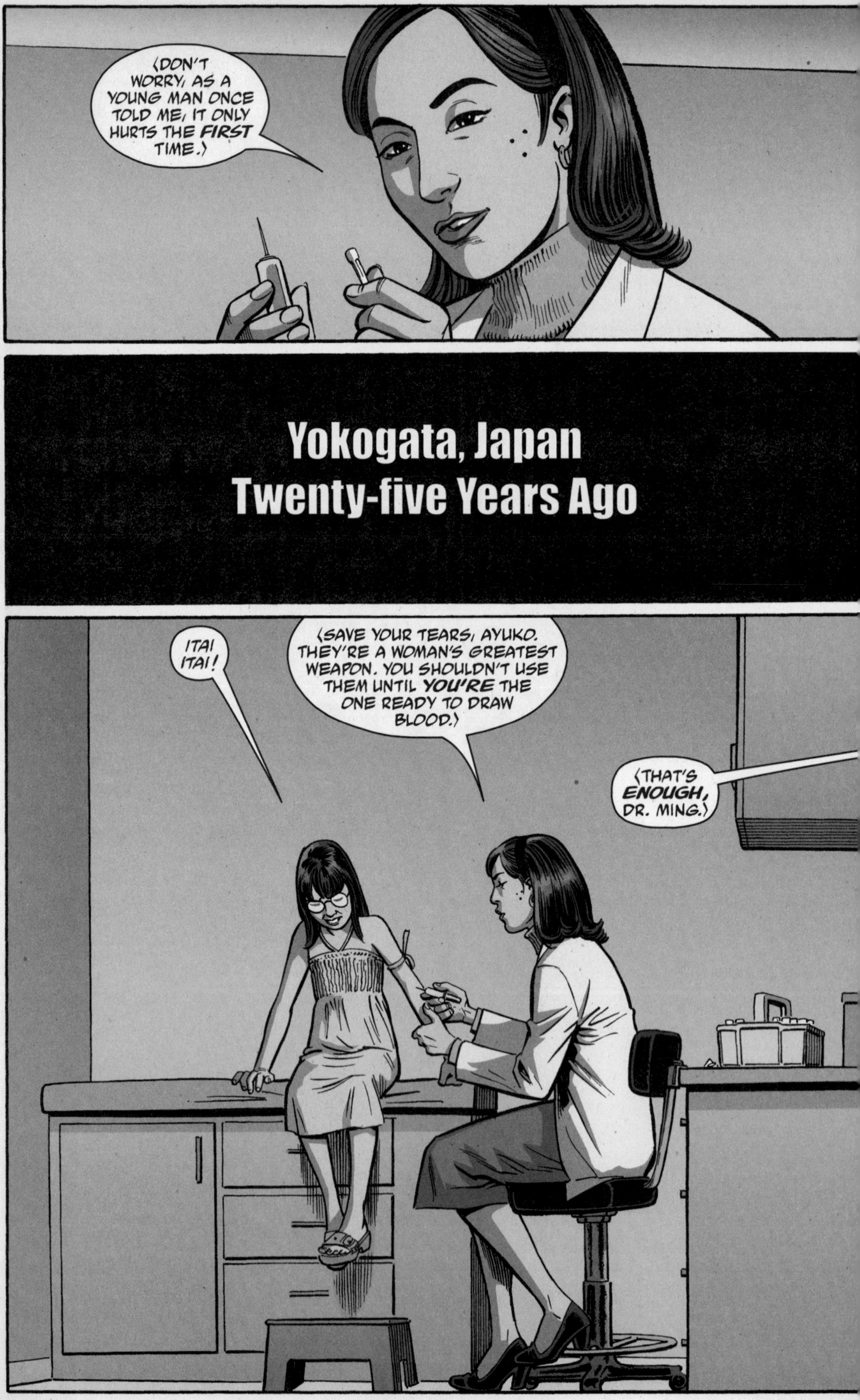
(DON'T WORRY, AS A YOUNG MAN ONCE TOLD ME, IT ONLY HURTS THE FIRST TIME.)
Yokogata, Japan
Twenty-five Years Ago
ITAI ITAI!
(SAVE YOUR TEARS, AYUKO. THEY'RE A WOMAN'S GREATEST WEAPON. YOU SHOULDN'T USE THEM UNTIL YOU'RE THE ONE READY TO DRAW BLOOD.)
(THAT'S ENOUGH, DR. MING.)

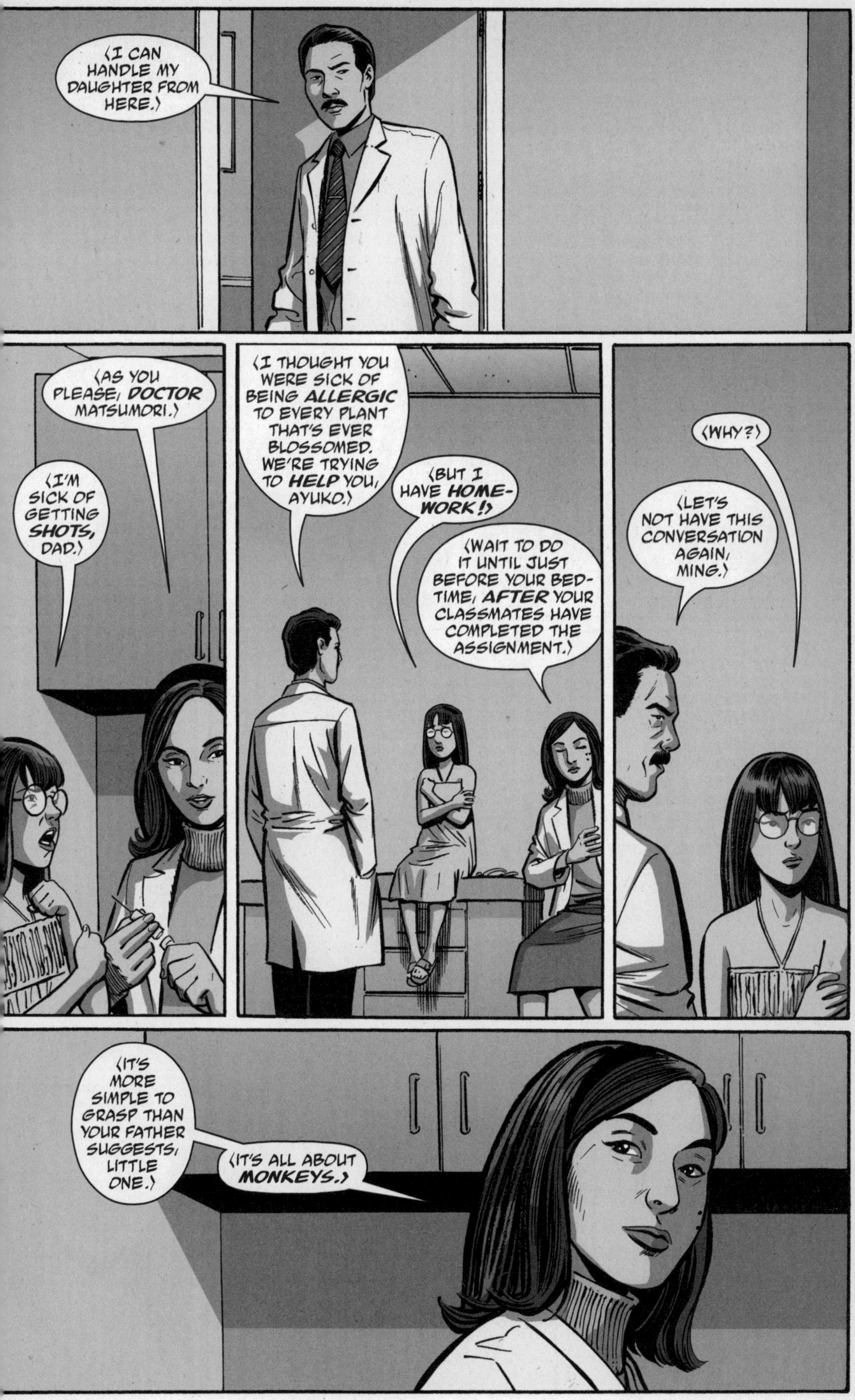
⟨I CAN HANDLE MY DAUGHTER FROM HERE.⟩
⟨AS YOU PLEASE, DOCTOR MATSUMORI.⟩
⟨I'M SICK OF GETTING SHOTS, DAD.⟩
⟨I THOUGHT YOU WERE SICK OF BEING ALLERGIC TO EVERY PLANT THAT'S EVER BLOSSOMED. WE'RE TRYING TO HELP YOU, AYUKO.⟩
⟨BUT I HAVE HOME-WORK!⟩
⟨WAIT TO DO IT UNTIL JUST BEFORE YOUR BED-TIME, AFTER YOUR CLASSMATES HAVE COMPLETED THE ASSIGNMENT.⟩
⟨WHY?⟩
⟨LET'S NOT HAVE THIS CONVERSATION AGAIN, MING.⟩
⟨IT'S MORE SIMPLE TO GRASP THAN YOUR FATHER SUGGESTS, LITTLE ONE.⟩
⟨IT'S ALL ABOUT MONKEYS.⟩

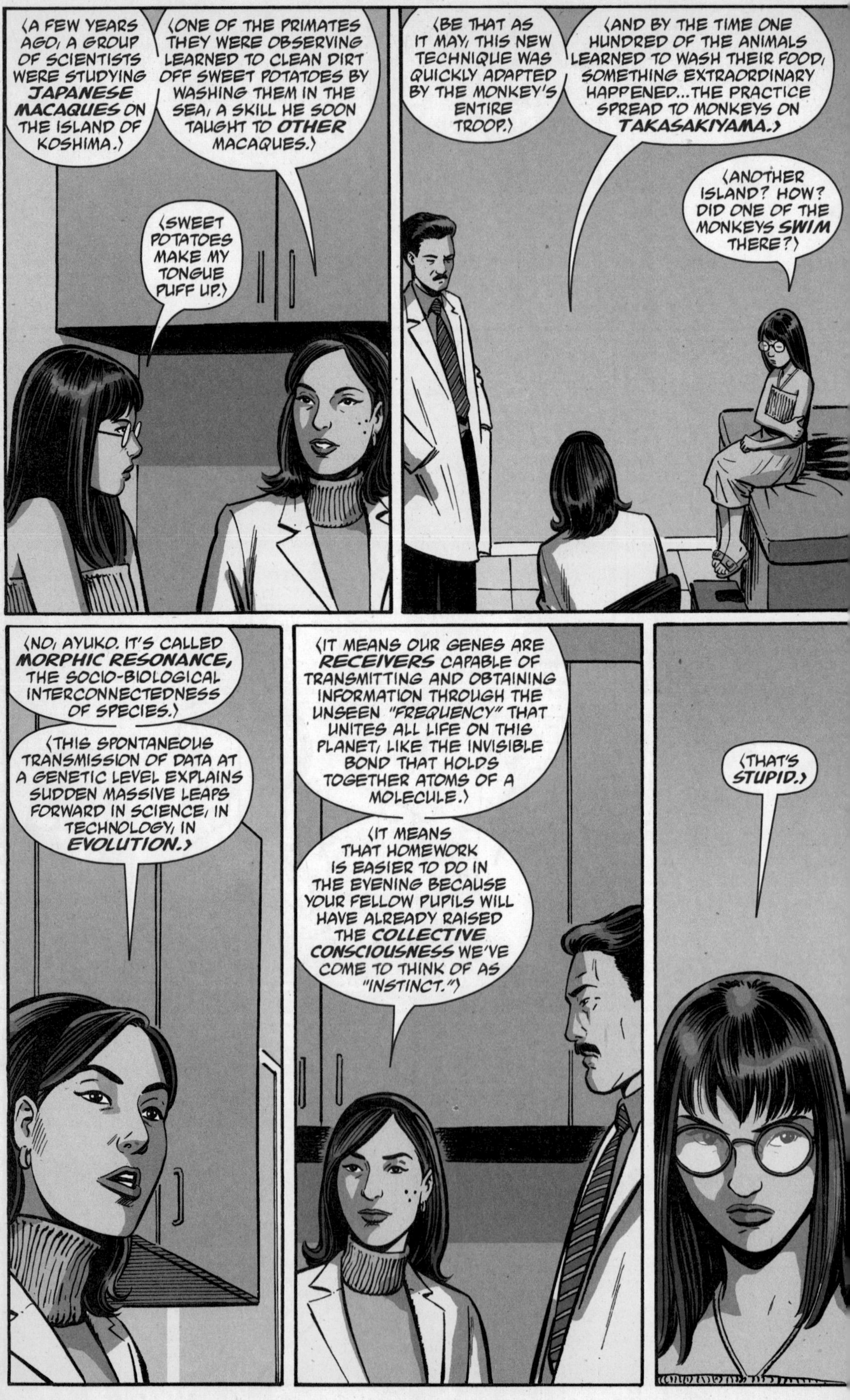

⟨A FEW YEARS AGO, A GROUP OF SCIENTISTS WERE STUDYING **JAPANESE MACAQUES** ON THE ISLAND OF KOSHIMA.⟩
⟨ONE OF THE PRIMATES THEY WERE OBSERVING LEARNED TO CLEAN DIRT OFF SWEET POTATOES BY WASHING THEM IN THE SEA, A SKILL HE SOON TAUGHT TO **OTHER** MACAQUES.⟩
⟨SWEET POTATOES MAKE MY TONGUE PUFF UP.⟩
⟨BE THAT AS IT MAY, THIS NEW TECHNIQUE WAS QUICKLY ADAPTED BY THE MONKEY'S ENTIRE TROOP.⟩
⟨AND BY THE TIME ONE HUNDRED OF THE ANIMALS LEARNED TO WASH THEIR FOOD, SOMETHING EXTRAORDINARY HAPPENED...THE PRACTICE SPREAD TO MONKEYS ON **TAKASAKIYAMA.**⟩
⟨ANOTHER ISLAND? HOW? DID ONE OF THE MONKEYS **SWIM** THERE?⟩
⟨NO, AYUKO. IT'S CALLED **MORPHIC RESONANCE,** THE SOCIO-BIOLOGICAL INTERCONNECTEDNESS OF SPECIES.⟩
⟨THIS SPONTANEOUS TRANSMISSION OF DATA AT A GENETIC LEVEL EXPLAINS SUDDEN MASSIVE LEAPS FORWARD IN SCIENCE, IN TECHNOLOGY, IN **EVOLUTION.**⟩
⟨IT MEANS OUR GENES ARE **RECEIVERS** CAPABLE OF TRANSMITTING AND OBTAINING INFORMATION THROUGH THE UNSEEN "FREQUENCY" THAT UNITES ALL LIFE ON THIS PLANET, LIKE THE INVISIBLE BOND THAT HOLDS TOGETHER ATOMS OF A MOLECULE.⟩
⟨IT MEANS THAT HOMEWORK IS EASIER TO DO IN THE EVENING BECAUSE YOUR FELLOW PUPILS WILL HAVE ALREADY RAISED THE **COLLECTIVE CONSCIOUSNESS** WE'VE COME TO THINK OF AS "INSTINCT."⟩
⟨THAT'S **STUPID.**⟩

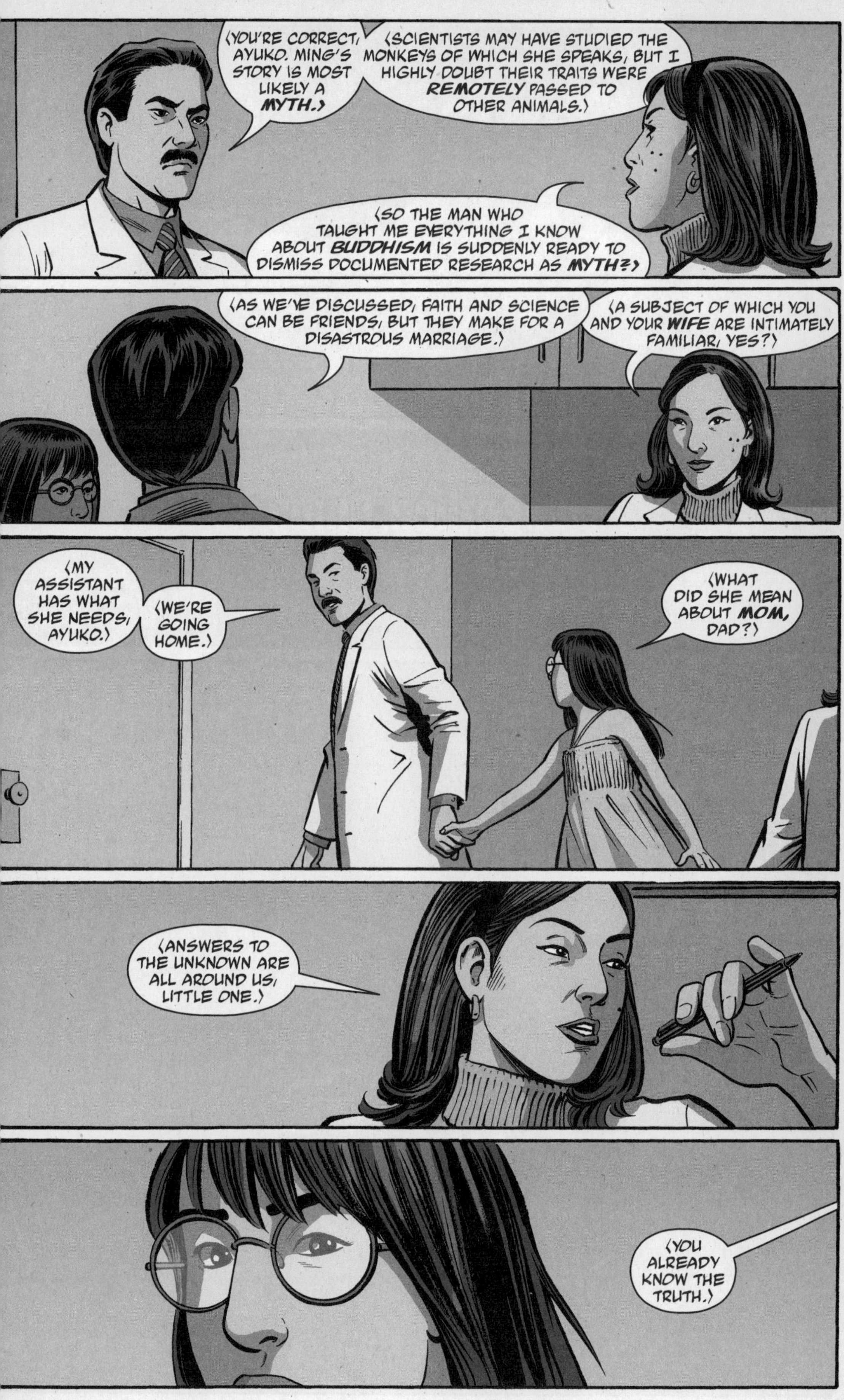
⟨YOU'RE CORRECT, AYUKO. MING'S STORY IS MOST LIKELY A **MYTH.**⟩
⟨SCIENTISTS MAY HAVE STUDIED THE MONKEYS OF WHICH SHE SPEAKS, BUT I HIGHLY DOUBT THEIR TRAITS WERE ***REMOTELY*** PASSED TO OTHER ANIMALS.⟩
⟨SO THE MAN WHO TAUGHT ME EVERYTHING I KNOW ABOUT ***BUDDHISM*** IS SUDDENLY READY TO DISMISS DOCUMENTED RESEARCH AS ***MYTH?***⟩
⟨AS WE'VE DISCUSSED, FAITH AND SCIENCE CAN BE FRIENDS, BUT THEY MAKE FOR A DISASTROUS MARRIAGE.⟩
⟨A SUBJECT OF WHICH YOU AND YOUR ***WIFE*** ARE INTIMATELY FAMILIAR, YES?⟩
⟨MY ASSISTANT HAS WHAT SHE NEEDS, AYUKO.⟩
⟨WE'RE GOING HOME.⟩
⟨WHAT DID SHE MEAN ABOUT ***MOM,*** DAD?⟩
⟨ANSWERS TO THE UNKNOWN ARE ALL AROUND US, LITTLE ONE.⟩
⟨YOU ALREADY KNOW THE TRUTH.⟩

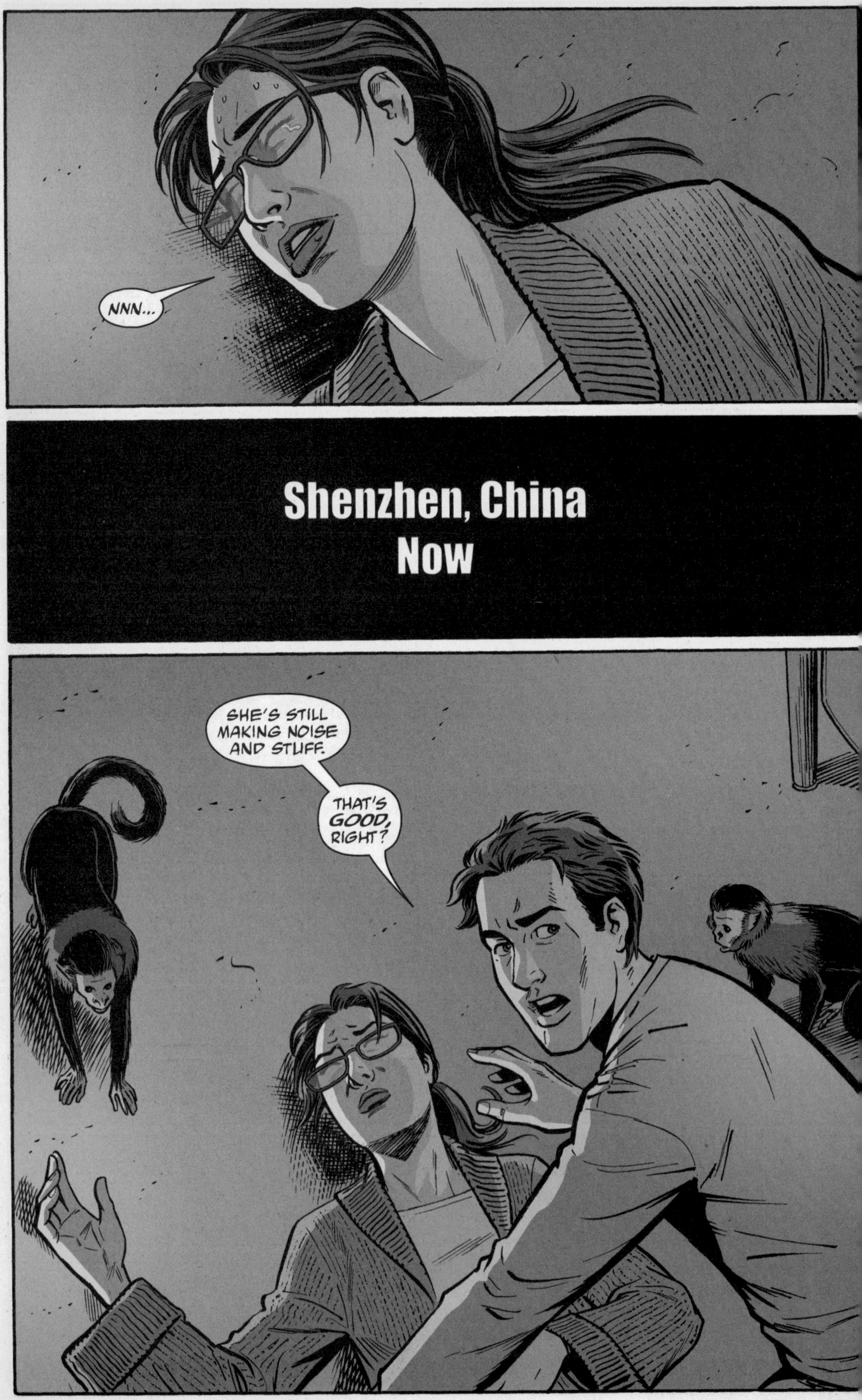
NNN...
Shenzhen, China
Now
SHE'S STILL MAKING NOISE AND STUFF.
THAT'S GOOD, RIGHT?

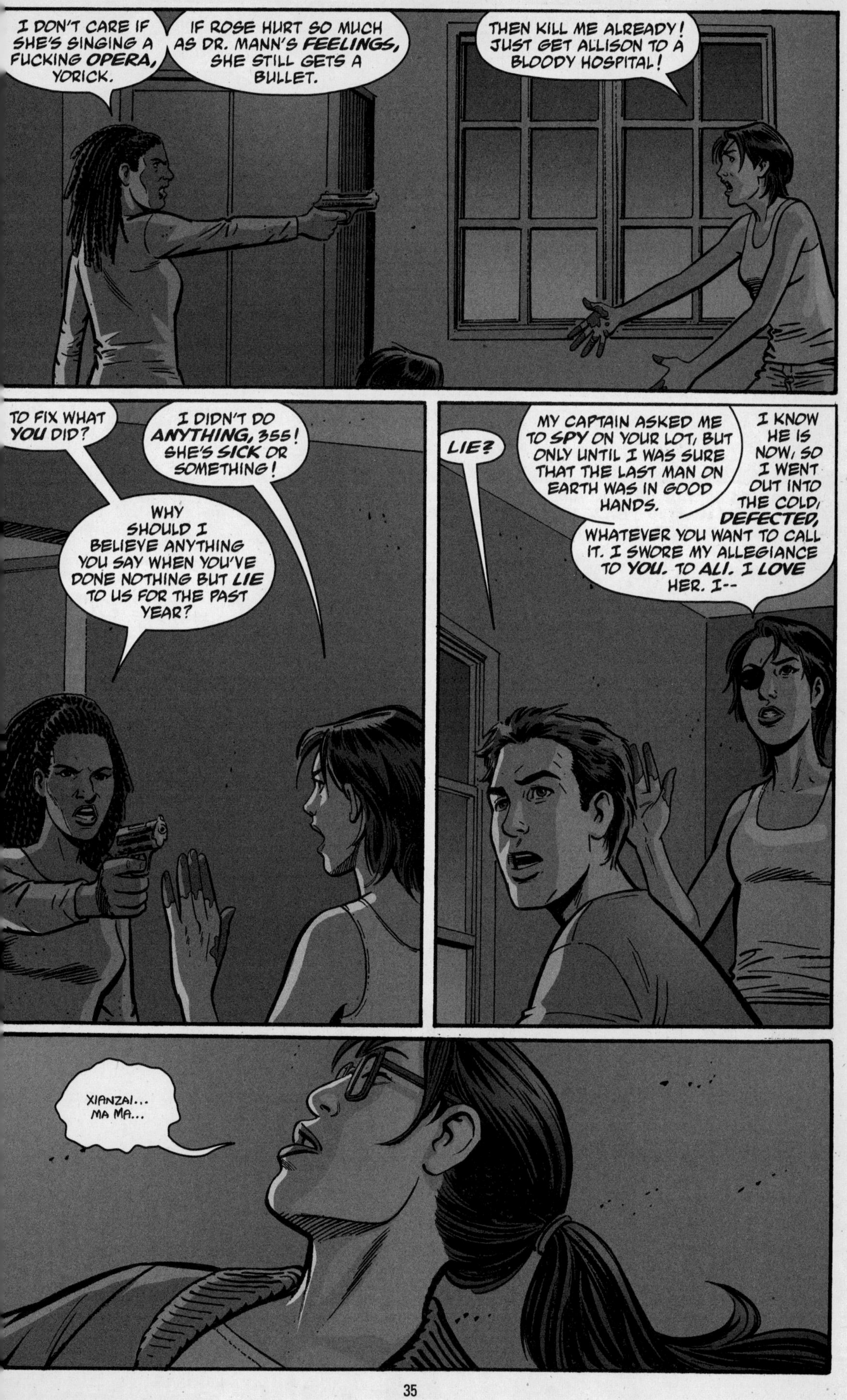

I DON'T CARE IF SHE'S SINGING A FUCKING OPERA, YORICK.
IF ROSE HURT SO MUCH AS DR. MANN'S FEELINGS, SHE STILL GETS A BULLET.
THEN KILL ME ALREADY! JUST GET ALLISON TO A BLOODY HOSPITAL!
TO FIX WHAT YOU DID?
I DIDN'T DO ANYTHING, 355! SHE'S SICK OR SOMETHING!
WHY SHOULD I BELIEVE ANYTHING YOU SAY WHEN YOU'VE DONE NOTHING BUT LIE TO US FOR THE PAST YEAR?
LIE?
MY CAPTAIN ASKED ME TO SPY ON YOUR LOT, BUT ONLY UNTIL I WAS SURE THAT THE LAST MAN ON EARTH WAS IN GOOD HANDS.
I KNOW HE IS NOW, SO I WENT OUT INTO THE COLD, DEFECTED, WHATEVER YOU WANT TO CALL IT. I SWORE MY ALLEGIANCE TO YOU. TO ALI. I LOVE HER. I--
XIANZAI... MA MA...

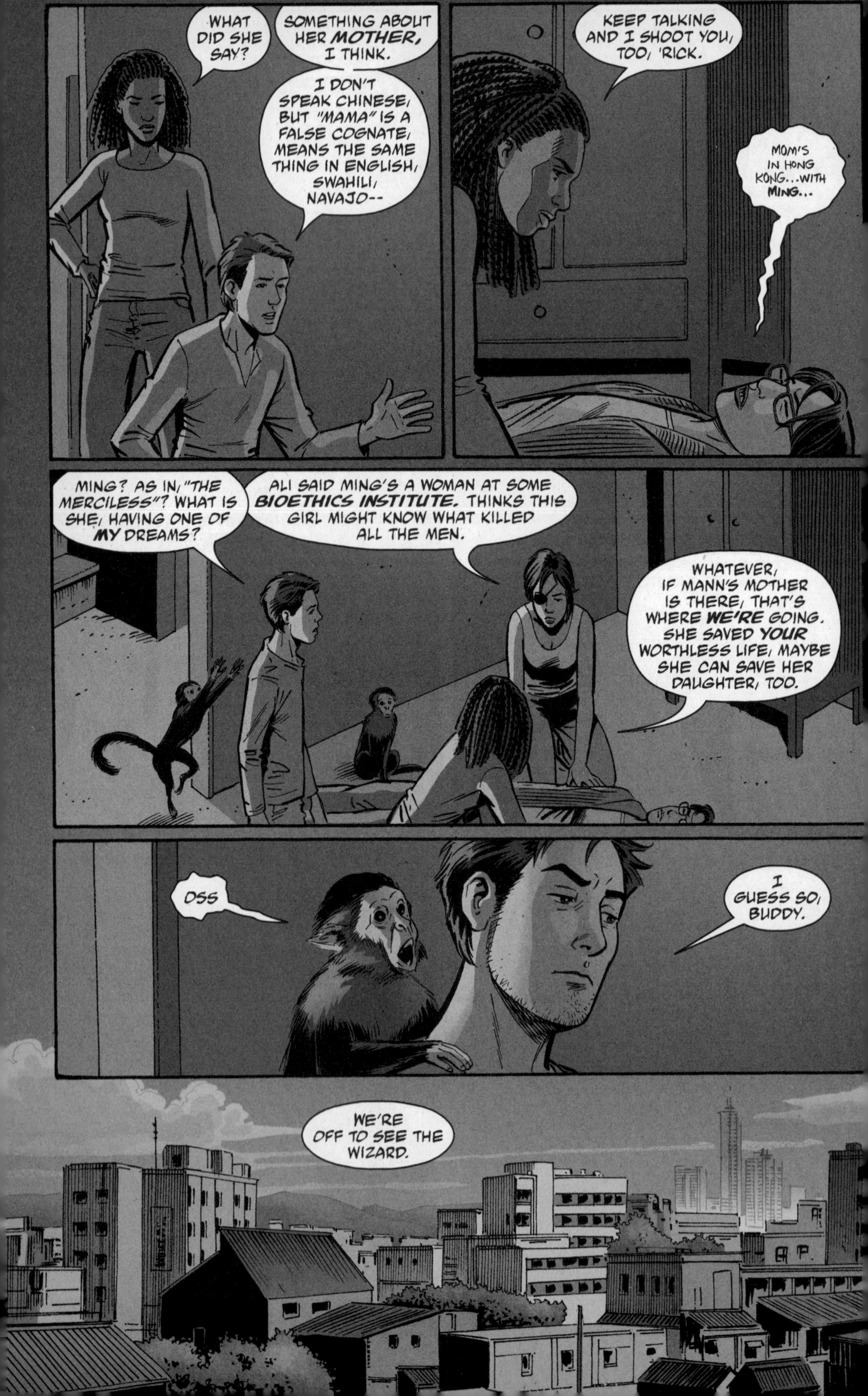
WHAT DID SHE SAY?
SOMETHING ABOUT HER MOTHER, I THINK.
I DON'T SPEAK CHINESE, BUT "MAMA" IS A FALSE COGNATE, MEANS THE SAME THING IN ENGLISH, SWAHILI, NAVAJO--
KEEP TALKING AND I SHOOT YOU, TOO, 'RICK.
MOM'S IN HONG KONG...WITH MING...
MING? AS IN, "THE MERCILESS"? WHAT IS SHE, HAVING ONE OF MY DREAMS?
ALI SAID MING'S A WOMAN AT SOME BIOETHICS INSTITUTE. THINKS THIS GIRL MIGHT KNOW WHAT KILLED ALL THE MEN.
WHATEVER, IF MANN'S MOTHER IS THERE, THAT'S WHERE WE'RE GOING. SHE SAVED YOUR WORTHLESS LIFE, MAYBE SHE CAN SAVE HER DAUGHTER, TOO.
OSS
I GUESS SO, BUDDY.
WE'RE OFF TO SEE THE WIZARD.

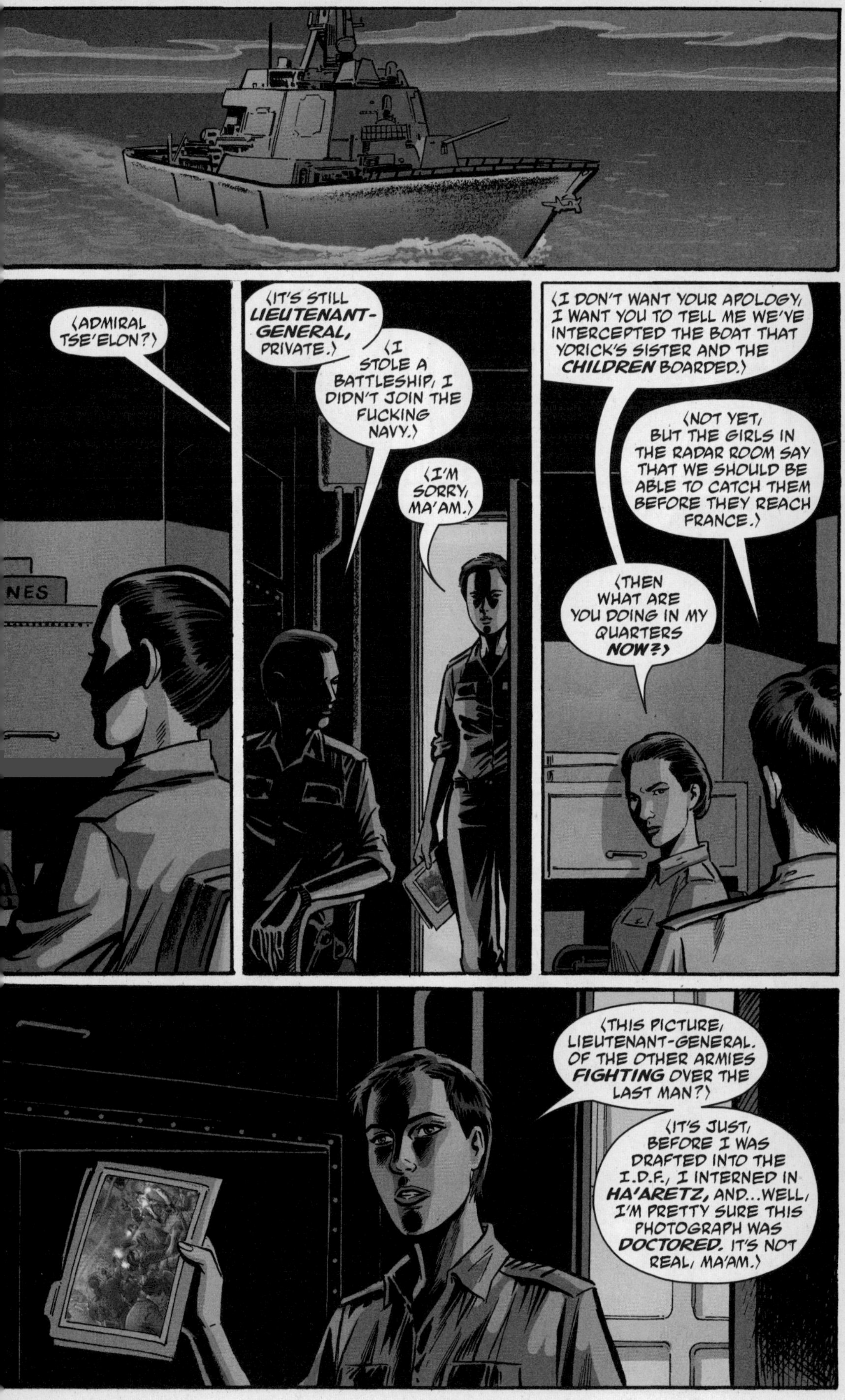

⟨ADMIRAL TSE'ELON?⟩
⟨IT'S STILL LIEUTENANT-GENERAL, PRIVATE.⟩
⟨I STOLE A BATTLESHIP, I DIDN'T JOIN THE FUCKING NAVY.⟩
⟨I'M SORRY, MA'AM.⟩
⟨I DON'T WANT YOUR APOLOGY, I WANT YOU TO TELL ME WE'VE INTERCEPTED THE BOAT THAT YORICK'S SISTER AND THE CHILDREN BOARDED.⟩
⟨NOT YET, BUT THE GIRLS IN THE RADAR ROOM SAY THAT WE SHOULD BE ABLE TO CATCH THEM BEFORE THEY REACH FRANCE.⟩
⟨THEN WHAT ARE YOU DOING IN MY QUARTERS NOW?!⟩
⟨THIS PICTURE, LIEUTENANT-GENERAL. OF THE OTHER ARMIES FIGHTING OVER THE LAST MAN?⟩
⟨IT'S JUST, BEFORE I WAS DRAFTED INTO THE I.D.F., I INTERNED IN HA'ARETZ, AND...WELL, I'M PRETTY SURE THIS PHOTOGRAPH WAS DOCTORED. IT'S NOT REAL, MA'AM.⟩

⟨ELIANA, ISN'T THAT EXACTLY WHAT THE PETTY CONSPIRACY THEORISTS SAID ABOUT THE PHOTO OF YORICK BROWN?⟩

⟨AND HAVEN'T I PROVED TO YOU THAT HE'S ABSOLUTELY REAL?⟩

⟨YES, BUT... WITH RESPECT, MOST OF THESE GIRLS DIDN'T JOIN YOUR MISSION TO CHASE SOME MAN. THEY DID IT TO HELP BRING PEACE TO--⟩

⟨HKK⟩

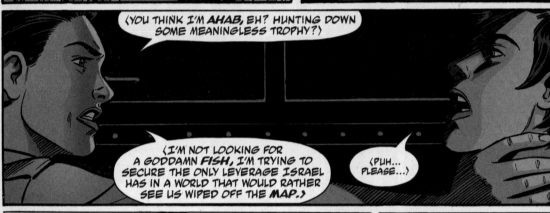

⟨YOU THINK I'M AHAB, EH? HUNTING DOWN SOME MEANINGLESS TROPHY?⟩

⟨I'M NOT LOOKING FOR A GODDAMN FISH, I'M TRYING TO SECURE THE ONLY LEVERAGE ISRAEL HAS IN A WORLD THAT WOULD RATHER SEE US WIPED OFF THE MAP.⟩

⟨PUH... PLEASE...⟩

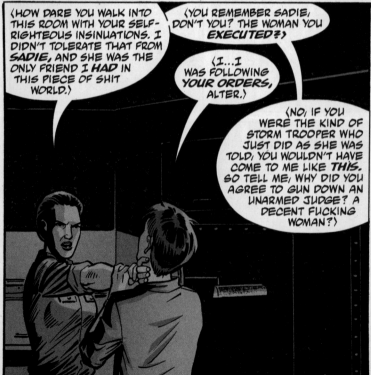

⟨HOW DARE YOU WALK INTO THIS ROOM WITH YOUR SELF-RIGHTEOUS INSINUATIONS. I DIDN'T TOLERATE THAT FROM SADIE, AND SHE WAS THE ONLY FRIEND I HAD IN THIS PIECE OF SHIT WORLD.⟩

⟨YOU REMEMBER SADIE, DON'T YOU? THE WOMAN YOU EXECUTED?⟩

⟨I...I WAS FOLLOWING YOUR ORDERS, ALTER.⟩

⟨NO, IF YOU WERE THE KIND OF STORM TROOPER WHO JUST DID AS SHE WAS TOLD, YOU WOULDN'T HAVE COME TO ME LIKE THIS. SO TELL ME, WHY DID YOU AGREE TO GUN DOWN AN UNARMED JUDGE? A DECENT FUCKING WOMAN?⟩

⟨WHY DID YOU DO THAT?⟩

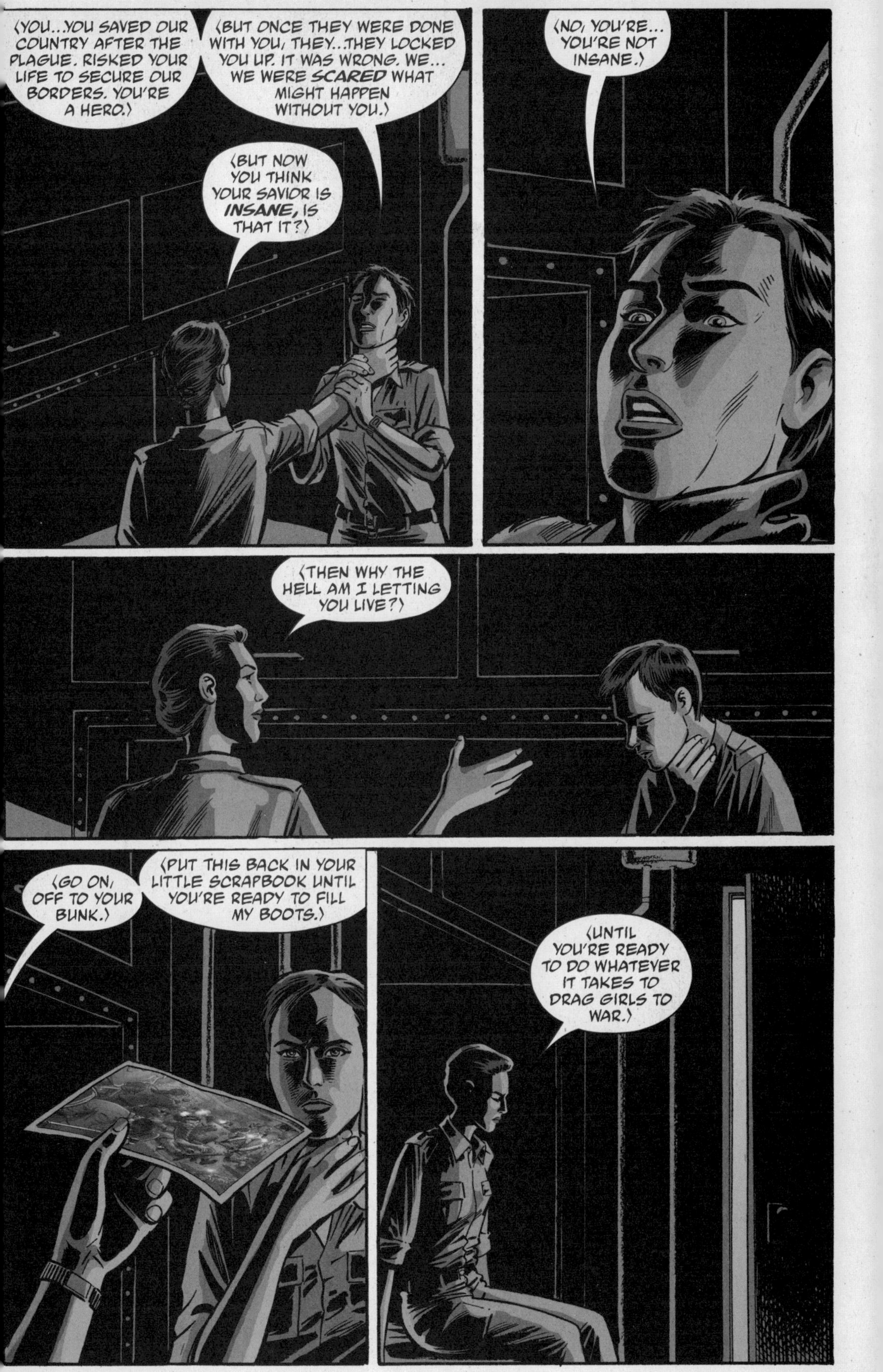
⟨YOU...YOU SAVED OUR COUNTRY AFTER THE PLAGUE. RISKED YOUR LIFE TO SECURE OUR BORDERS. YOU'RE A HERO.⟩
⟨BUT ONCE THEY WERE DONE WITH YOU, THEY...THEY LOCKED YOU UP. IT WAS WRONG. WE... WE WERE SCARED WHAT MIGHT HAPPEN WITHOUT YOU.⟩
⟨BUT NOW YOU THINK YOUR SAVIOR IS INSANE, IS THAT IT?⟩
⟨NO, YOU'RE... YOU'RE NOT INSANE.⟩
⟨THEN WHY THE HELL AM I LETTING YOU LIVE?⟩
⟨GO ON, OFF TO YOUR BUNK.⟩
⟨PUT THIS BACK IN YOUR LITTLE SCRAPBOOK UNTIL YOU'RE READY TO FILL MY BOOTS.⟩
⟨UNTIL YOU'RE READY TO DO WHATEVER IT TAKES TO DRAG GIRLS TO WAR.⟩

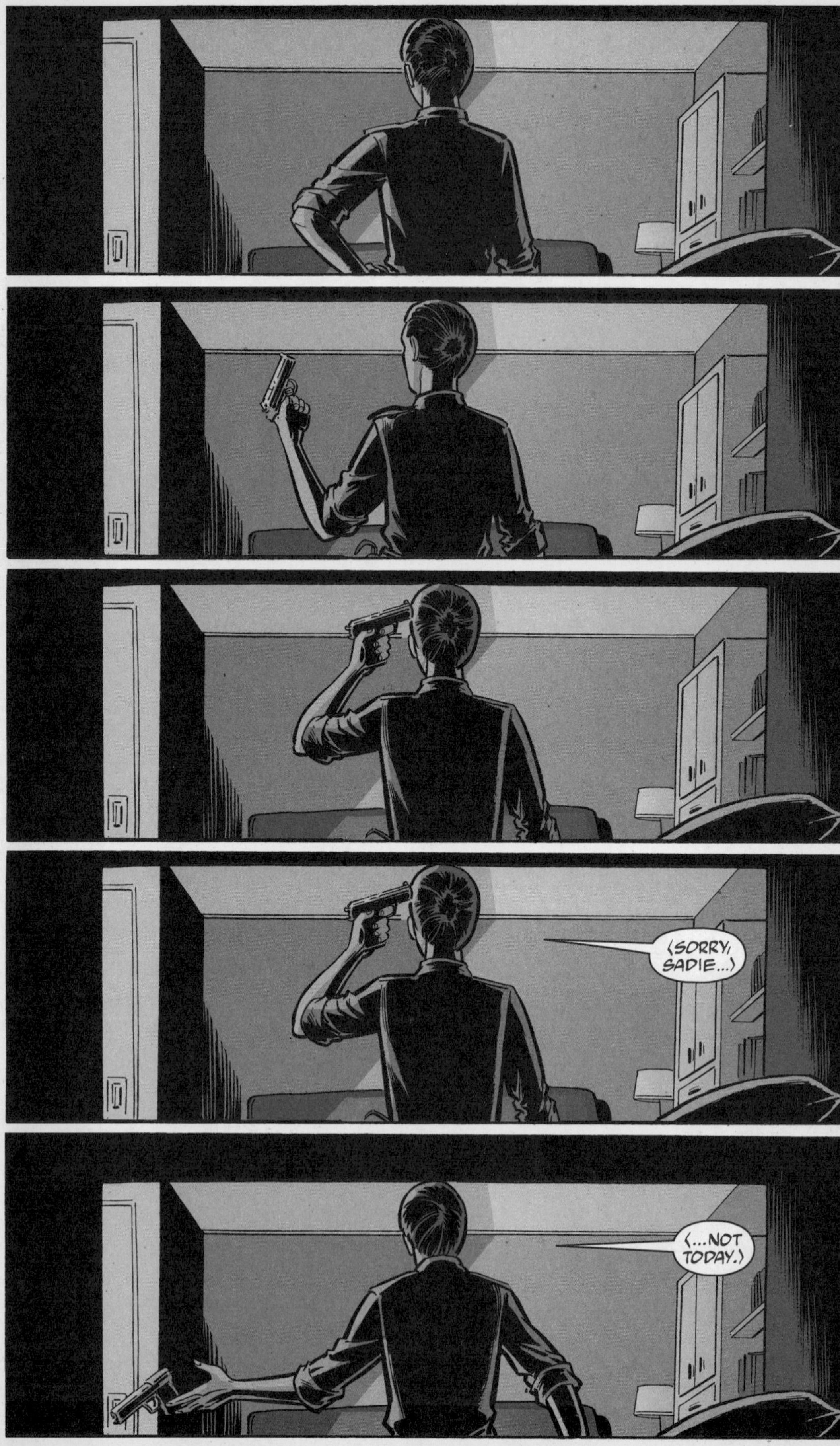
‹SORRY, SADIE...›
‹...NOT TODAY.›

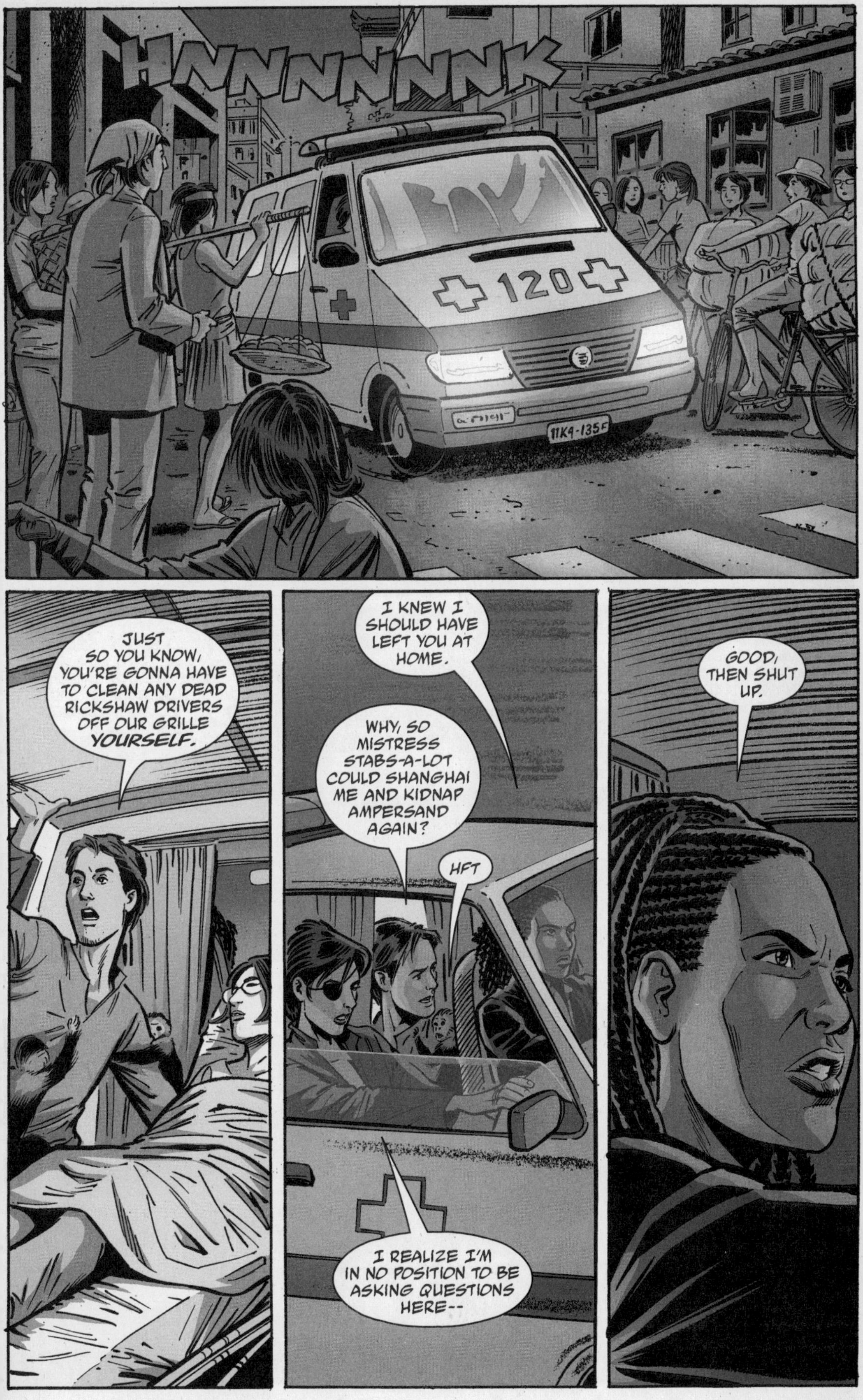
HNNNNNNK
JUST SO YOU KNOW, YOU'RE GONNA HAVE TO CLEAN ANY DEAD RICKSHAW DRIVERS OFF OUR GRILLE YOURSELF.
I KNEW I SHOULD HAVE LEFT YOU AT HOME.
WHY, SO MISTRESS STABS-A-LOT COULD SHANGHAI ME AND KIDNAP AMPERSAND AGAIN?
HFT
I REALIZE I'M IN NO POSITION TO BE ASKING QUESTIONS HERE--
GOOD, THEN SHUT UP.

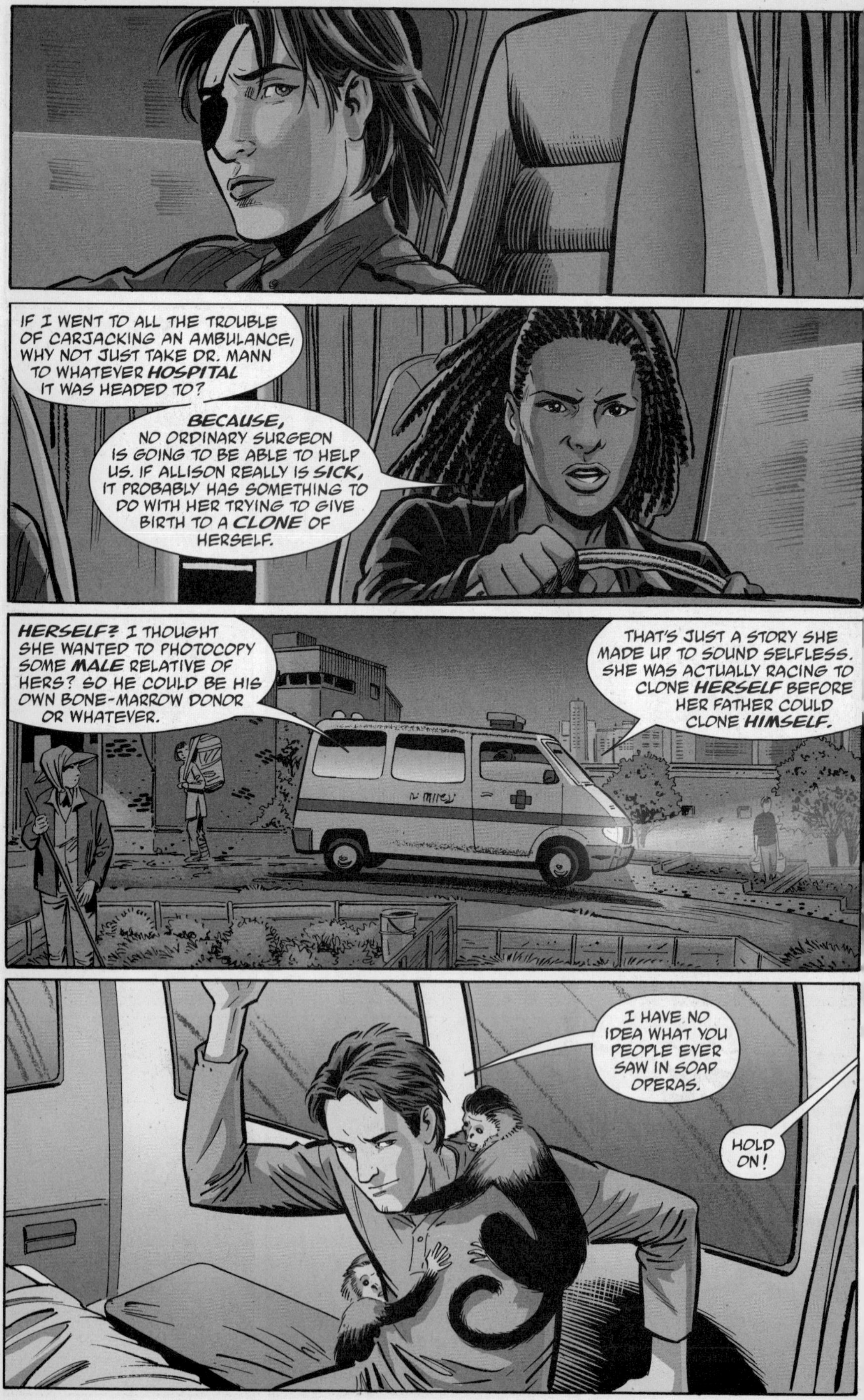
IF I WENT TO ALL THE TROUBLE OF CARJACKING AN AMBULANCE, WHY NOT JUST TAKE DR. MANN TO WHATEVER HOSPITAL IT WAS HEADED TO?
BECAUSE, NO ORDINARY SURGEON IS GOING TO BE ABLE TO HELP US. IF ALLISON REALLY IS SICK, IT PROBABLY HAS SOMETHING TO DO WITH HER TRYING TO GIVE BIRTH TO A CLONE OF HERSELF.
HERSELF? I THOUGHT SHE WANTED TO PHOTOCOPY SOME MALE RELATIVE OF HERS? SO HE COULD BE HIS OWN BONE-MARROW DONOR OR WHATEVER.
THAT'S JUST A STORY SHE MADE UP TO SOUND SELFLESS. SHE WAS ACTUALLY RACING TO CLONE HERSELF BEFORE HER FATHER COULD CLONE HIMSELF.
I HAVE NO IDEA WHAT YOU PEOPLE EVER SAW IN SOAP OPERAS.
HOLD ON!

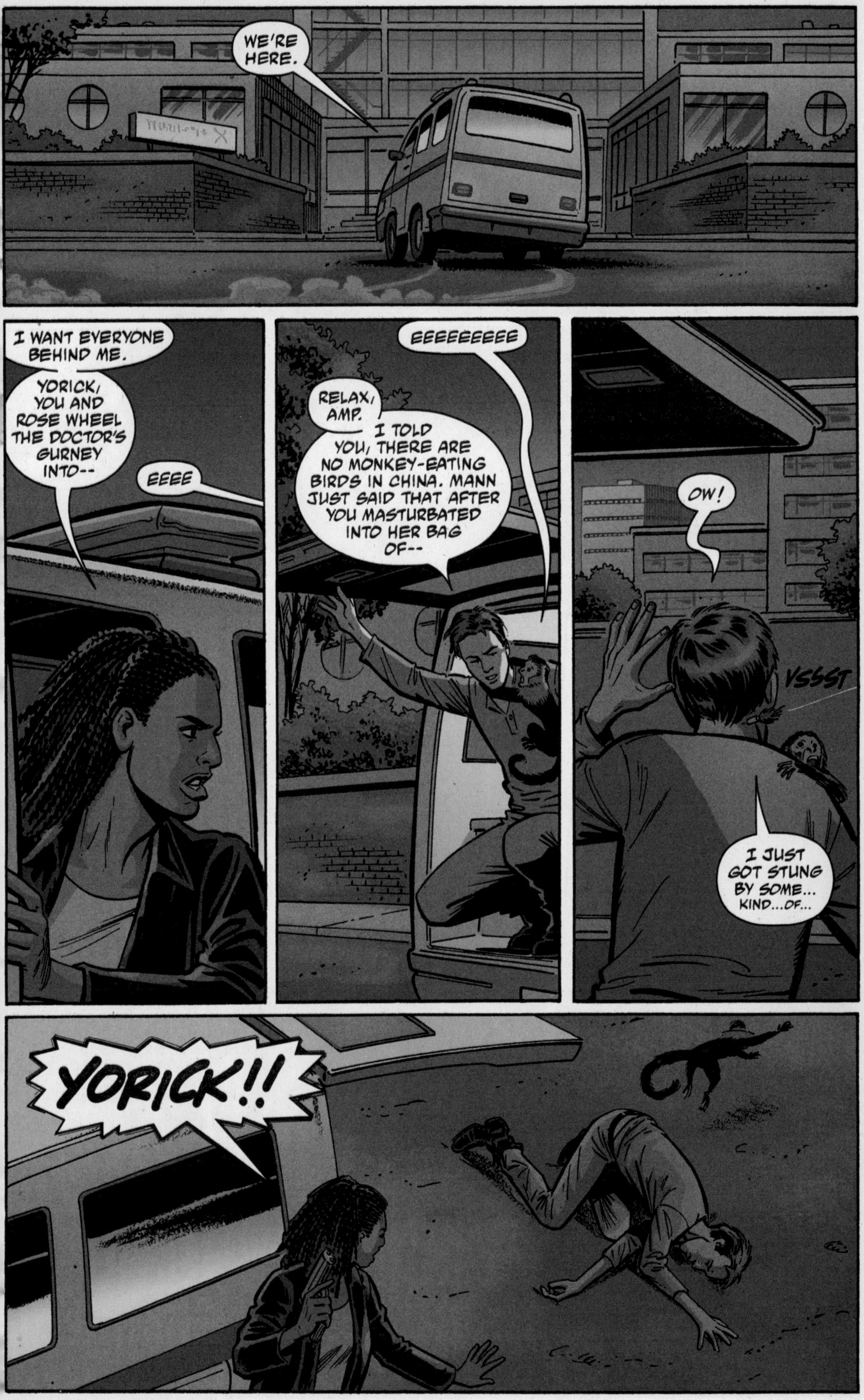
WE'RE HERE.
I WANT EVERYONE BEHIND ME.
YORICK, YOU AND ROSE WHEEL THE DOCTOR'S GURNEY INTO--
EEEE
EEEEEEEEE
RELAX, AMP.
I TOLD YOU, THERE ARE NO MONKEY-EATING BIRDS IN CHINA. MANN JUST SAID THAT AFTER YOU MASTURBATED INTO HER BAG OF--
OW!
VSSST
I JUST GOT STUNG BY SOME... KIND...OF...
YORICK!!

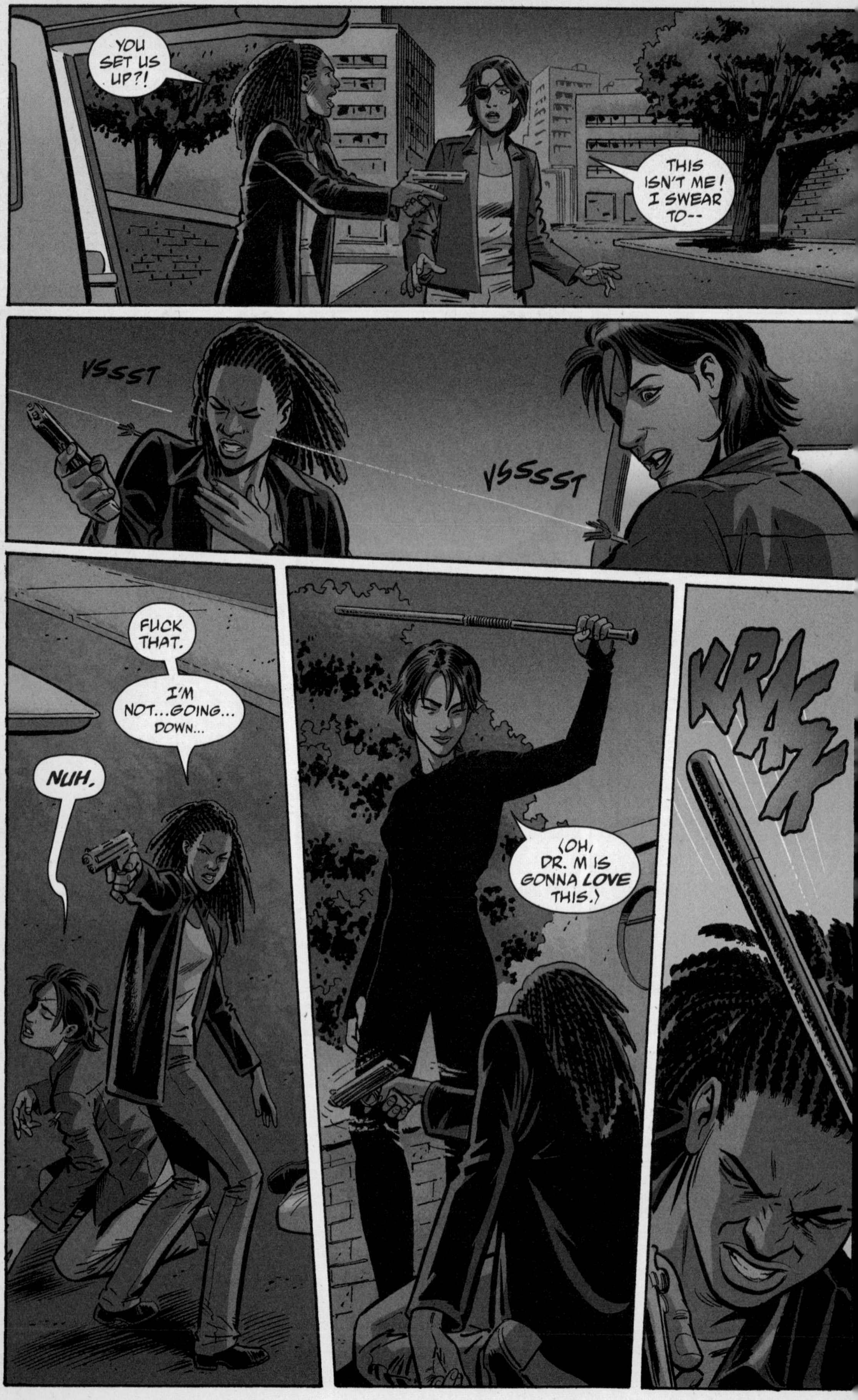
YOU SET US UP?!
THIS ISN'T ME! I SWEAR TO--
VSSST
VSSSST
FUCK THAT.
I'M NOT...GOING... DOWN...
NUH.
(OH, DR. M IS GONNA LOVE THIS.)
KRAK

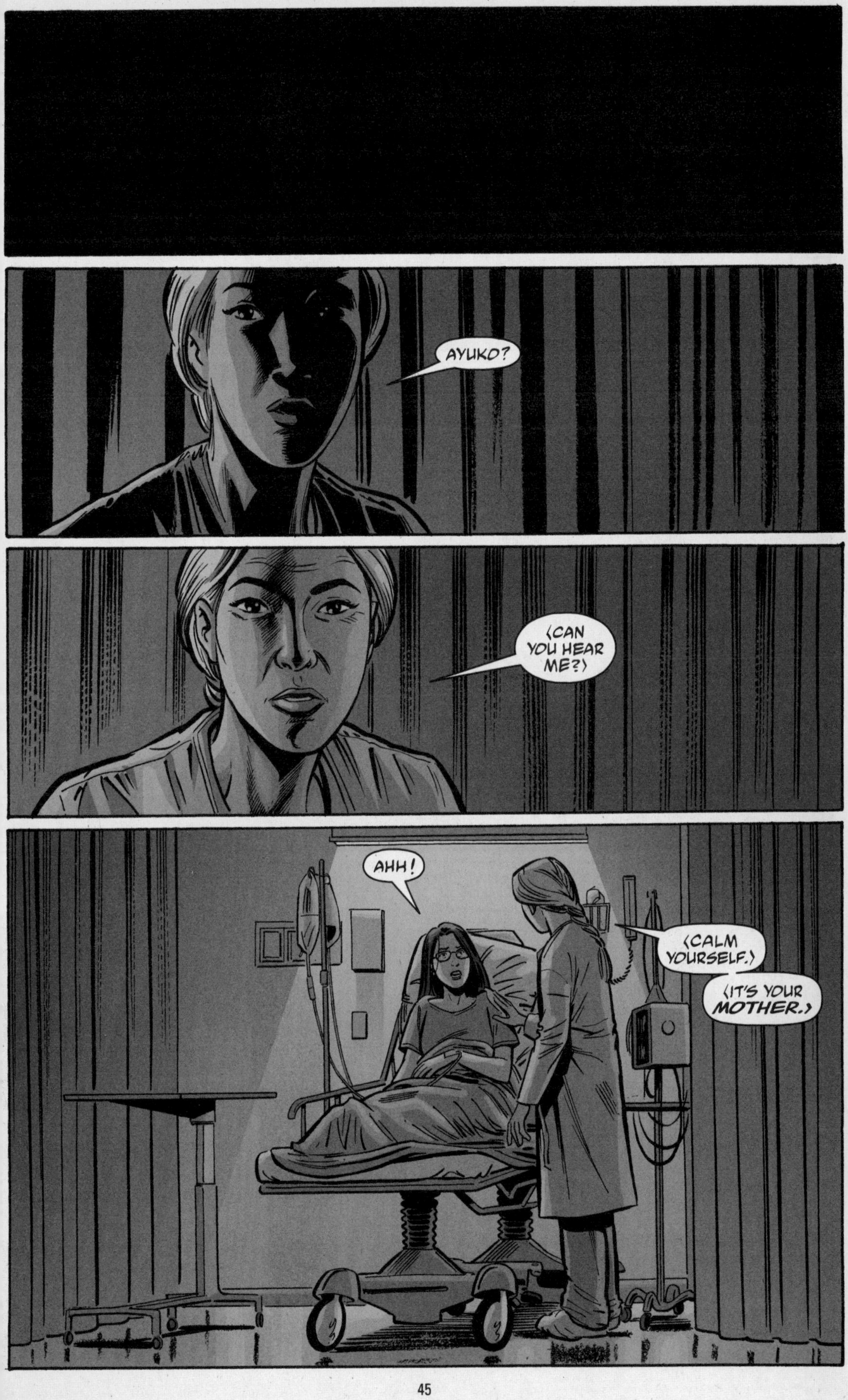
AYUKO?
⟨CAN YOU HEAR ME?⟩
AHH!
⟨CALM YOURSELF.⟩
⟨IT'S YOUR *MOTHER.*⟩

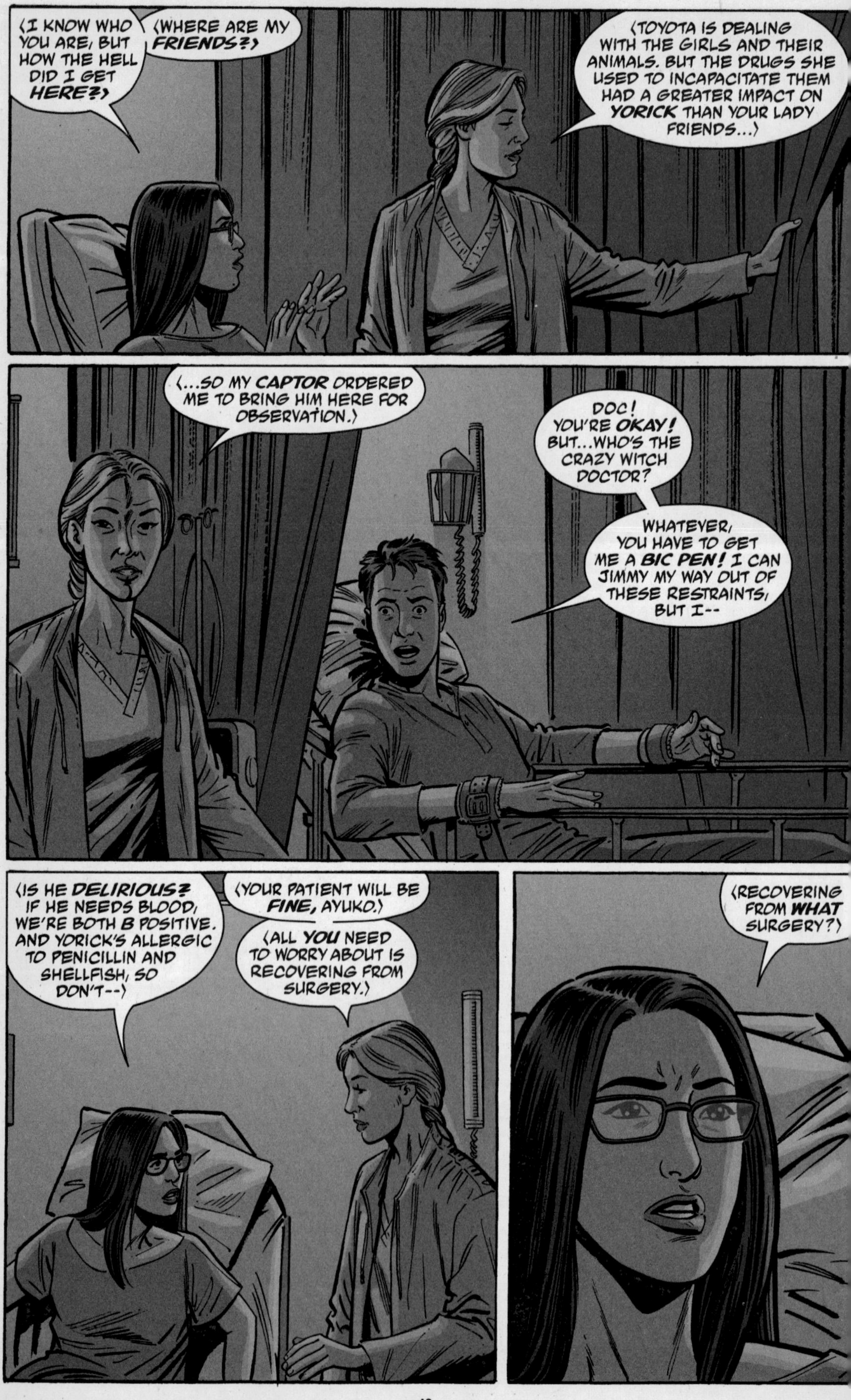
⟨I KNOW WHO YOU ARE, BUT HOW THE HELL DID I GET HERE?⟩
⟨WHERE ARE MY FRIENDS?⟩
⟨TOYOTA IS DEALING WITH THE GIRLS AND THEIR ANIMALS. BUT THE DRUGS SHE USED TO INCAPACITATE THEM HAD A GREATER IMPACT ON YORICK THAN YOUR LADY FRIENDS...⟩
⟨...SO MY CAPTOR ORDERED ME TO BRING HIM HERE FOR OBSERVATION.⟩
DOC! YOU'RE OKAY! BUT...WHO'S THE CRAZY WITCH DOCTOR?
WHATEVER, YOU HAVE TO GET ME A BIC PEN! I CAN JIMMY MY WAY OUT OF THESE RESTRAINTS, BUT I--
⟨IS HE DELIRIOUS? IF HE NEEDS BLOOD, WE'RE BOTH B POSITIVE. AND YORICK'S ALLERGIC TO PENICILLIN AND SHELLFISH, SO DON'T--⟩
⟨YOUR PATIENT WILL BE FINE, AYUKO.⟩
⟨ALL YOU NEED TO WORRY ABOUT IS RECOVERING FROM SURGERY.⟩
⟨RECOVERING FROM WHAT SURGERY?⟩

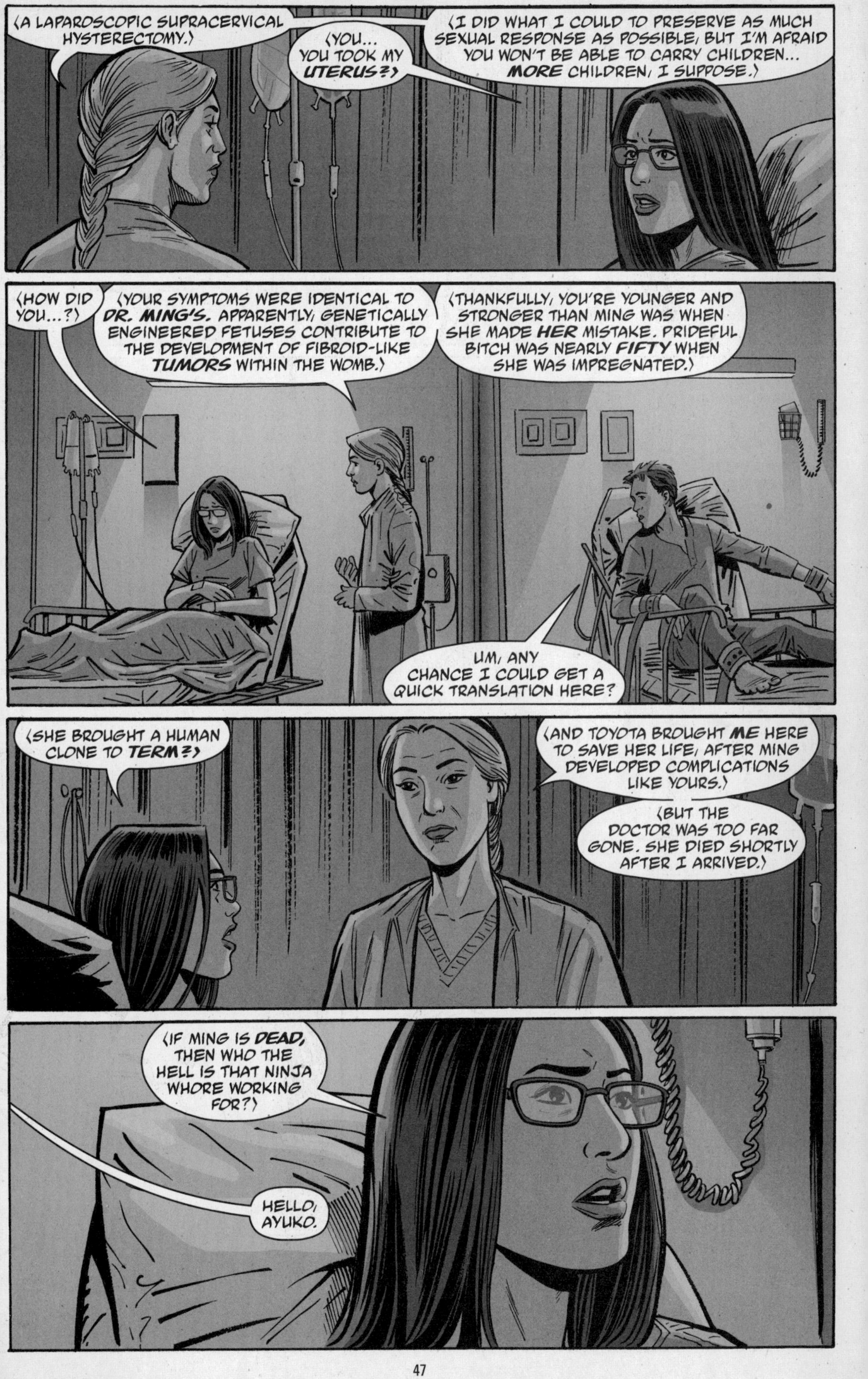
<A LAPAROSCOPIC SUPRACERVICAL HYSTERECTOMY.>
<YOU... YOU TOOK MY UTERUS?!>
<I DID WHAT I COULD TO PRESERVE AS MUCH SEXUAL RESPONSE AS POSSIBLE, BUT I'M AFRAID YOU WON'T BE ABLE TO CARRY CHILDREN... MORE CHILDREN, I SUPPOSE.>
<HOW DID YOU...?>
<YOUR SYMPTOMS WERE IDENTICAL TO DR. MING'S. APPARENTLY, GENETICALLY ENGINEERED FETUSES CONTRIBUTE TO THE DEVELOPMENT OF FIBROID-LIKE TUMORS WITHIN THE WOMB.>
<THANKFULLY, YOU'RE YOUNGER AND STRONGER THAN MING WAS WHEN SHE MADE HER MISTAKE. PRIDEFUL BITCH WAS NEARLY FIFTY WHEN SHE WAS IMPREGNATED.>
UM, ANY CHANCE I COULD GET A QUICK TRANSLATION HERE?
<SHE BROUGHT A HUMAN CLONE TO TERM?!>
<AND TOYOTA BROUGHT ME HERE TO SAVE HER LIFE, AFTER MING DEVELOPED COMPLICATIONS LIKE YOURS.>
<BUT THE DOCTOR WAS TOO FAR GONE. SHE DIED SHORTLY AFTER I ARRIVED.>
<IF MING IS DEAD, THEN WHO THE HELL IS THAT NINJA WHORE WORKING FOR?>
HELLO, AYUKO.

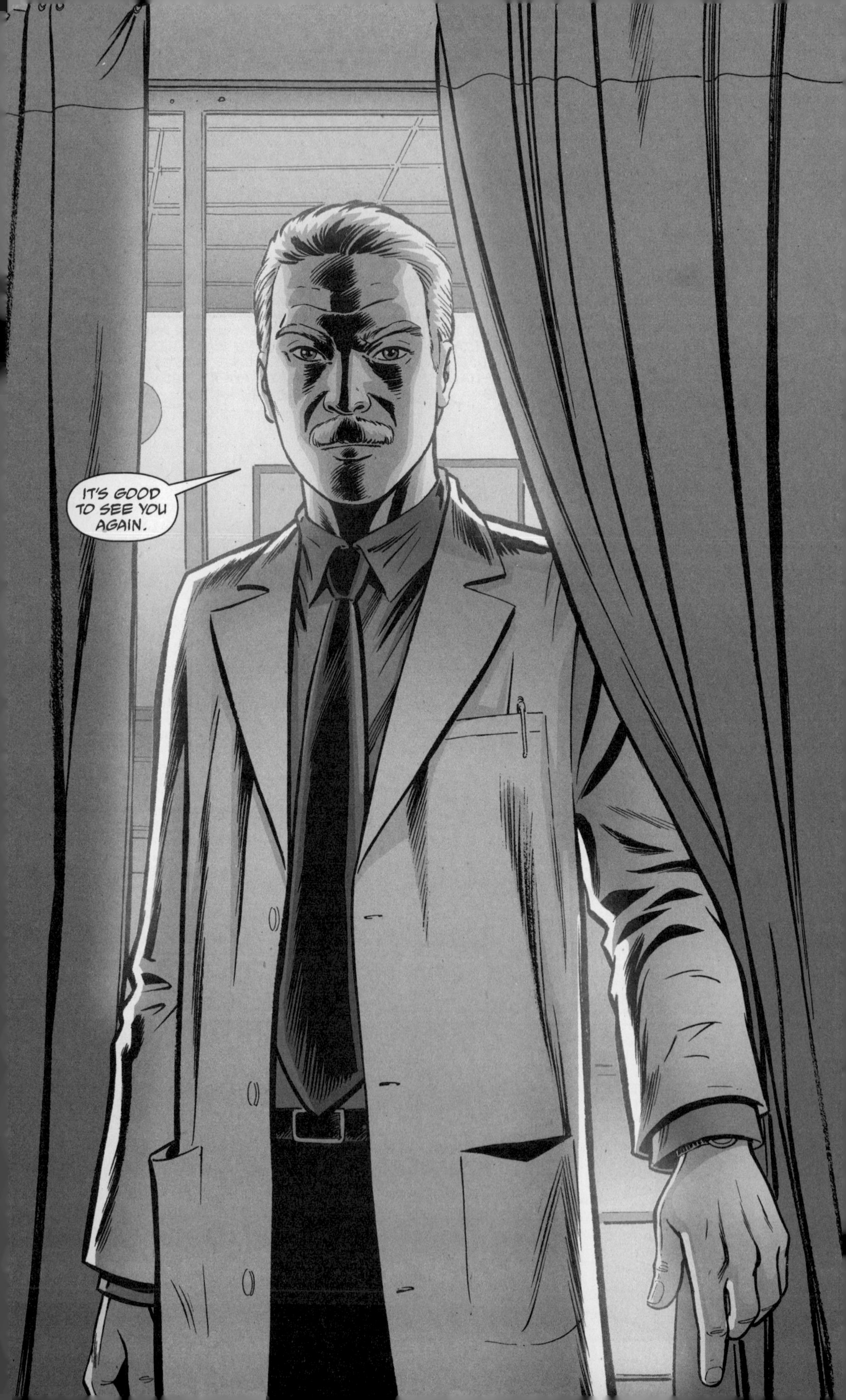
IT'S GOOD TO SEE YOU AGAIN.

OH, MAN. NOT ANOTHER FUCKING ROBOT.

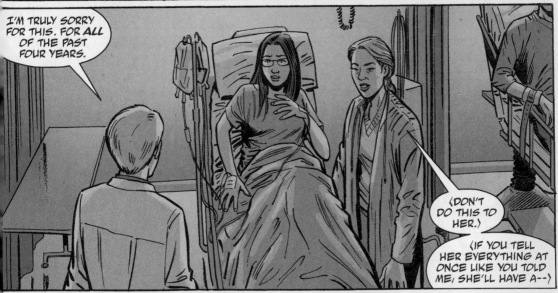

I'M TRULY SORRY FOR THIS. FOR ALL OF THE PAST FOUR YEARS.

⟨DON'T DO THIS TO HER.⟩

⟨IF YOU TELL HER EVERYTHING AT ONCE LIKE YOU TOLD ME, SHE'LL HAVE A--⟩

⟨I'LL SPEAK TO OUR DAUGHTER AS I PLEASE.⟩

BACK UP, IS THIS...?

I MEAN, IS HE REALLY...?

HOW ARE YOU STILL ALIVE, DAD?

THE SAME WAY THAT MR. BROWN IS, THOUGH THIS ISN'T ABOUT HIM OR HIS ANIMAL.

IT'S ABOUT THE PEOPLE RESPONSIBLE FOR THE PLAGUE...NAMELY ME AND MY OFFSPRING.

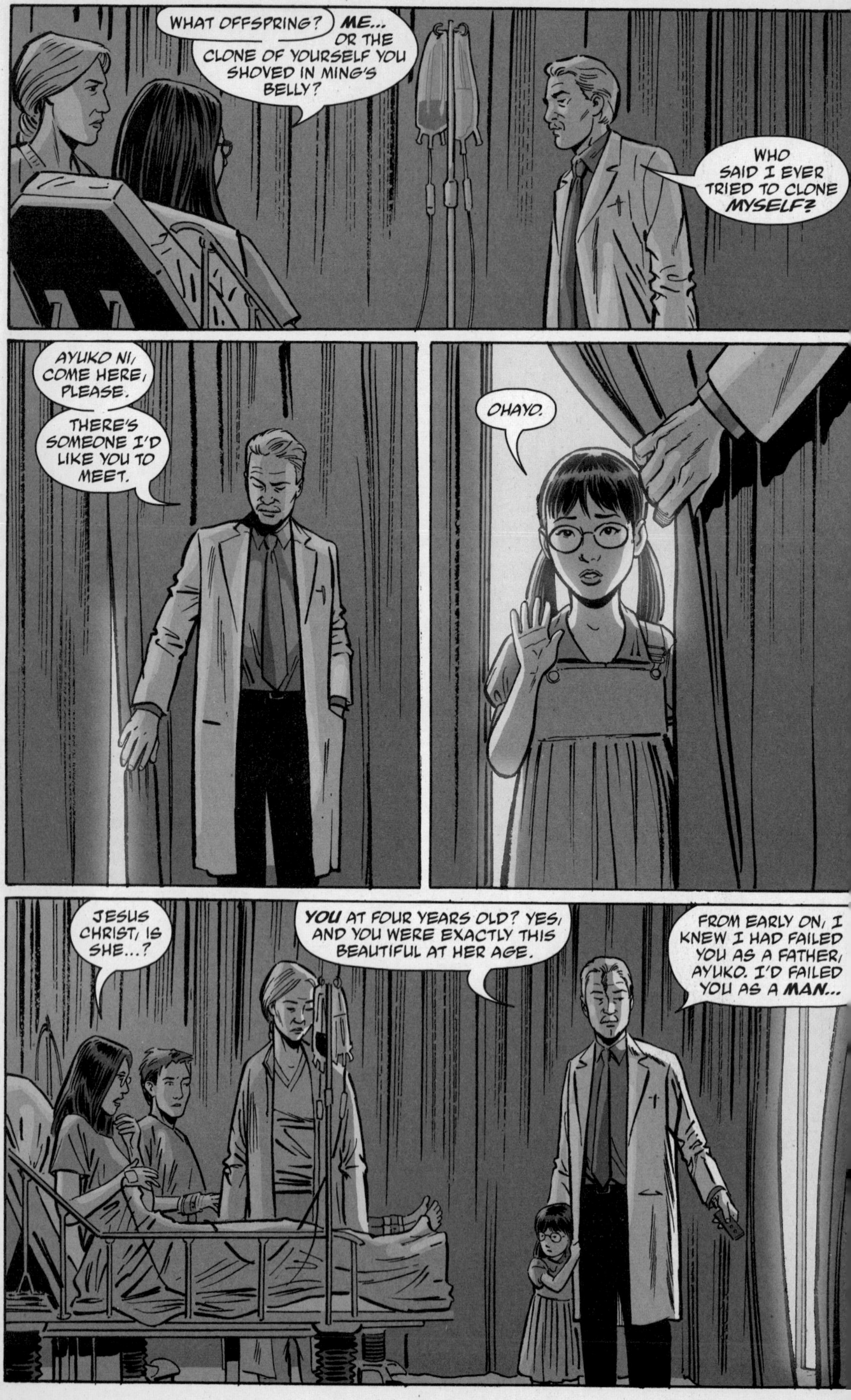
WHAT OFFSPRING?
ME... OR THE CLONE OF YOURSELF YOU SHOVED IN MING'S BELLY?
WHO SAID I EVER TRIED TO CLONE MYSELF?
AYUKO NI, COME HERE, PLEASE.
THERE'S SOMEONE I'D LIKE YOU TO MEET.
OHAYO.
JESUS CHRIST, IS SHE...?
YOU AT FOUR YEARS OLD? YES, AND YOU WERE EXACTLY THIS BEAUTIFUL AT HER AGE.
FROM EARLY ON, I KNEW I HAD FAILED YOU AS A FATHER, AYUKO. I'D FAILED YOU AS A MAN...

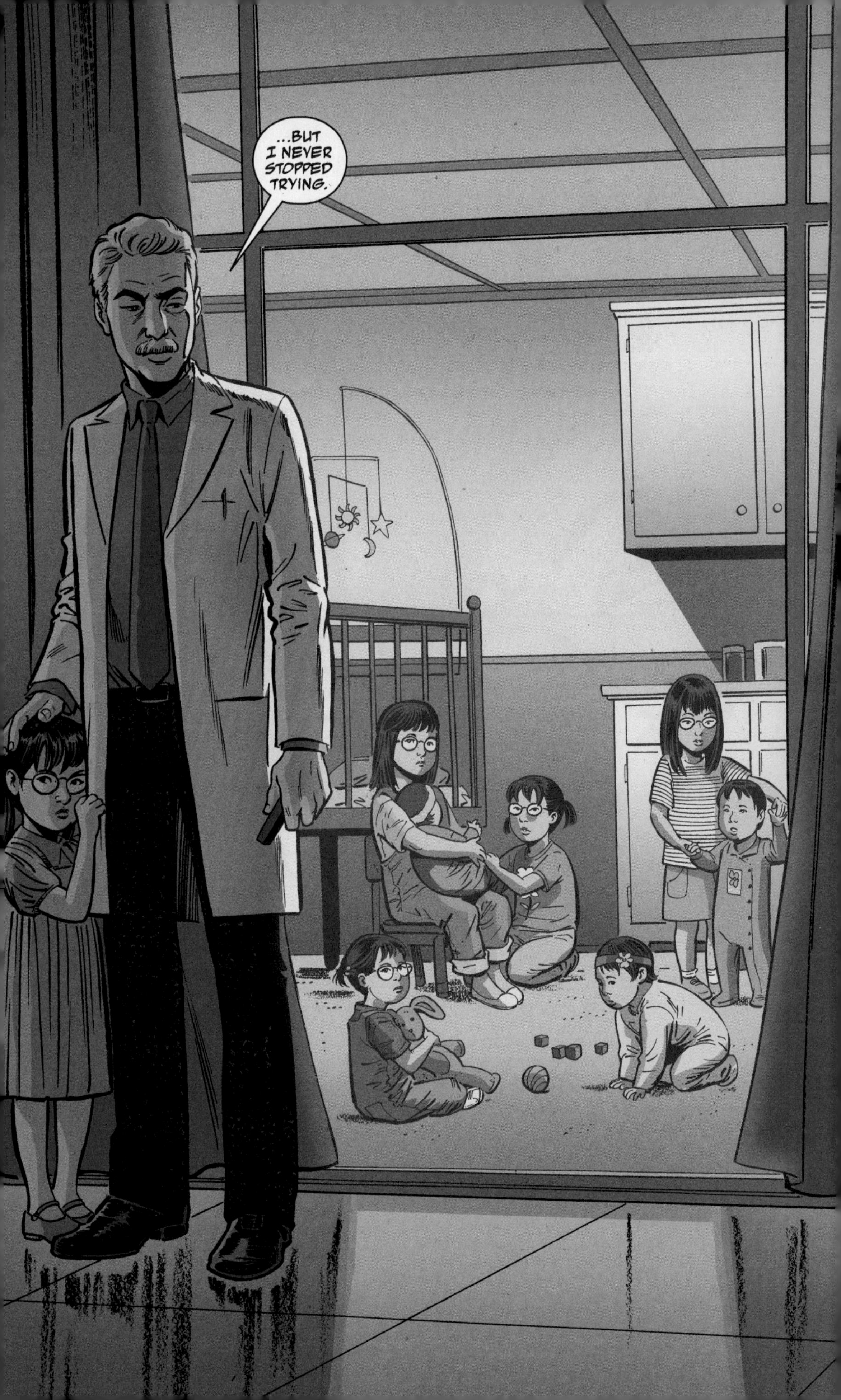
...BUT I NEVER STOPPED TRYING.

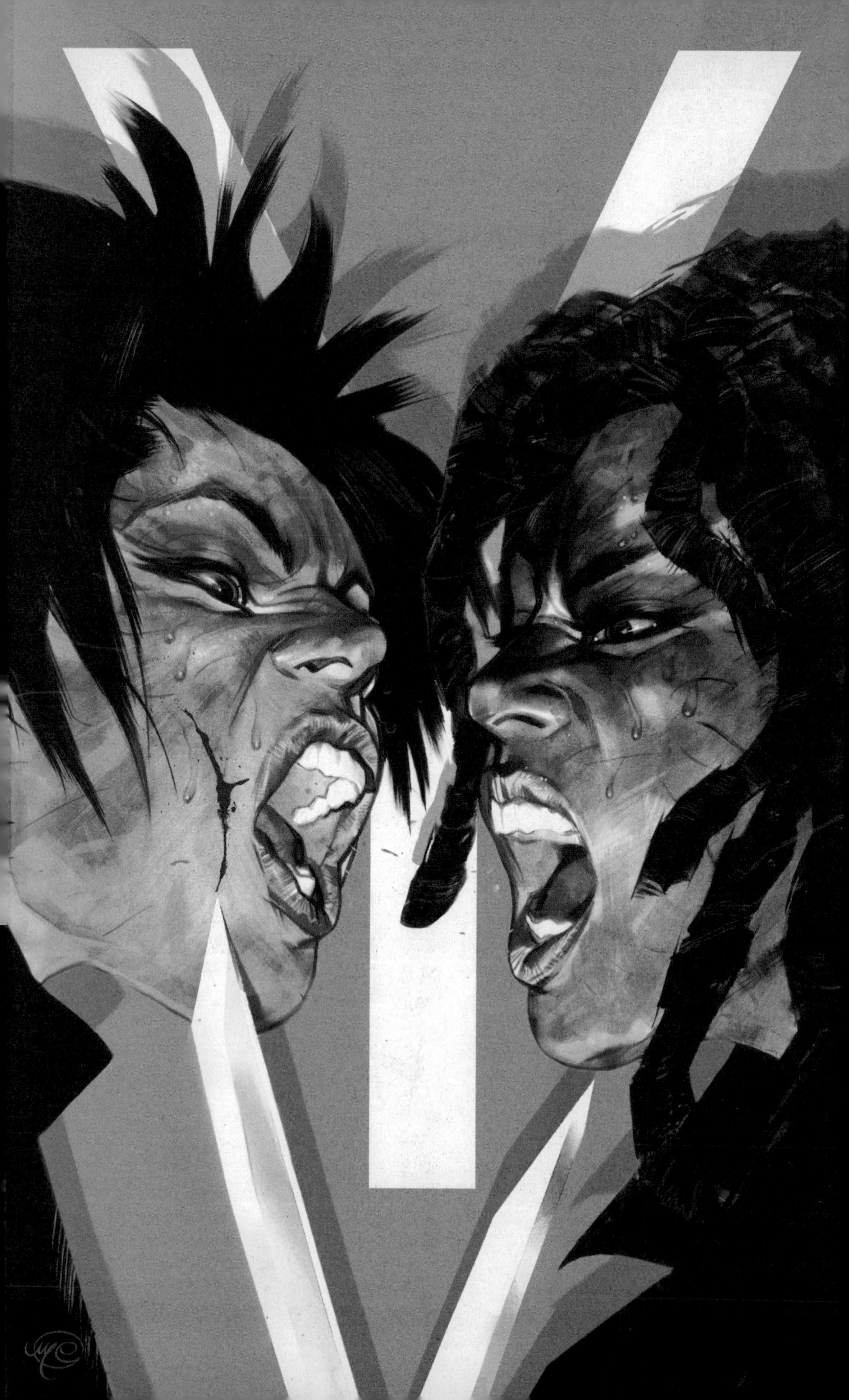

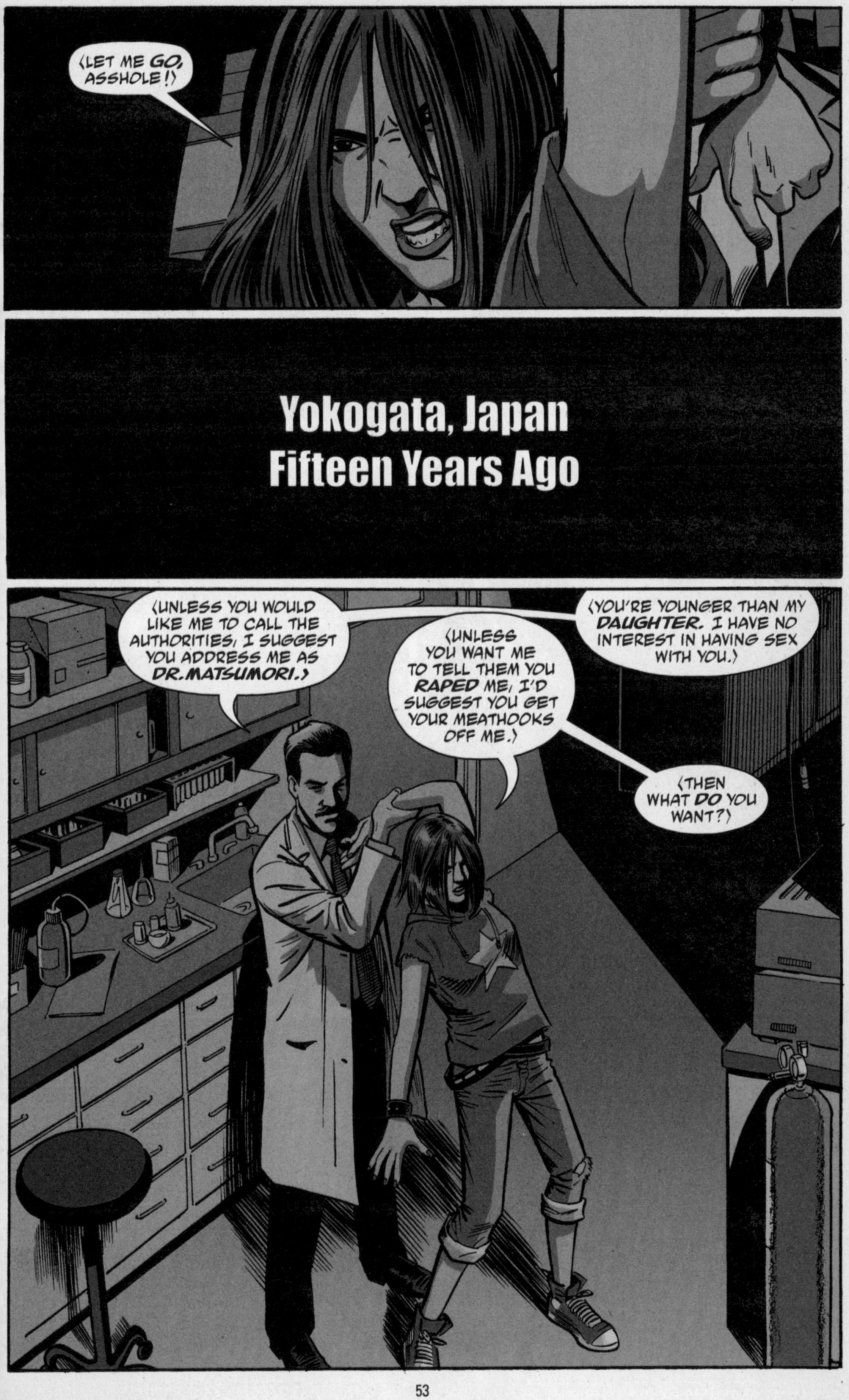
⟨LET ME GO, ASSHOLE!⟩
Yokogata, Japan
Fifteen Years Ago
⟨UNLESS YOU WOULD LIKE ME TO CALL THE AUTHORITIES, I SUGGEST YOU ADDRESS ME AS DR.MATSUMORI.⟩
⟨UNLESS YOU WANT ME TO TELL THEM YOU RAPED ME, I'D SUGGEST YOU GET YOUR MEATHOOKS OFF ME.⟩
⟨YOU'RE YOUNGER THAN MY DAUGHTER. I HAVE NO INTEREST IN HAVING SEX WITH YOU.⟩
⟨THEN WHAT DO YOU WANT?⟩

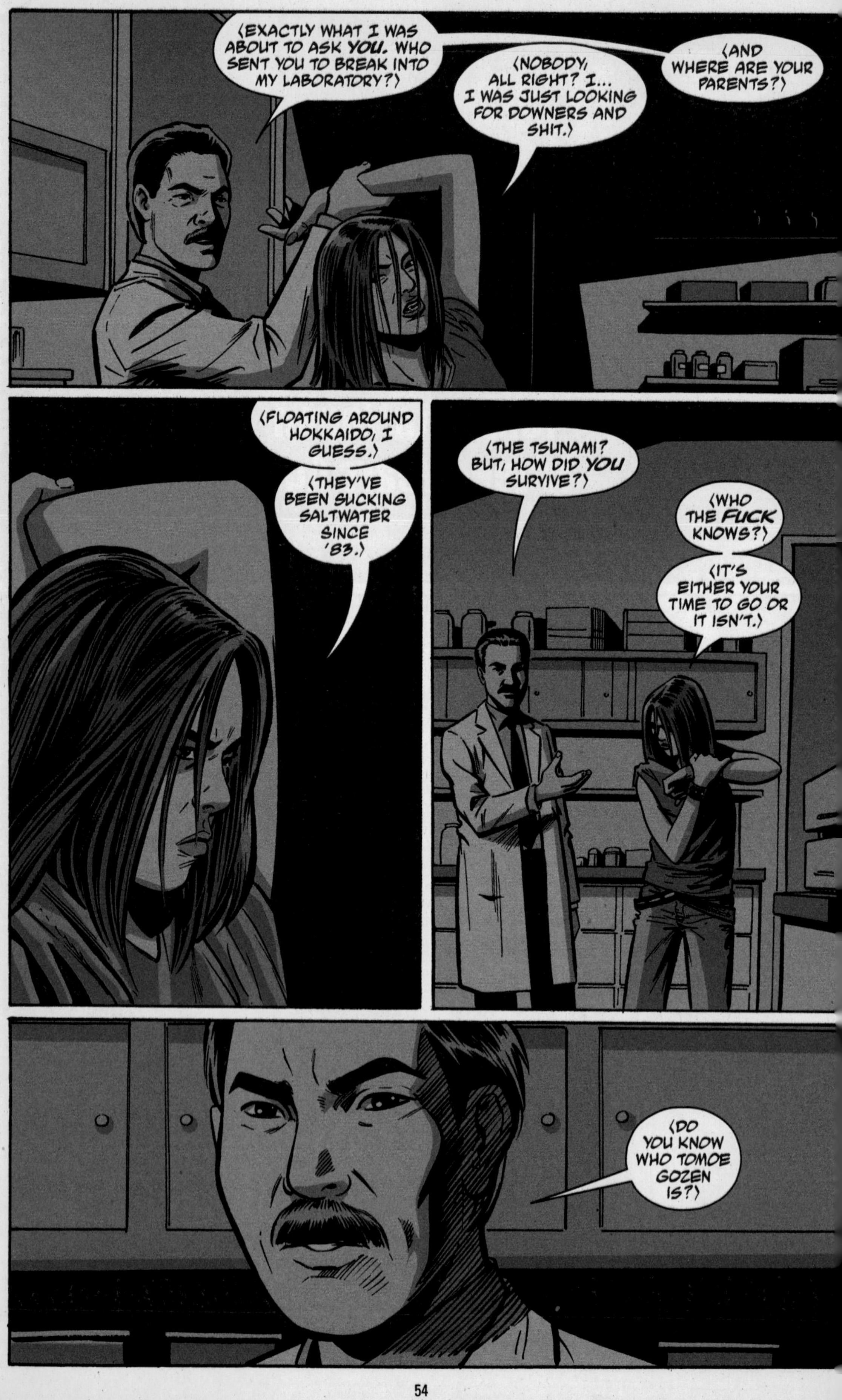
⟨EXACTLY WHAT I WAS ABOUT TO ASK YOU. WHO SENT YOU TO BREAK INTO MY LABORATORY?⟩
⟨NOBODY, ALL RIGHT? I... I WAS JUST LOOKING FOR DOWNERS AND SHIT.⟩
⟨AND WHERE ARE YOUR PARENTS?⟩
⟨FLOATING AROUND HOKKAIDO, I GUESS.⟩
⟨THEY'VE BEEN SUCKING SALTWATER SINCE '83.⟩
⟨THE TSUNAMI? BUT, HOW DID YOU SURVIVE?⟩
⟨WHO THE FUCK KNOWS?⟩
⟨IT'S EITHER YOUR TIME TO GO OR IT ISN'T.⟩
⟨DO YOU KNOW WHO TOMOE GOZEN IS?⟩

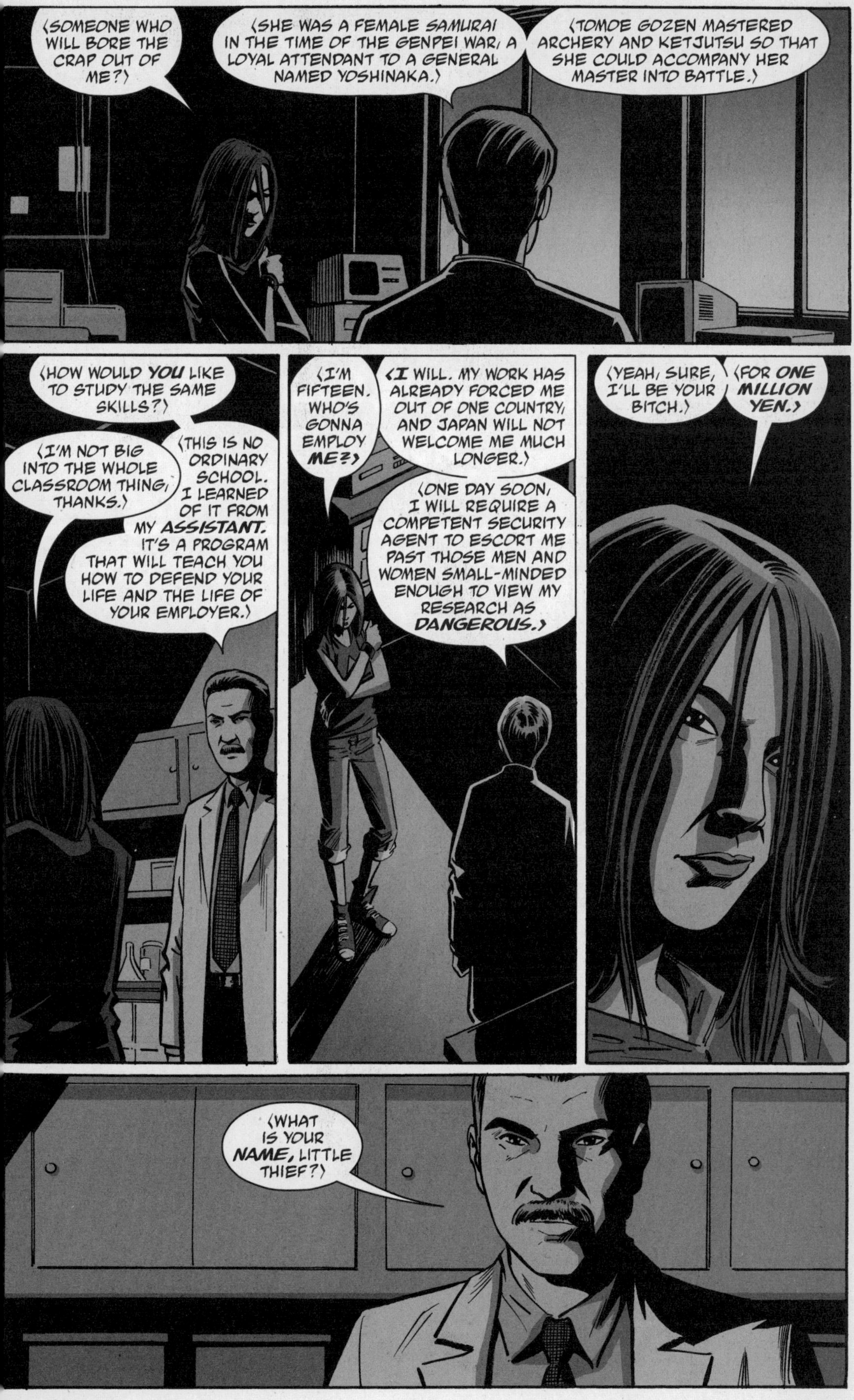
<SOMEONE WHO WILL BORE THE CRAP OUT OF ME?>
<SHE WAS A FEMALE SAMURAI IN THE TIME OF THE GENPEI WAR, A LOYAL ATTENDANT TO A GENERAL NAMED YOSHINAKA.>
<TOMOE GOZEN MASTERED ARCHERY AND KETJUTSU SO THAT SHE COULD ACCOMPANY HER MASTER INTO BATTLE.>
<HOW WOULD YOU LIKE TO STUDY THE SAME SKILLS?>
<I'M NOT BIG INTO THE WHOLE CLASSROOM THING, THANKS.>
<THIS IS NO ORDINARY SCHOOL. I LEARNED OF IT FROM MY ASSISTANT. IT'S A PROGRAM THAT WILL TEACH YOU HOW TO DEFEND YOUR LIFE AND THE LIFE OF YOUR EMPLOYER.>
<I'M FIFTEEN. WHO'S GONNA EMPLOY ME?>
<I WILL. MY WORK HAS ALREADY FORCED ME OUT OF ONE COUNTRY, AND JAPAN WILL NOT WELCOME ME MUCH LONGER.>
<ONE DAY SOON, I WILL REQUIRE A COMPETENT SECURITY AGENT TO ESCORT ME PAST THOSE MEN AND WOMEN SMALL-MINDED ENOUGH TO VIEW MY RESEARCH AS DANGEROUS.>
<YEAH, SURE, I'LL BE YOUR BITCH.>
<FOR ONE MILLION YEN.>
<WHAT IS YOUR NAME, LITTLE THIEF?>

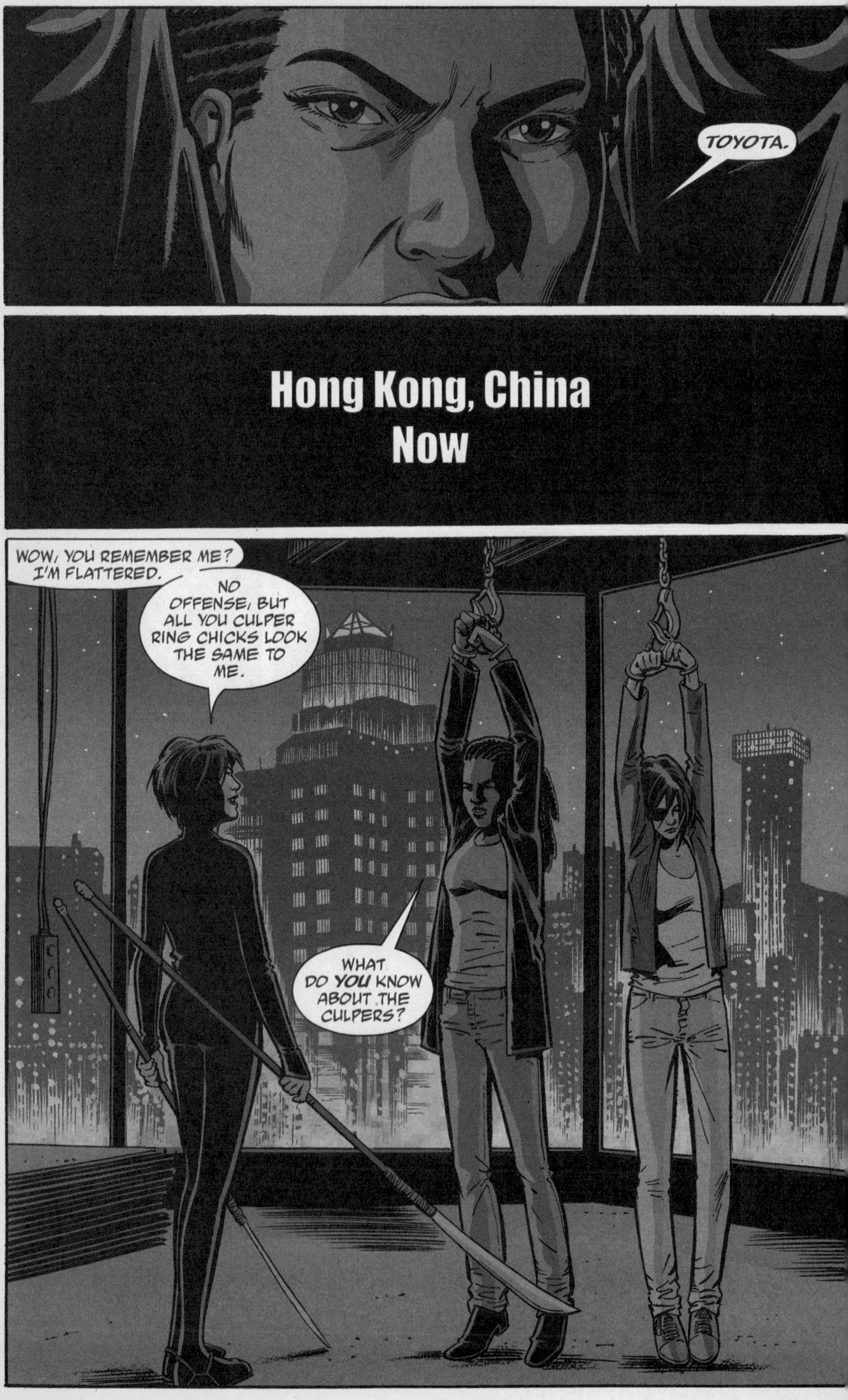
TOYOTA.
Hong Kong, China
Now
WOW, YOU REMEMBER ME? I'M FLATTERED.
NO OFFENSE, BUT ALL YOU CULPER RING CHICKS LOOK THE SAME TO ME.
WHAT DO YOU KNOW ABOUT THE CULPERS?

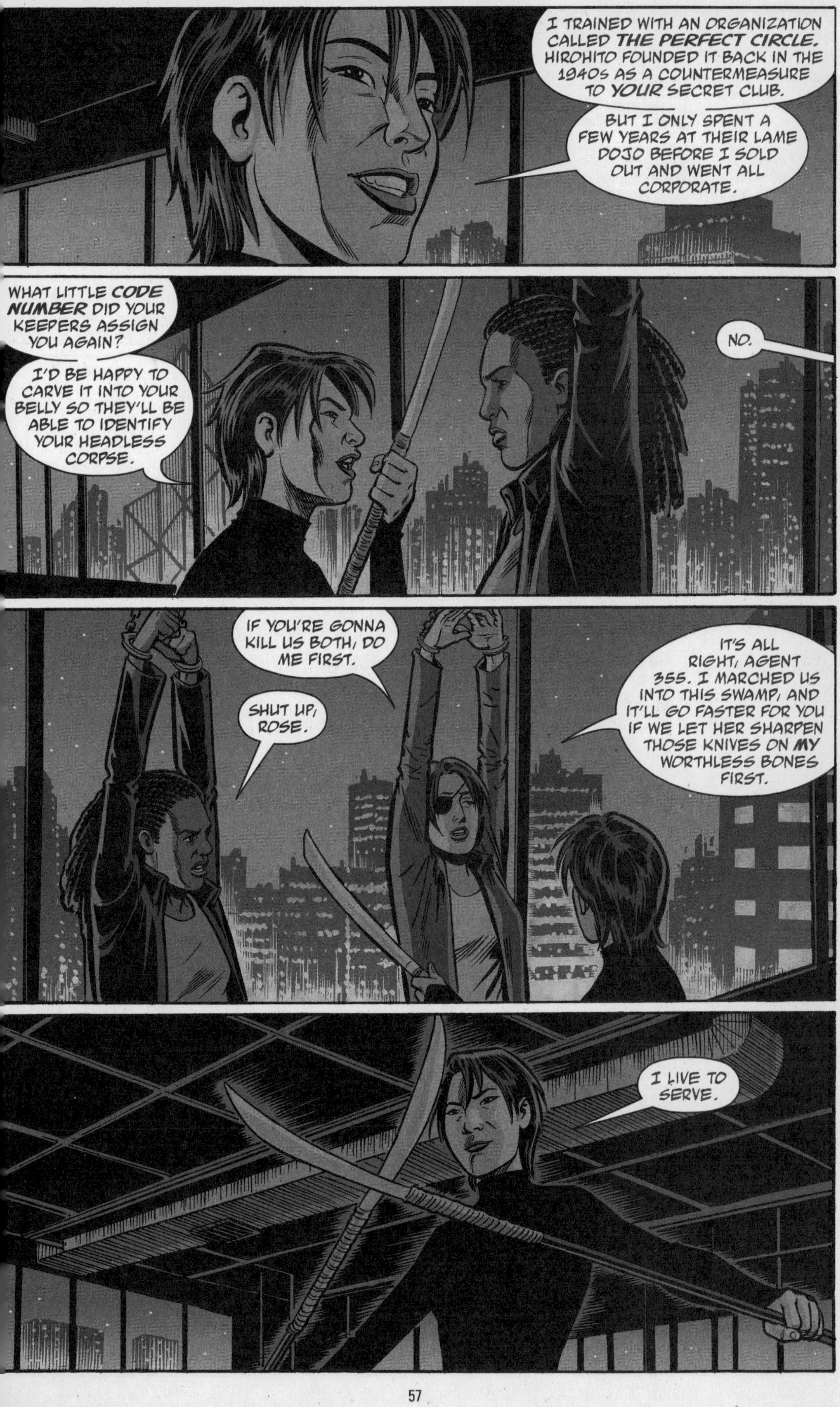

I TRAINED WITH AN ORGANIZATION CALLED THE PERFECT CIRCLE. HIROHITO FOUNDED IT BACK IN THE 1940s AS A COUNTERMEASURE TO YOUR SECRET CLUB.
BUT I ONLY SPENT A FEW YEARS AT THEIR LAME DOJO BEFORE I SOLD OUT AND WENT ALL CORPORATE.
WHAT LITTLE CODE NUMBER DID YOUR KEEPERS ASSIGN YOU AGAIN?
I'D BE HAPPY TO CARVE IT INTO YOUR BELLY SO THEY'LL BE ABLE TO IDENTIFY YOUR HEADLESS CORPSE.
NO.
IF YOU'RE GONNA KILL US BOTH, DO ME FIRST.
SHUT UP, ROSE.
IT'S ALL RIGHT, AGENT 355. I MARCHED US INTO THIS SWAMP, AND IT'LL GO FASTER FOR YOU IF WE LET HER SHARPEN THOSE KNIVES ON MY WORTHLESS BONES FIRST.
I LIVE TO SERVE.

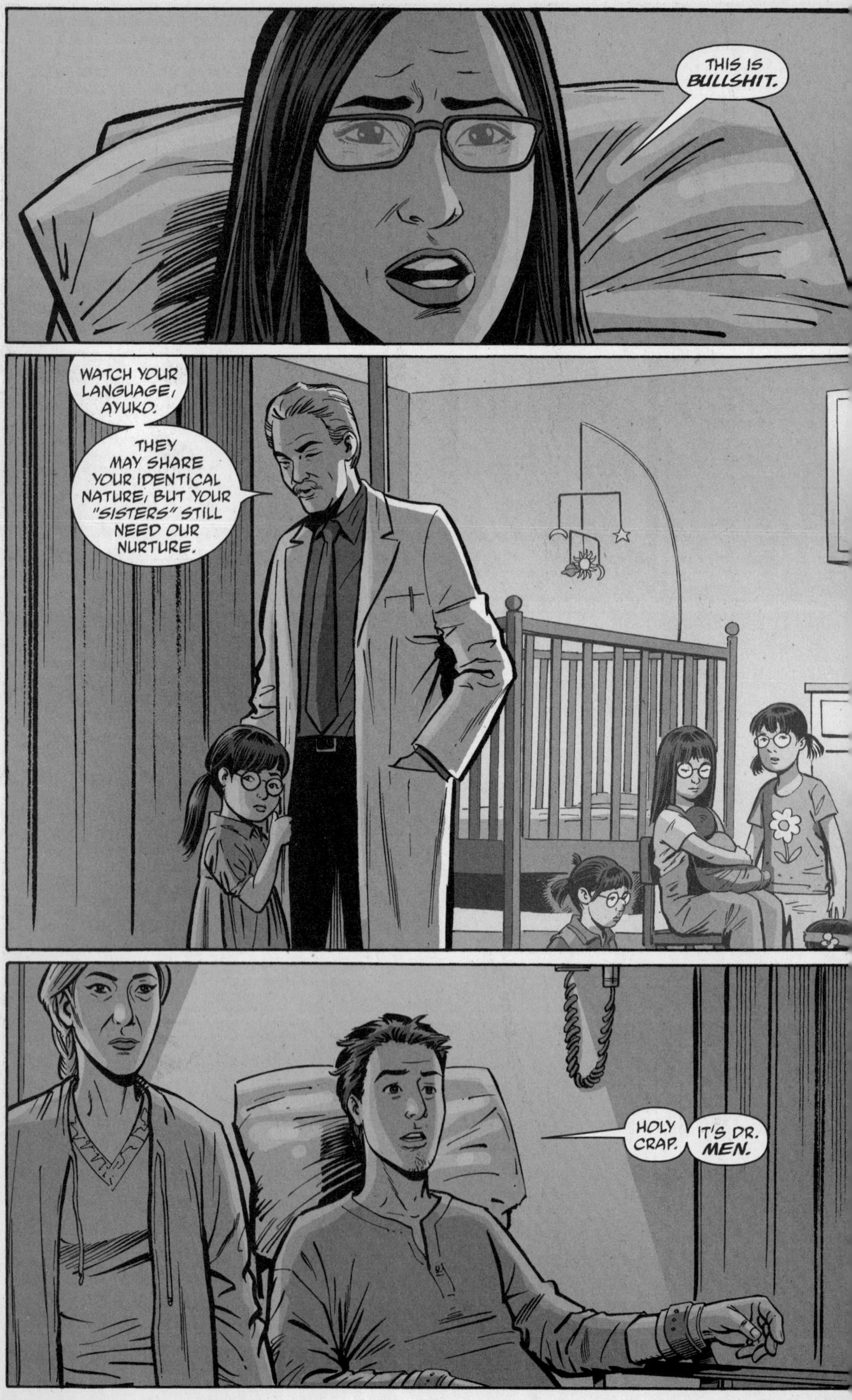
THIS IS BULLSHIT.
WATCH YOUR LANGUAGE, AYUKO.
THEY MAY SHARE YOUR IDENTICAL NATURE, BUT YOUR "SISTERS" STILL NEED OUR NURTURE.
HOLY CRAP.
IT'S DR. MEN.

BE SILENT, YORICK.

MY HUSBAND IS A VERY SICK MAN. HE--

⟨THAT'S ENOUGH.⟩

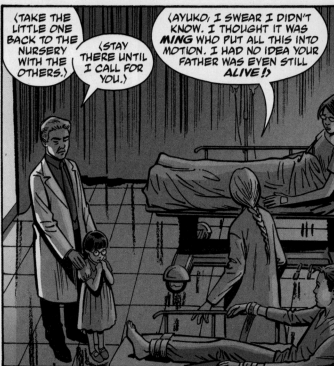

⟨TAKE THE LITTLE ONE BACK TO THE NURSERY WITH THE OTHERS.⟩

⟨STAY THERE UNTIL I CALL FOR YOU.⟩

⟨AYUKO, I SWEAR I DIDN'T KNOW. I THOUGHT IT WAS *MING* WHO PUT ALL THIS INTO MOTION. I HAD NO IDEA YOUR FATHER WAS EVEN STILL *ALIVE!*⟩

⟨GO.⟩ ⟨YOU'VE INTERFERED WITH MY RELATIONSHIPS LONG ENOUGH.⟩

I DON'T KNOW WHAT THE *FUCK* IS HAPPENING, BUT IF YOU DON'T TELL ME WHERE MY FRIENDS ARE, I'M GOING TO BUST OUT OF THESE RESTRAINTS AND KICK YOUR MUSTACHIOED *ASS.*

RIGHT AFTER I FIND MY STUPID *PEN...*

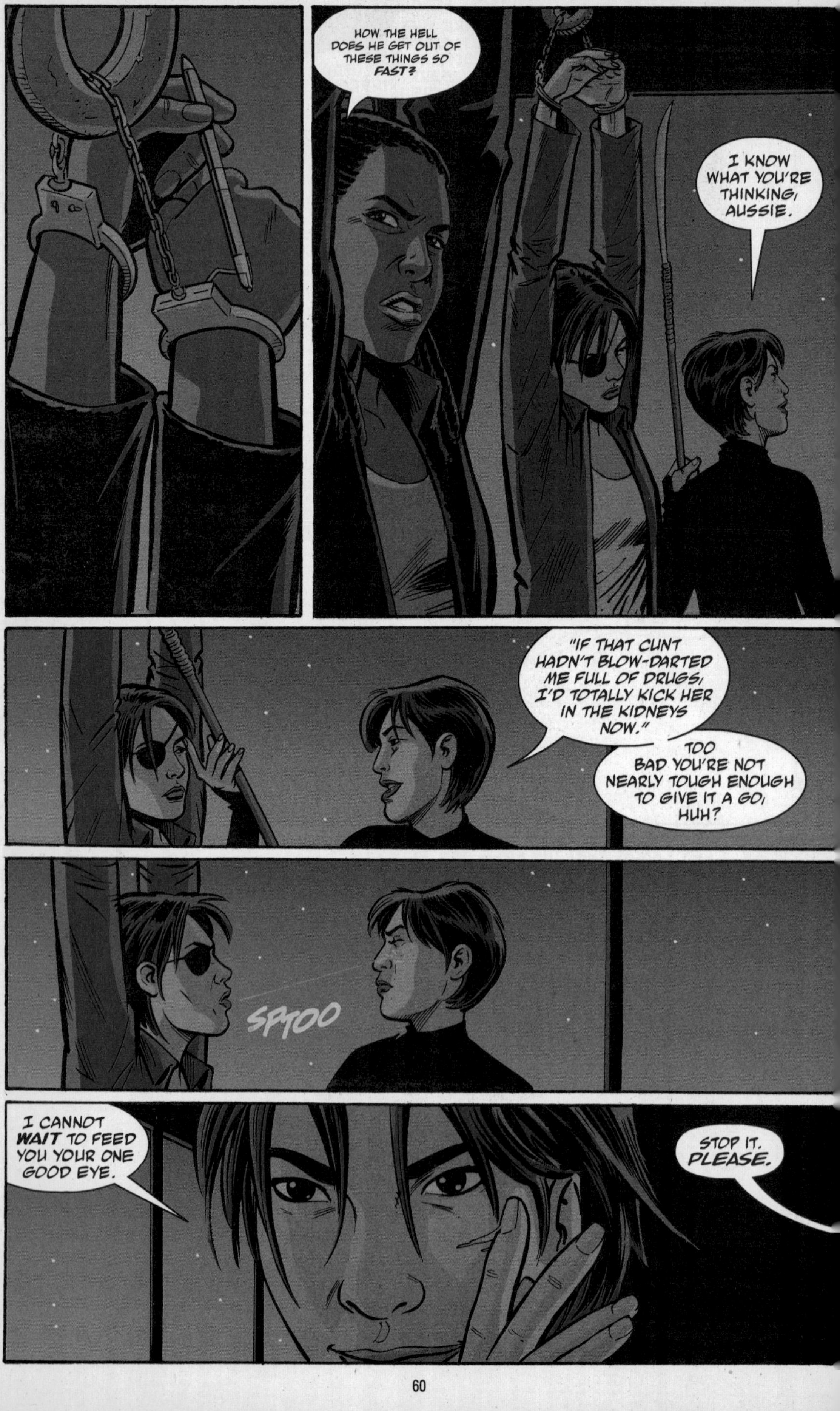
HOW THE HELL DOES HE GET OUT OF THESE THINGS SO FAST?
I KNOW WHAT YOU'RE THINKING, AUSSIE.
"IF THAT CUNT HADN'T BLOW-DARTED ME FULL OF DRUGS, I'D TOTALLY KICK HER IN THE KIDNEYS NOW."
TOO BAD YOU'RE NOT NEARLY TOUGH ENOUGH TO GIVE IT A GO, HUH?
SPTOO
I CANNOT WAIT TO FEED YOU YOUR ONE GOOD EYE.
STOP IT. PLEASE.

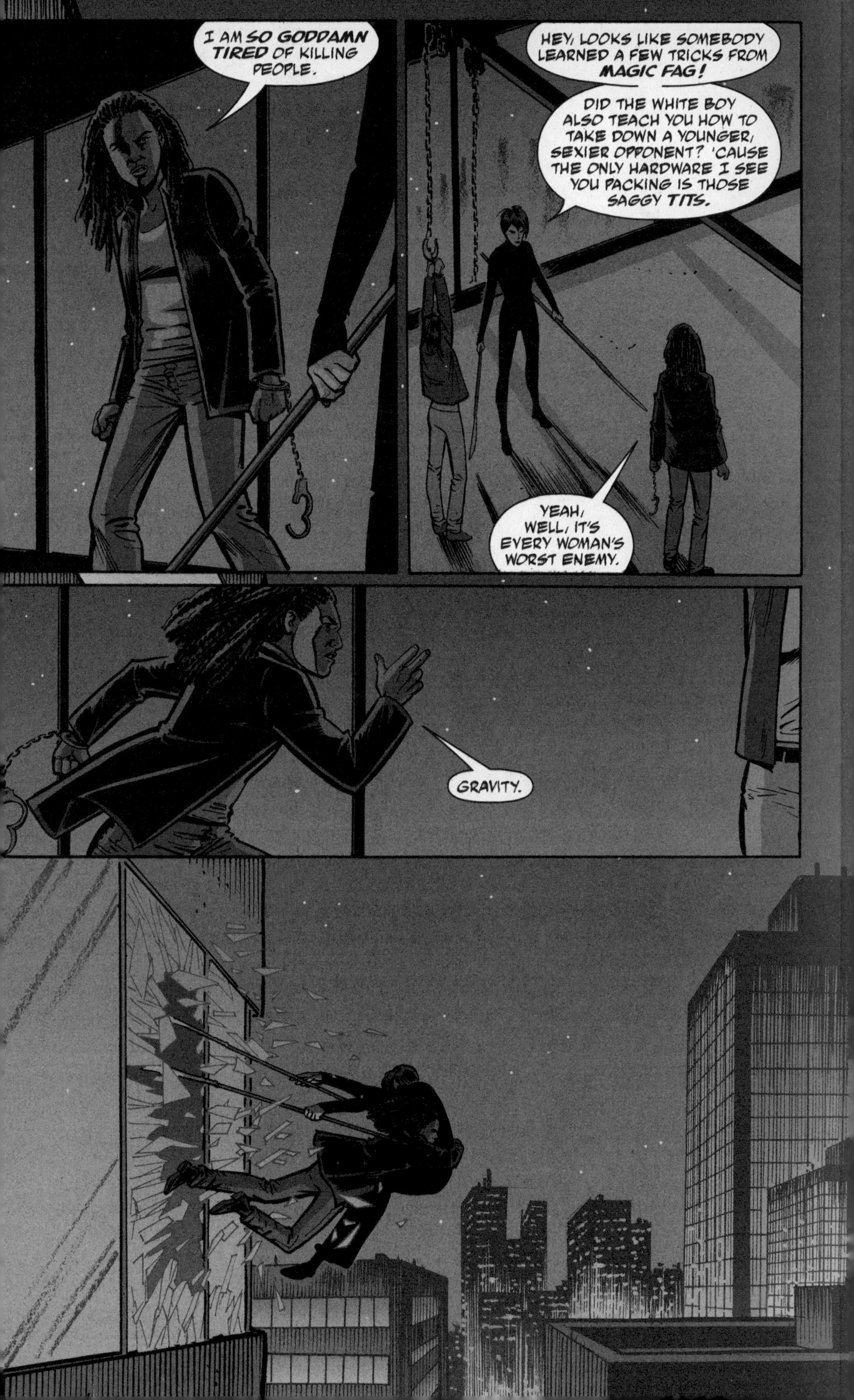

I AM SO GODDAMN TIRED OF KILLING PEOPLE.
HEY, LOOKS LIKE SOMEBODY LEARNED A FEW TRICKS FROM MAGIC FAG!
DID THE WHITE BOY ALSO TEACH YOU HOW TO TAKE DOWN A YOUNGER, SEXIER OPPONENT? 'CAUSE THE ONLY HARDWARE I SEE YOU PACKING IS THOSE SAGGY TITS.
YEAH, WELL, IT'S EVERY WOMAN'S WORST ENEMY.
GRAVITY.

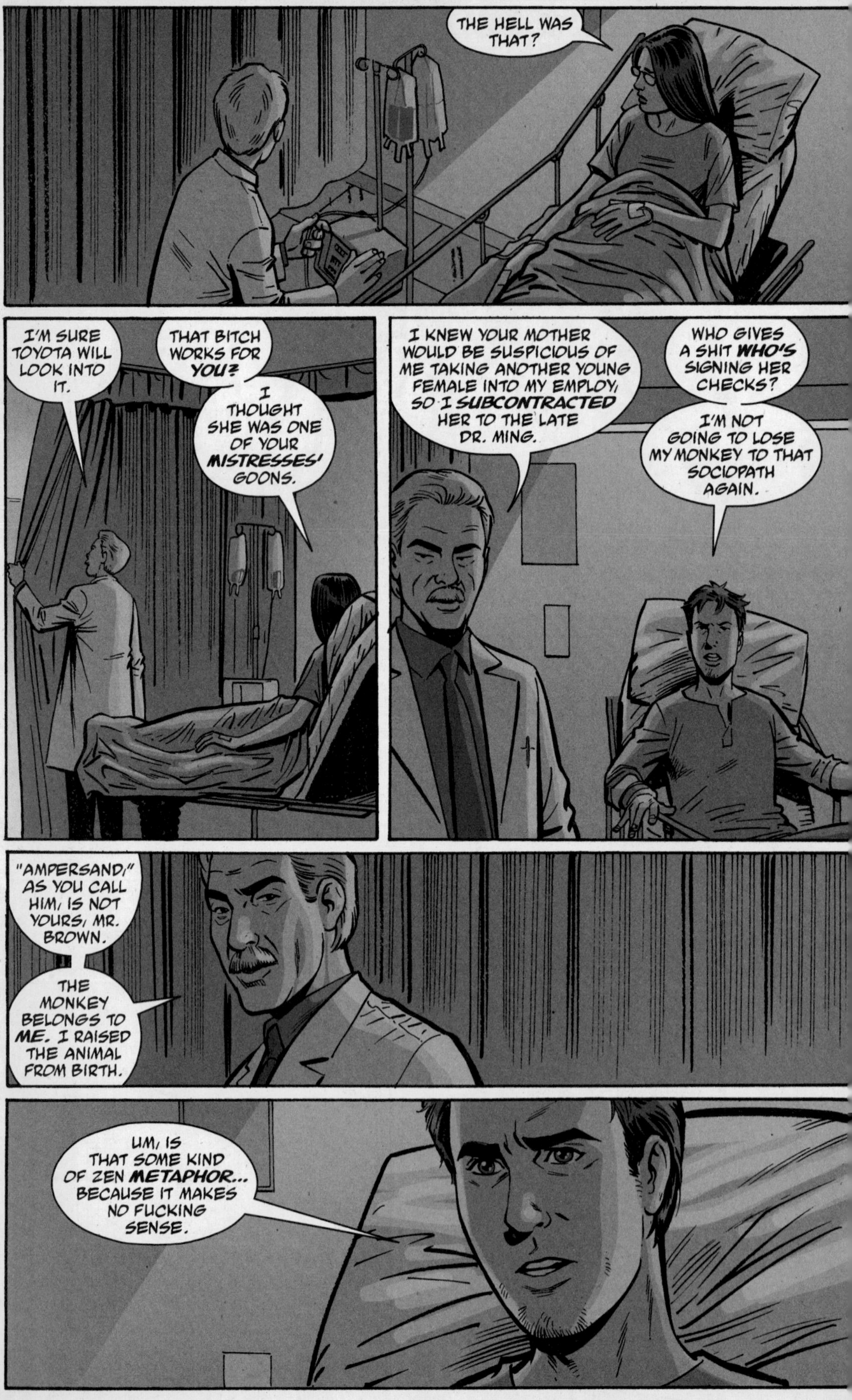

THE HELL WAS THAT?
I'M SURE TOYOTA WILL LOOK INTO IT.
THAT BITCH WORKS FOR YOU?
I THOUGHT SHE WAS ONE OF YOUR MISTRESSES' GOONS.
I KNEW YOUR MOTHER WOULD BE SUSPICIOUS OF ME TAKING ANOTHER YOUNG FEMALE INTO MY EMPLOY, SO I SUBCONTRACTED HER TO THE LATE DR. MING.
WHO GIVES A SHIT WHO'S SIGNING HER CHECKS?
I'M NOT GOING TO LOSE MY MONKEY TO THAT SOCIOPATH AGAIN.
"AMPERSAND," AS YOU CALL HIM, IS NOT YOURS, MR. BROWN.
THE MONKEY BELONGS TO ME. I RAISED THE ANIMAL FROM BIRTH.
UM, IS THAT SOME KIND OF ZEN METAPHOR... BECAUSE IT MAKES NO FUCKING SENSE.

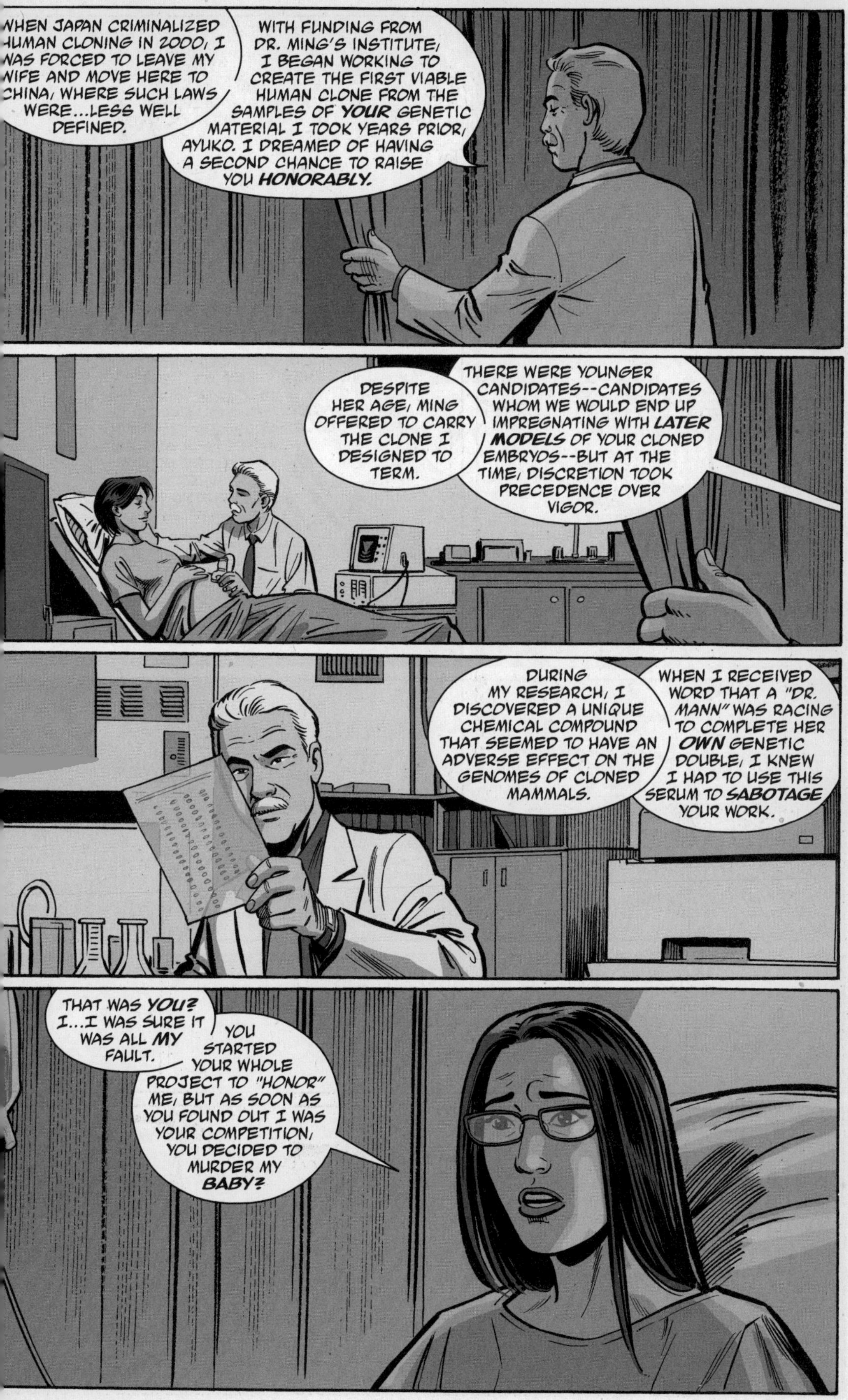
WHEN JAPAN CRIMINALIZED HUMAN CLONING IN 2000, I WAS FORCED TO LEAVE MY WIFE AND MOVE HERE TO CHINA, WHERE SUCH LAWS WERE...LESS WELL DEFINED.
WITH FUNDING FROM DR. MING'S INSTITUTE, I BEGAN WORKING TO CREATE THE FIRST VIABLE HUMAN CLONE FROM THE SAMPLES OF YOUR GENETIC MATERIAL I TOOK YEARS PRIOR, AYUKO. I DREAMED OF HAVING A SECOND CHANCE TO RAISE YOU HONORABLY.
DESPITE HER AGE, MING OFFERED TO CARRY THE CLONE I DESIGNED TO TERM.
THERE WERE YOUNGER CANDIDATES--CANDIDATES WHOM WE WOULD END UP IMPREGNATING WITH LATER MODELS OF YOUR CLONED EMBRYOS--BUT AT THE TIME, DISCRETION TOOK PRECEDENCE OVER VIGOR.
DURING MY RESEARCH, I DISCOVERED A UNIQUE CHEMICAL COMPOUND THAT SEEMED TO HAVE AN ADVERSE EFFECT ON THE GENOMES OF CLONED MAMMALS.
WHEN I RECEIVED WORD THAT A "DR. MANN" WAS RACING TO COMPLETE HER OWN GENETIC DOUBLE, I KNEW I HAD TO USE THIS SERUM TO SABOTAGE YOUR WORK.
THAT WAS YOU? I...I WAS SURE IT WAS ALL MY FAULT.
YOU STARTED YOUR WHOLE PROJECT TO "HONOR" ME, BUT AS SOON AS YOU FOUND OUT I WAS YOUR COMPETITION, YOU DECIDED TO MURDER MY BABY?

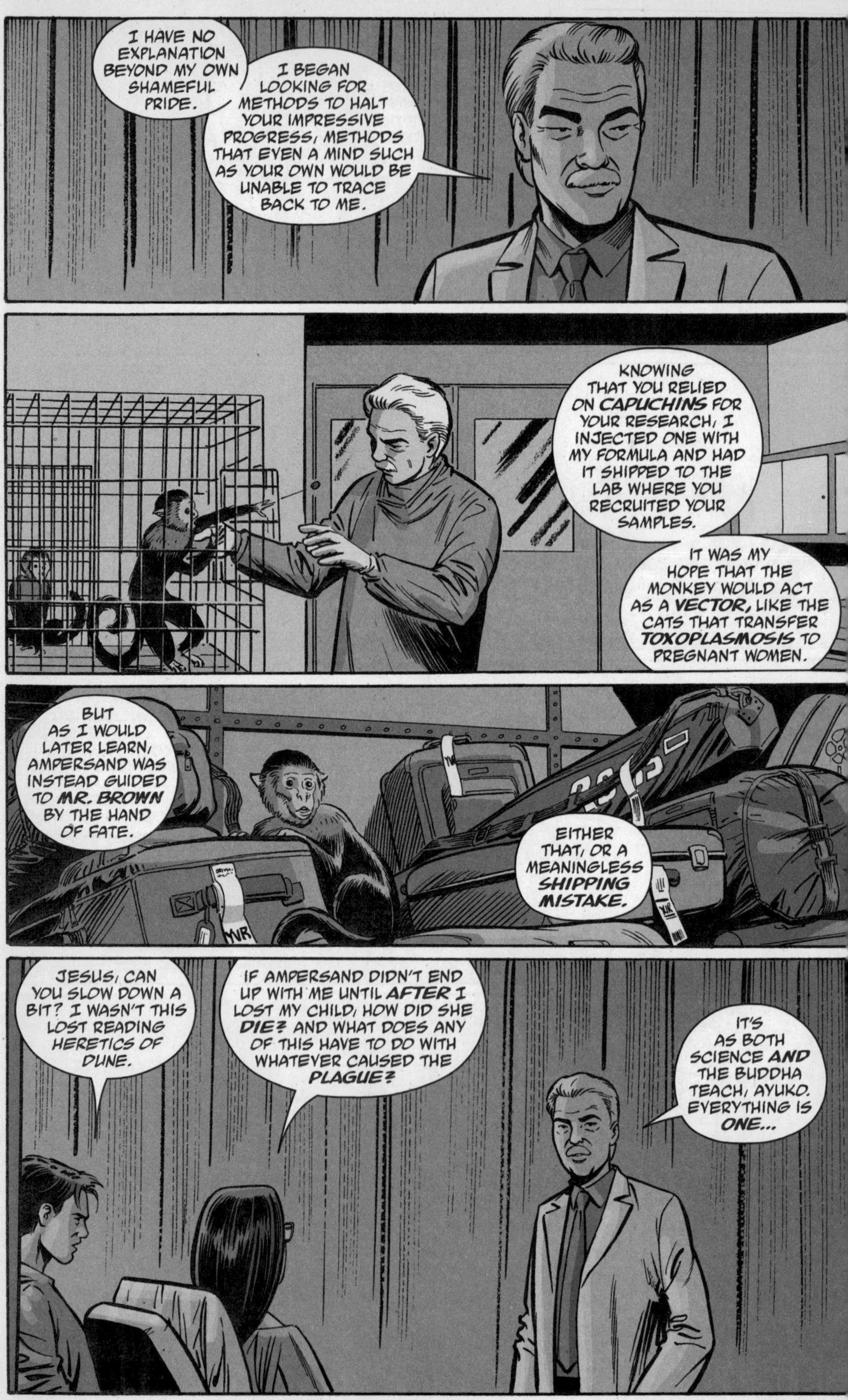

I HAVE NO EXPLANATION BEYOND MY OWN SHAMEFUL PRIDE.
I BEGAN LOOKING FOR METHODS TO HALT YOUR IMPRESSIVE PROGRESS, METHODS THAT EVEN A MIND SUCH AS YOUR OWN WOULD BE UNABLE TO TRACE BACK TO ME.
KNOWING THAT YOU RELIED ON CAPUCHINS FOR YOUR RESEARCH, I INJECTED ONE WITH MY FORMULA AND HAD IT SHIPPED TO THE LAB WHERE YOU RECRUITED YOUR SAMPLES.
IT WAS MY HOPE THAT THE MONKEY WOULD ACT AS A VECTOR, LIKE THE CATS THAT TRANSFER TOXOPLASMOSIS TO PREGNANT WOMEN.
BUT AS I WOULD LATER LEARN, AMPERSAND WAS INSTEAD GUIDED TO MR. BROWN BY THE HAND OF FATE.
EITHER THAT, OR A MEANINGLESS SHIPPING MISTAKE.
JESUS, CAN YOU SLOW DOWN A BIT? I WASN'T THIS LOST READING HERETICS OF DUNE.
IF AMPERSAND DIDN'T END UP WITH ME UNTIL AFTER I LOST MY CHILD, HOW DID SHE DIE? AND WHAT DOES ANY OF THIS HAVE TO DO WITH WHATEVER CAUSED THE PLAGUE?
IT'S AS BOTH SCIENCE AND THE BUDDHA TEACH, AYUKO. EVERYTHING IS ONE...

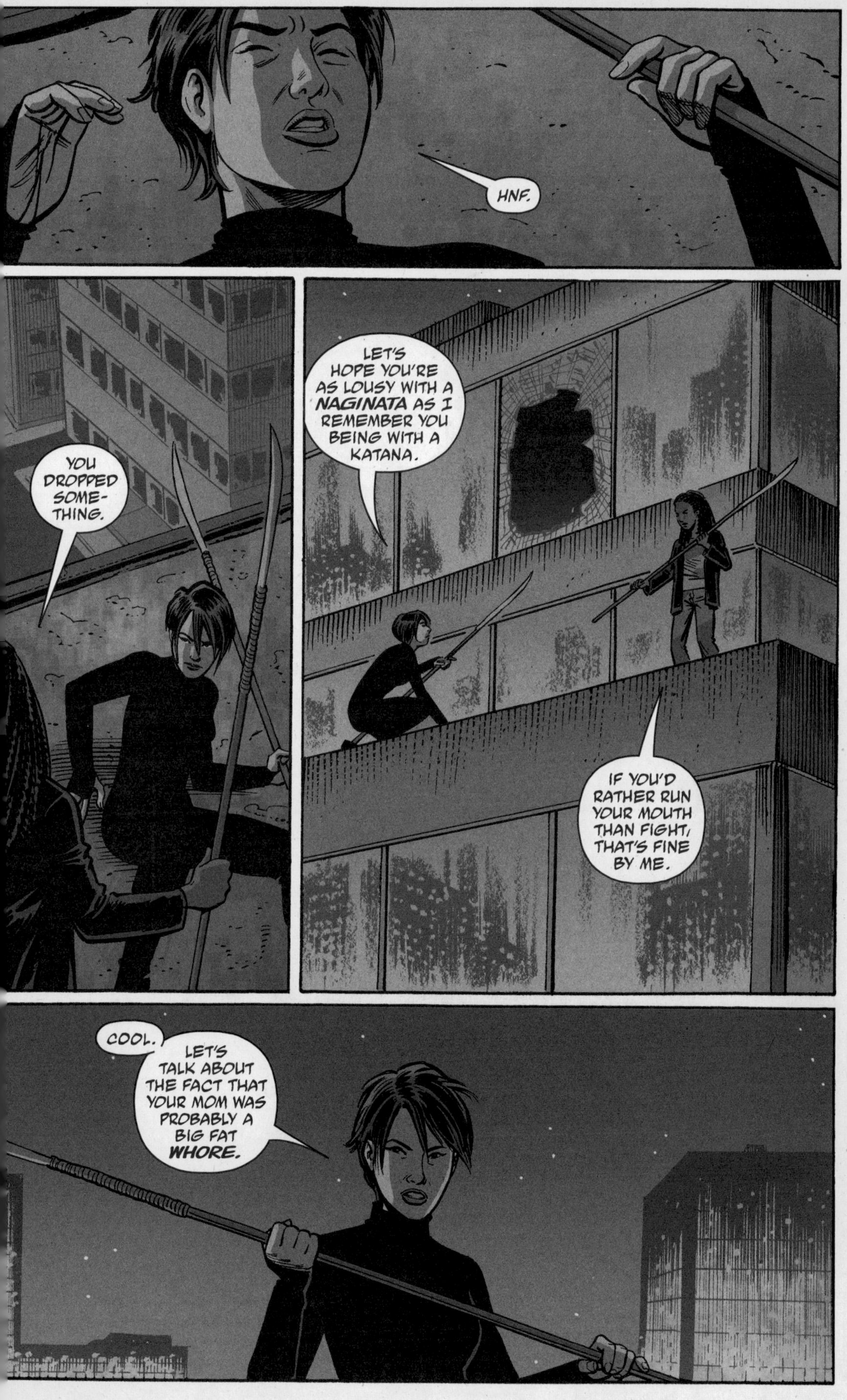
HNF.
YOU DROPPED SOME-THING.
LET'S HOPE YOU'RE AS LOUSY WITH A NAGINATA AS I REMEMBER YOU BEING WITH A KATANA.
IF YOU'D RATHER RUN YOUR MOUTH THAN FIGHT, THAT'S FINE BY ME.
COOL.
LET'S TALK ABOUT THE FACT THAT YOUR MOM WAS PROBABLY A BIG FAT WHORE.

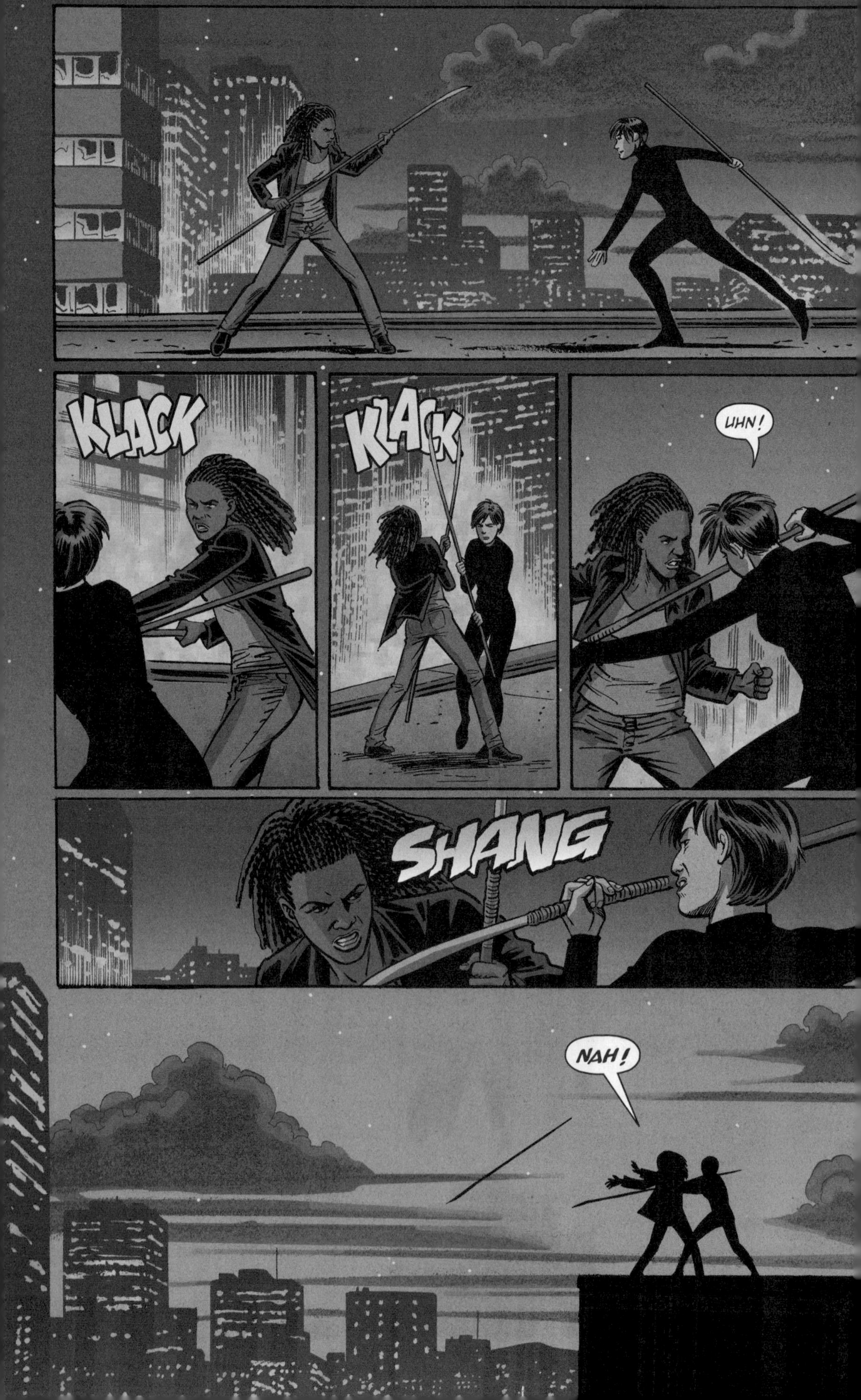
KLACK
KLACK
UHN!
SHANG
NAH!

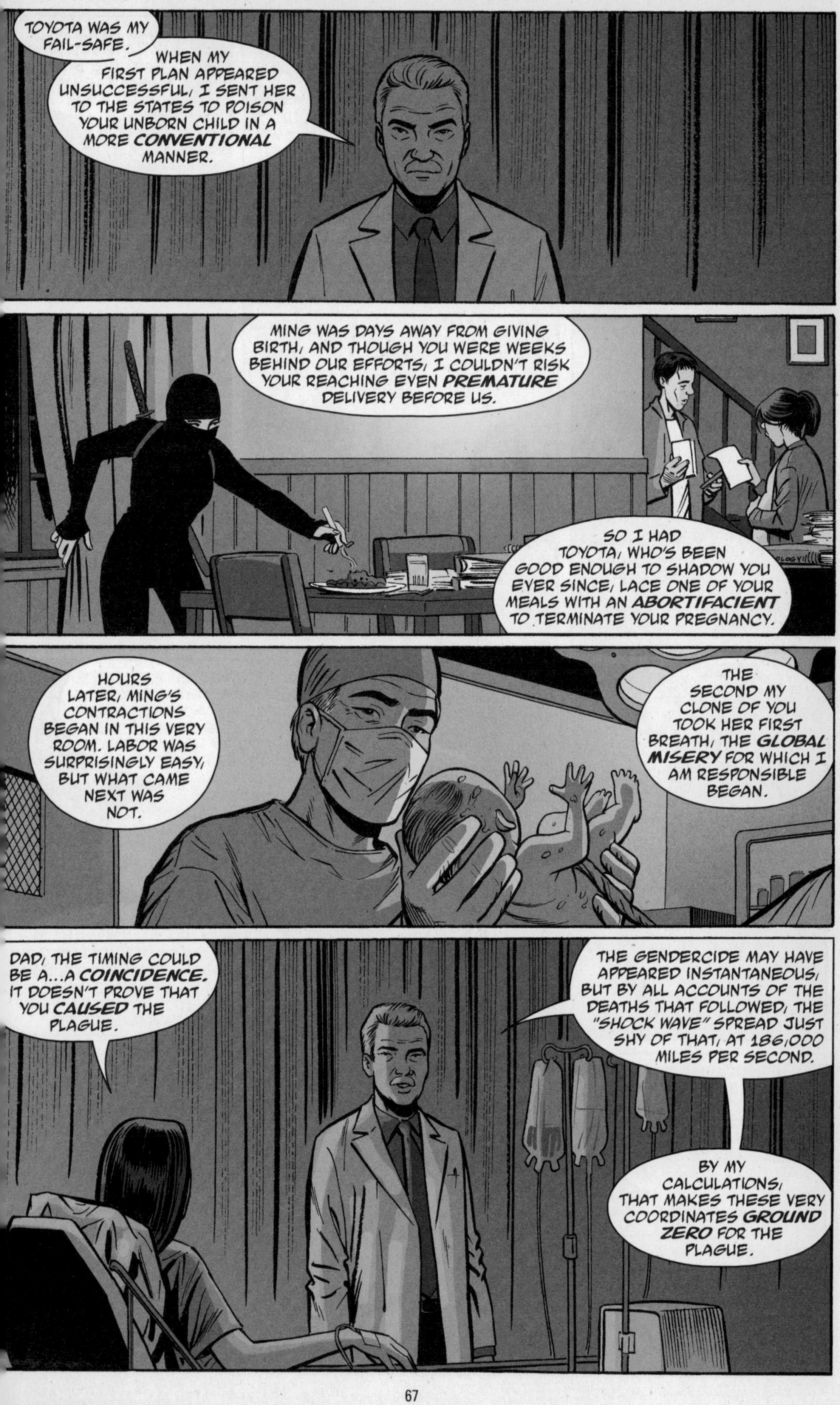
TOYOTA WAS MY FAIL-SAFE.
WHEN MY FIRST PLAN APPEARED UNSUCCESSFUL, I SENT HER TO THE STATES TO POISON YOUR UNBORN CHILD IN A MORE CONVENTIONAL MANNER.
MING WAS DAYS AWAY FROM GIVING BIRTH, AND THOUGH YOU WERE WEEKS BEHIND OUR EFFORTS, I COULDN'T RISK YOUR REACHING EVEN PREMATURE DELIVERY BEFORE US.
SO I HAD TOYOTA, WHO'S BEEN GOOD ENOUGH TO SHADOW YOU EVER SINCE, LACE ONE OF YOUR MEALS WITH AN ABORTIFACIENT TO TERMINATE YOUR PREGNANCY.
HOURS LATER, MING'S CONTRACTIONS BEGAN IN THIS VERY ROOM. LABOR WAS SURPRISINGLY EASY, BUT WHAT CAME NEXT WAS NOT.
THE SECOND MY CLONE OF YOU TOOK HER FIRST BREATH, THE GLOBAL MISERY FOR WHICH I AM RESPONSIBLE BEGAN.
DAD, THE TIMING COULD BE A...A COINCIDENCE. IT DOESN'T PROVE THAT YOU CAUSED THE PLAGUE.
THE GENDERCIDE MAY HAVE APPEARED INSTANTANEOUS, BUT BY ALL ACCOUNTS OF THE DEATHS THAT FOLLOWED, THE "SHOCK WAVE" SPREAD JUST SHY OF THAT, AT 186,000 MILES PER SECOND.
BY MY CALCULATIONS, THAT MAKES THESE VERY COORDINATES GROUND ZERO FOR THE PLAGUE.

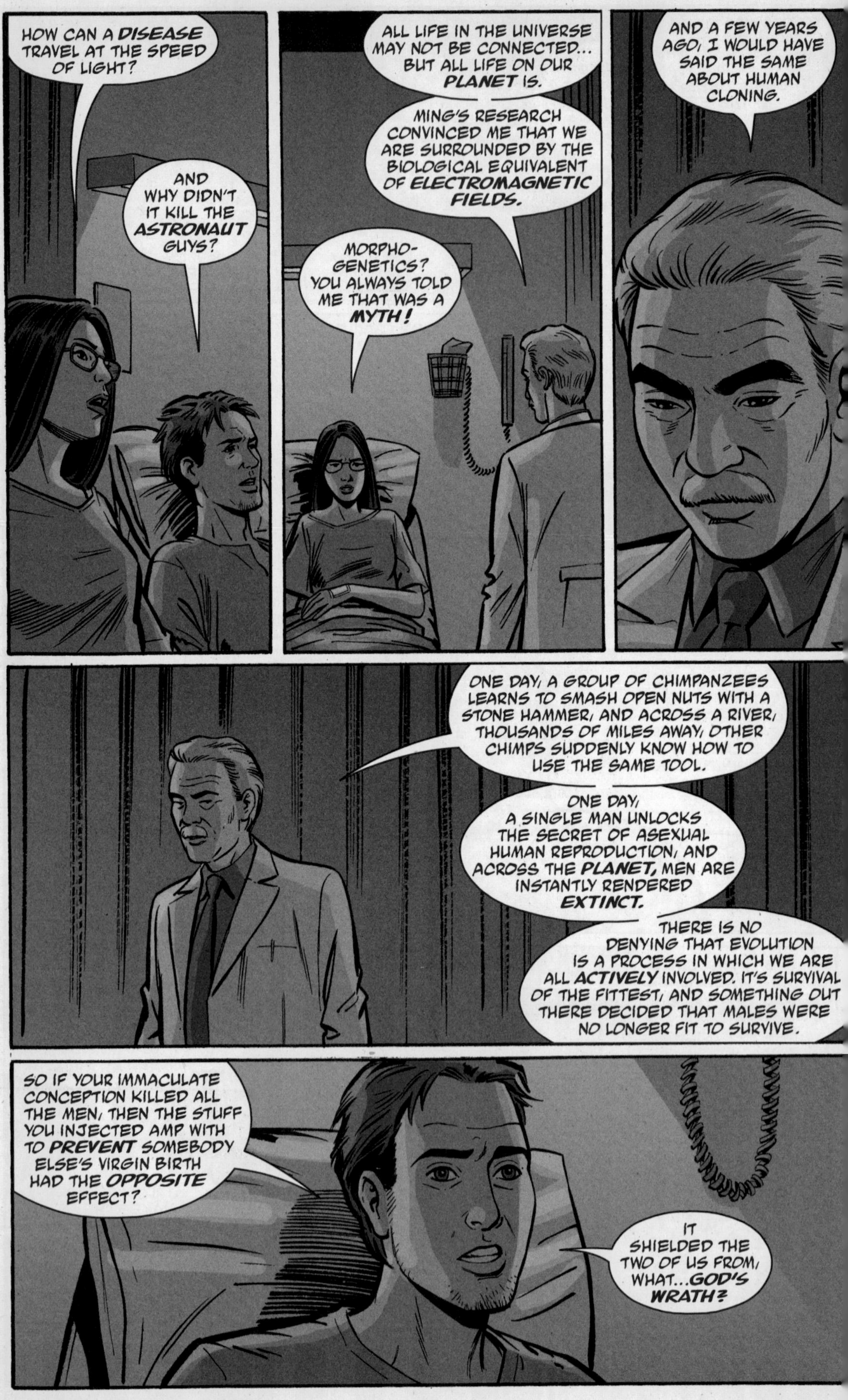
HOW CAN A DISEASE TRAVEL AT THE SPEED OF LIGHT?
AND WHY DIDN'T IT KILL THE ASTRONAUT GUYS?
ALL LIFE IN THE UNIVERSE MAY NOT BE CONNECTED... BUT ALL LIFE ON OUR PLANET IS.
MING'S RESEARCH CONVINCED ME THAT WE ARE SURROUNDED BY THE BIOLOGICAL EQUIVALENT OF ELECTROMAGNETIC FIELDS.
MORPHO-GENETICS? YOU ALWAYS TOLD ME THAT WAS A MYTH!
AND A FEW YEARS AGO, I WOULD HAVE SAID THE SAME ABOUT HUMAN CLONING.
ONE DAY, A GROUP OF CHIMPANZEES LEARNS TO SMASH OPEN NUTS WITH A STONE HAMMER, AND ACROSS A RIVER, THOUSANDS OF MILES AWAY, OTHER CHIMPS SUDDENLY KNOW HOW TO USE THE SAME TOOL.
ONE DAY, A SINGLE MAN UNLOCKS THE SECRET OF ASEXUAL HUMAN REPRODUCTION, AND ACROSS THE PLANET, MEN ARE INSTANTLY RENDERED EXTINCT.
THERE IS NO DENYING THAT EVOLUTION IS A PROCESS IN WHICH WE ARE ALL ACTIVELY INVOLVED. IT'S SURVIVAL OF THE FITTEST, AND SOMETHING OUT THERE DECIDED THAT MALES WERE NO LONGER FIT TO SURVIVE.
SO IF YOUR IMMACULATE CONCEPTION KILLED ALL THE MEN, THEN THE STUFF YOU INJECTED AMP WITH TO PREVENT SOMEBODY ELSE'S VIRGIN BIRTH HAD THE OPPOSITE EFFECT?
IT SHIELDED THE TWO OF US FROM, WHAT...GOD'S WRATH?

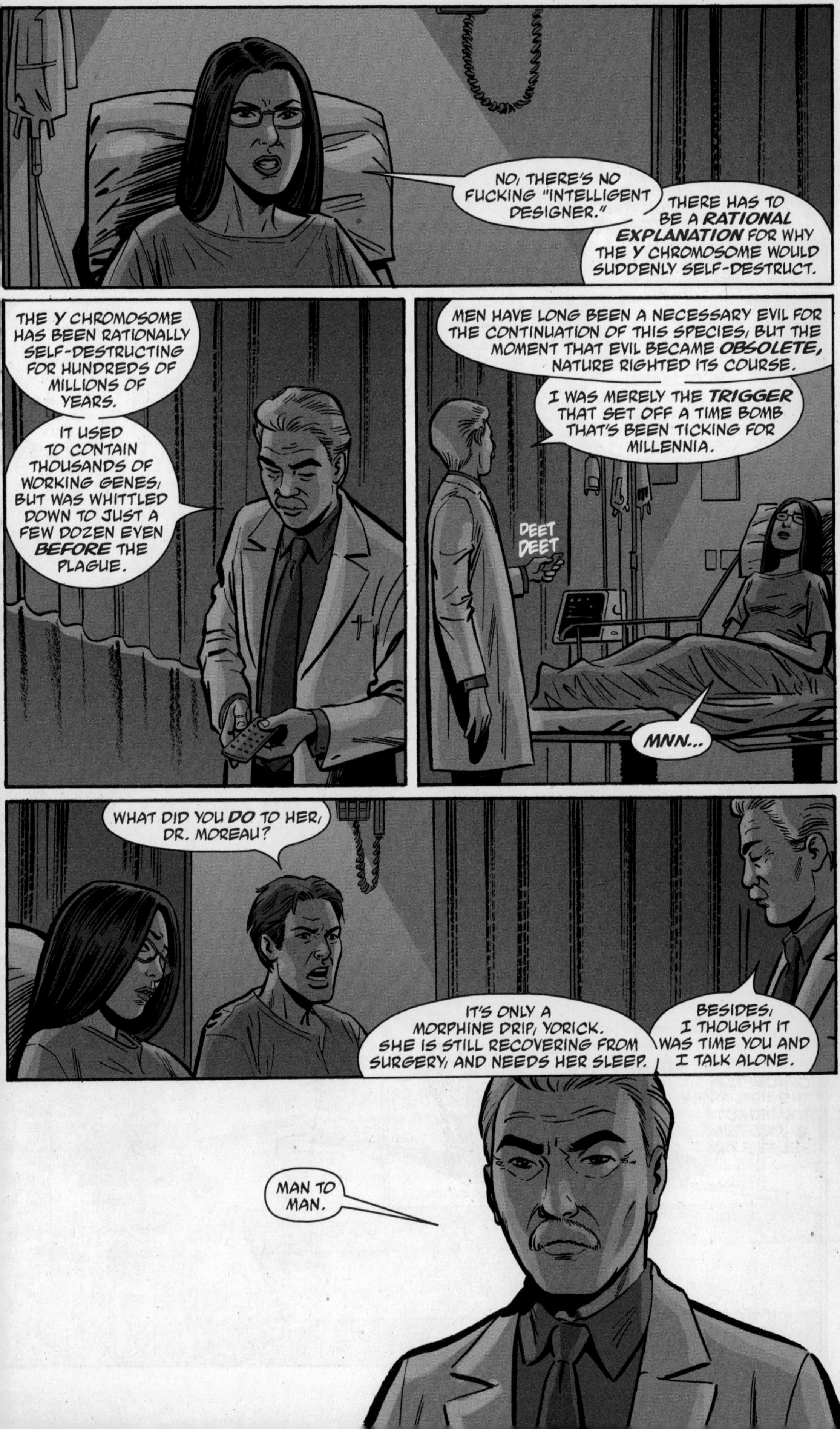
NO, THERE'S NO FUCKING "INTELLIGENT DESIGNER."
THERE HAS TO BE A **RATIONAL EXPLANATION** FOR WHY THE Y CHROMOSOME WOULD SUDDENLY SELF-DESTRUCT.
THE Y CHROMOSOME HAS BEEN RATIONALLY SELF-DESTRUCTING FOR HUNDREDS OF MILLIONS OF YEARS.
IT USED TO CONTAIN THOUSANDS OF WORKING GENES, BUT WAS WHITTLED DOWN TO JUST A FEW DOZEN EVEN **BEFORE** THE PLAGUE.
MEN HAVE LONG BEEN A NECESSARY EVIL FOR THE CONTINUATION OF THIS SPECIES, BUT THE MOMENT THAT EVIL BECAME **OBSOLETE,** NATURE RIGHTED ITS COURSE.
I WAS MERELY THE **TRIGGER** THAT SET OFF A TIME BOMB THAT'S BEEN TICKING FOR MILLENNIA.
DEET DEET
MNN...
WHAT DID YOU **DO** TO HER, DR. MOREAU?
IT'S ONLY A MORPHINE DRIP, YORICK. SHE IS STILL RECOVERING FROM SURGERY, AND NEEDS HER SLEEP.
BESIDES, I THOUGHT IT WAS TIME YOU AND I TALK ALONE.
MAN TO MAN.

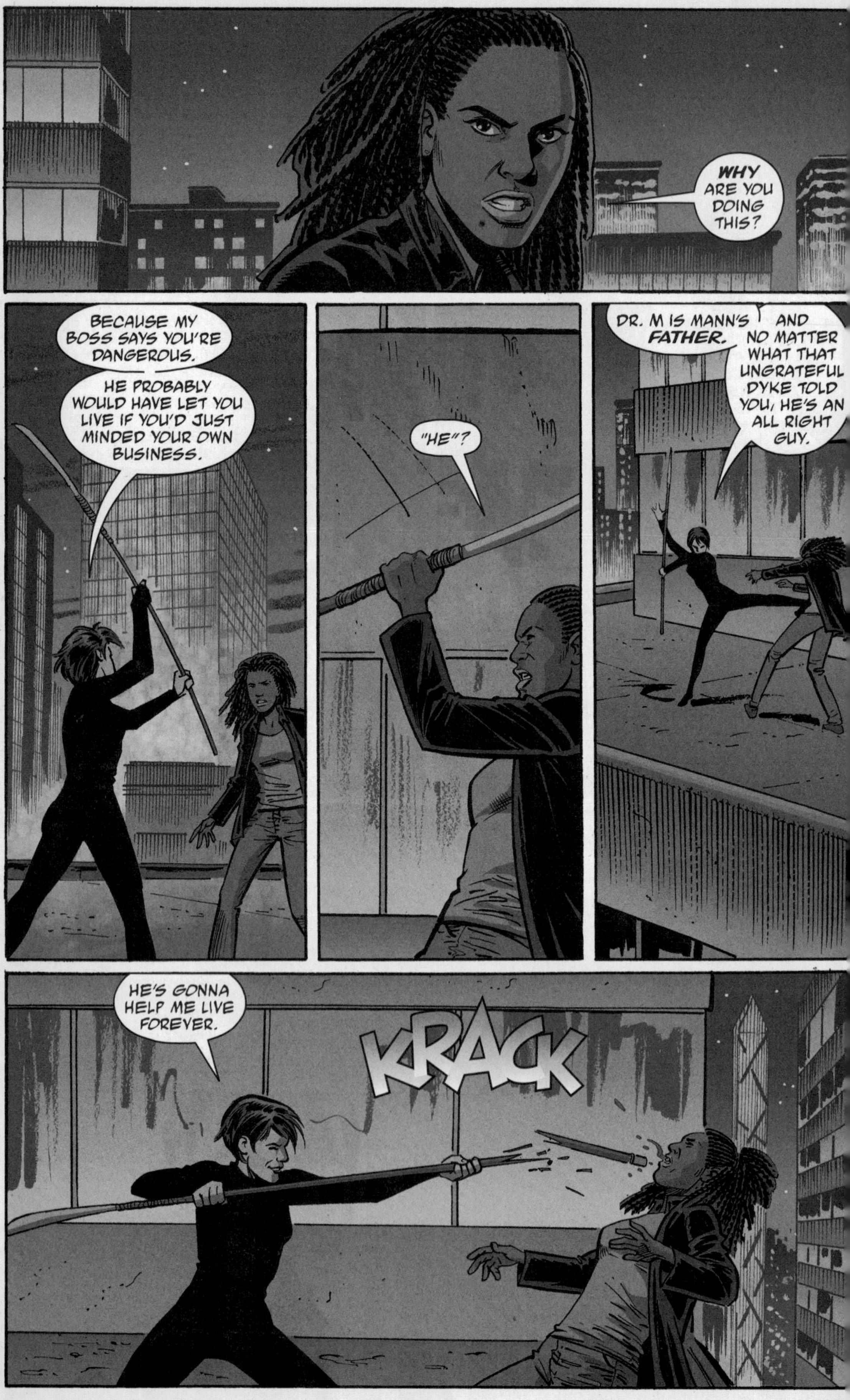
WHY ARE YOU DOING THIS?
BECAUSE MY BOSS SAYS YOU'RE DANGEROUS.
HE PROBABLY WOULD HAVE LET YOU LIVE IF YOU'D JUST MINDED YOUR OWN BUSINESS.
"HE"?
DR. M IS MANN'S FATHER.
AND NO MATTER WHAT THAT UNGRATEFUL DYKE TOLD YOU, HE'S AN ALL RIGHT GUY.
HE'S GONNA HELP ME LIVE FOREVER.
KRACK

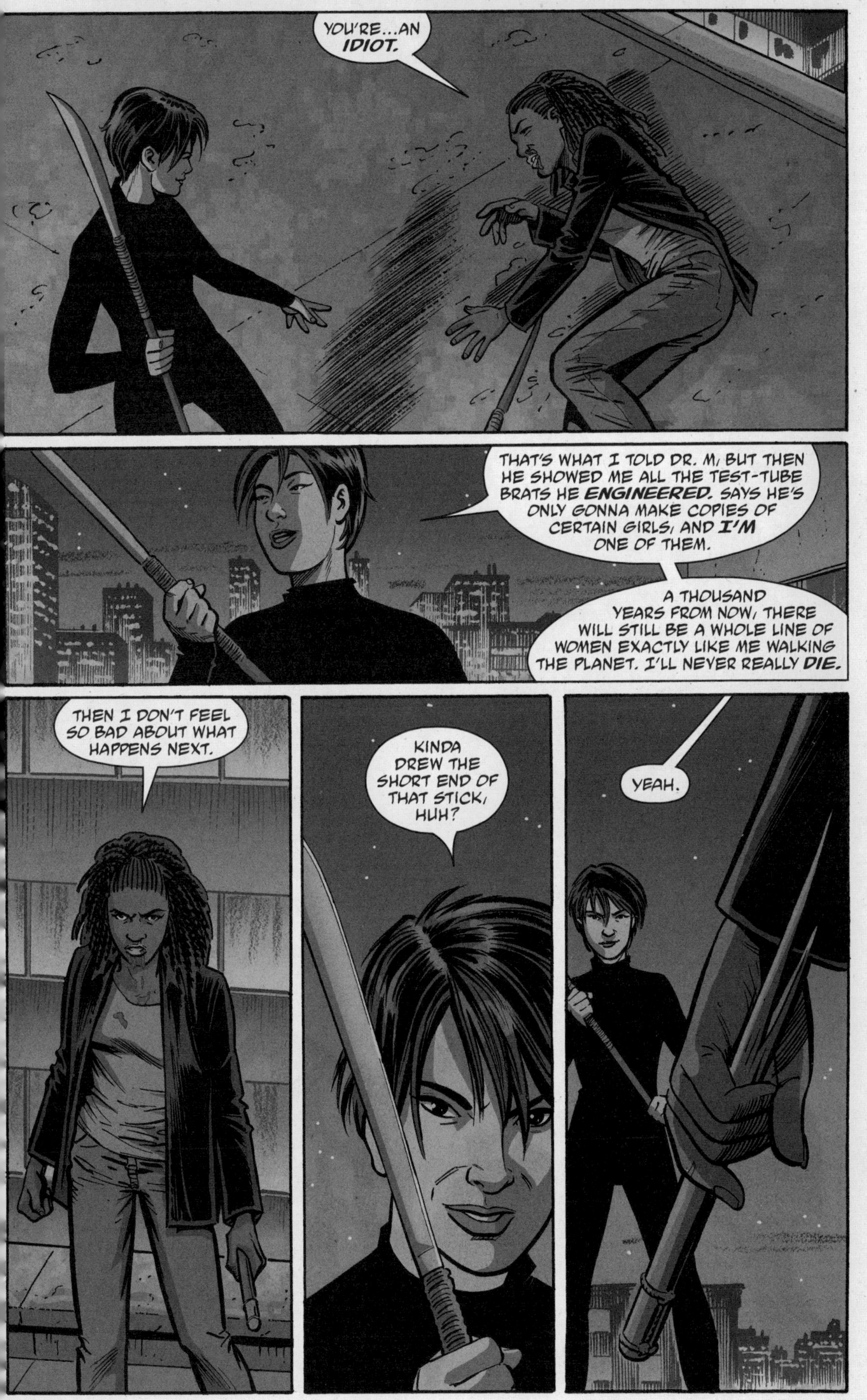
YOU'RE...AN **IDIOT.**
THAT'S WHAT I TOLD DR. M, BUT THEN HE SHOWED ME ALL THE TEST-TUBE BRATS HE **ENGINEERED.** SAYS HE'S ONLY GONNA MAKE COPIES OF CERTAIN GIRLS, AND **I'M** ONE OF THEM.
A THOUSAND YEARS FROM NOW, THERE WILL STILL BE A WHOLE LINE OF WOMEN EXACTLY LIKE ME WALKING THE PLANET. I'LL NEVER REALLY **DIE.**
THEN I DON'T FEEL SO BAD ABOUT WHAT HAPPENS NEXT.
KINDA DREW THE SHORT END OF THAT STICK, HUH?
YEAH.

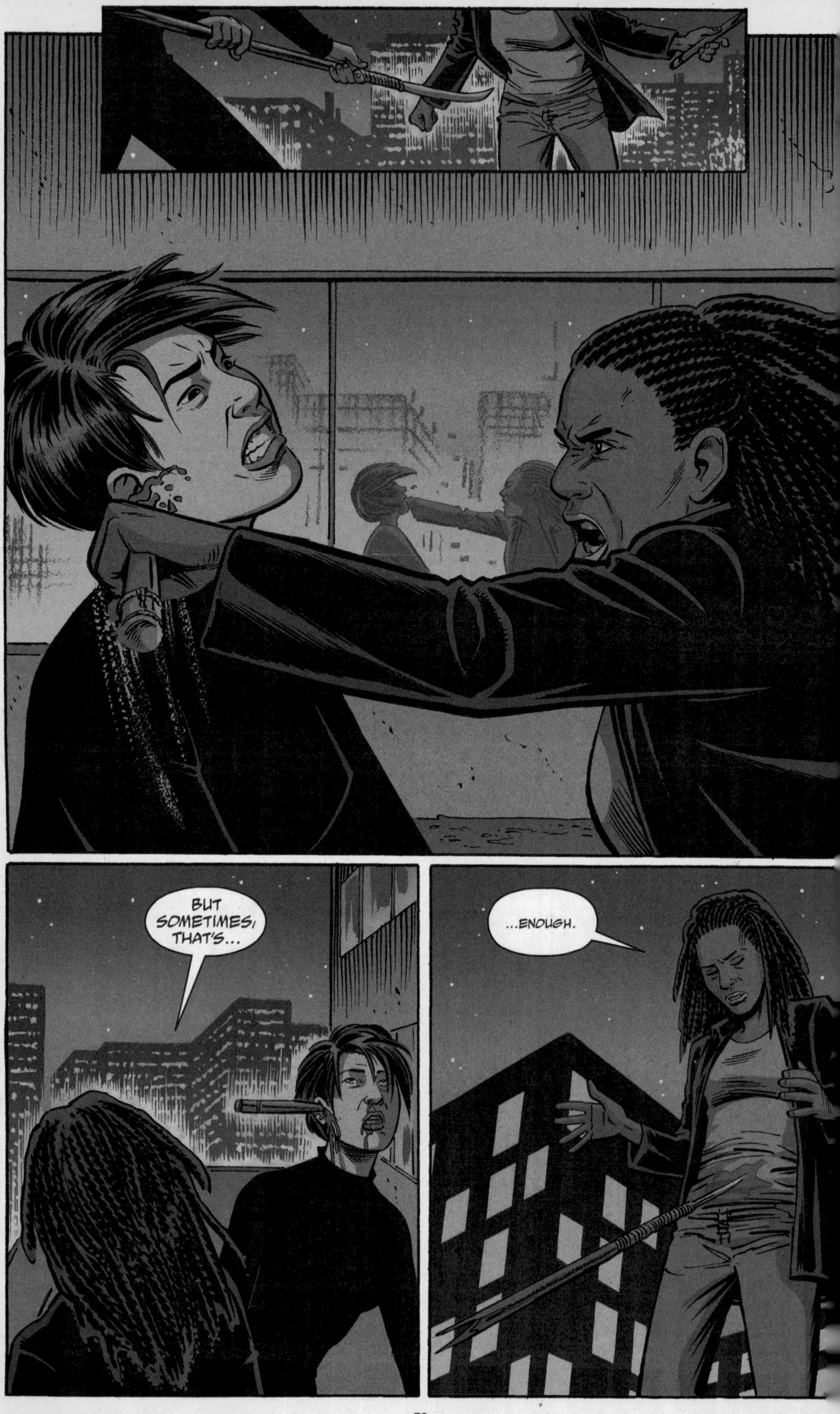
BUT SOMETIMES, THAT'S...
...ENOUGH.

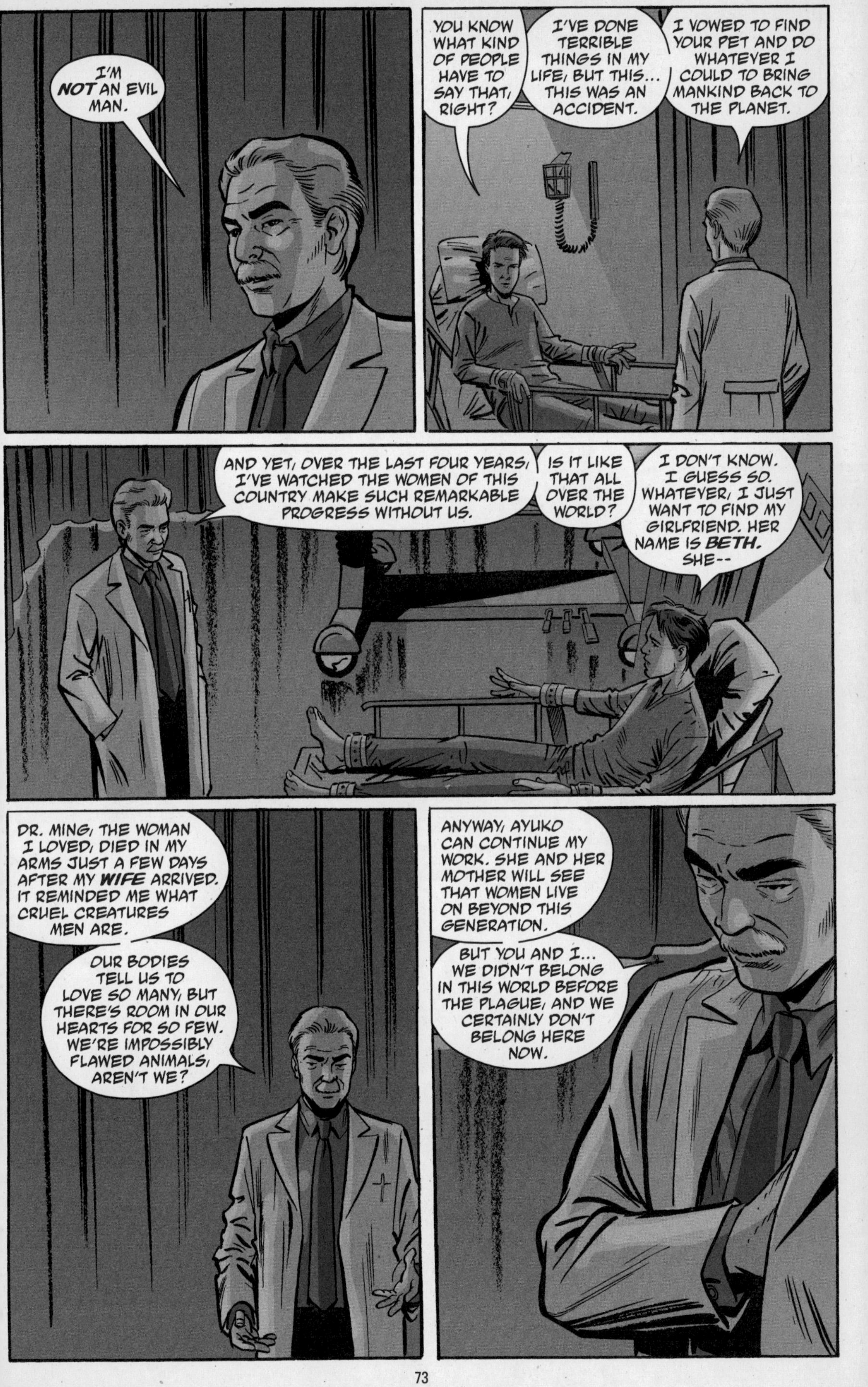
I'M NOT AN EVIL MAN.
YOU KNOW WHAT KIND OF PEOPLE HAVE TO SAY THAT, RIGHT?
I'VE DONE TERRIBLE THINGS IN MY LIFE, BUT THIS... THIS WAS AN ACCIDENT.
I VOWED TO FIND YOUR PET AND DO WHATEVER I COULD TO BRING MANKIND BACK TO THE PLANET.
AND YET, OVER THE LAST FOUR YEARS, I'VE WATCHED THE WOMEN OF THIS COUNTRY MAKE SUCH REMARKABLE PROGRESS WITHOUT US.
IS IT LIKE THAT ALL OVER THE WORLD?
I DON'T KNOW. I GUESS SO. WHATEVER, I JUST WANT TO FIND MY GIRLFRIEND. HER NAME IS BETH. SHE--
DR. MING, THE WOMAN I LOVED, DIED IN MY ARMS JUST A FEW DAYS AFTER MY WIFE ARRIVED. IT REMINDED ME WHAT CRUEL CREATURES MEN ARE.
OUR BODIES TELL US TO LOVE SO MANY, BUT THERE'S ROOM IN OUR HEARTS FOR SO FEW. WE'RE IMPOSSIBLY FLAWED ANIMALS, AREN'T WE?
ANYWAY, AYUKO CAN CONTINUE MY WORK. SHE AND HER MOTHER WILL SEE THAT WOMEN LIVE ON BEYOND THIS GENERATION.
BUT YOU AND I... WE DIDN'T BELONG IN THIS WORLD BEFORE THE PLAGUE, AND WE CERTAINLY DON'T BELONG HERE NOW.

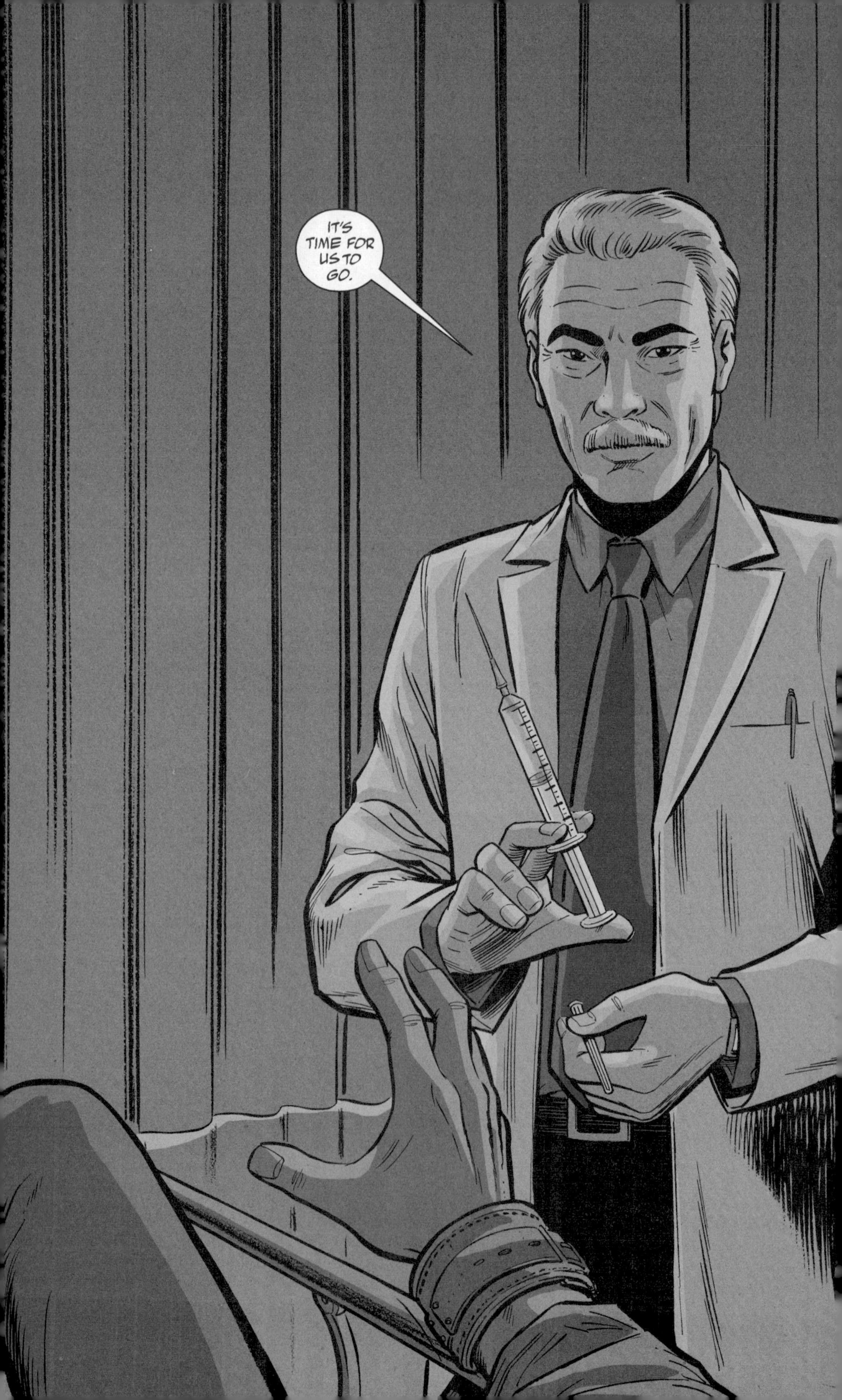
IT'S TIME FOR US TO GO.

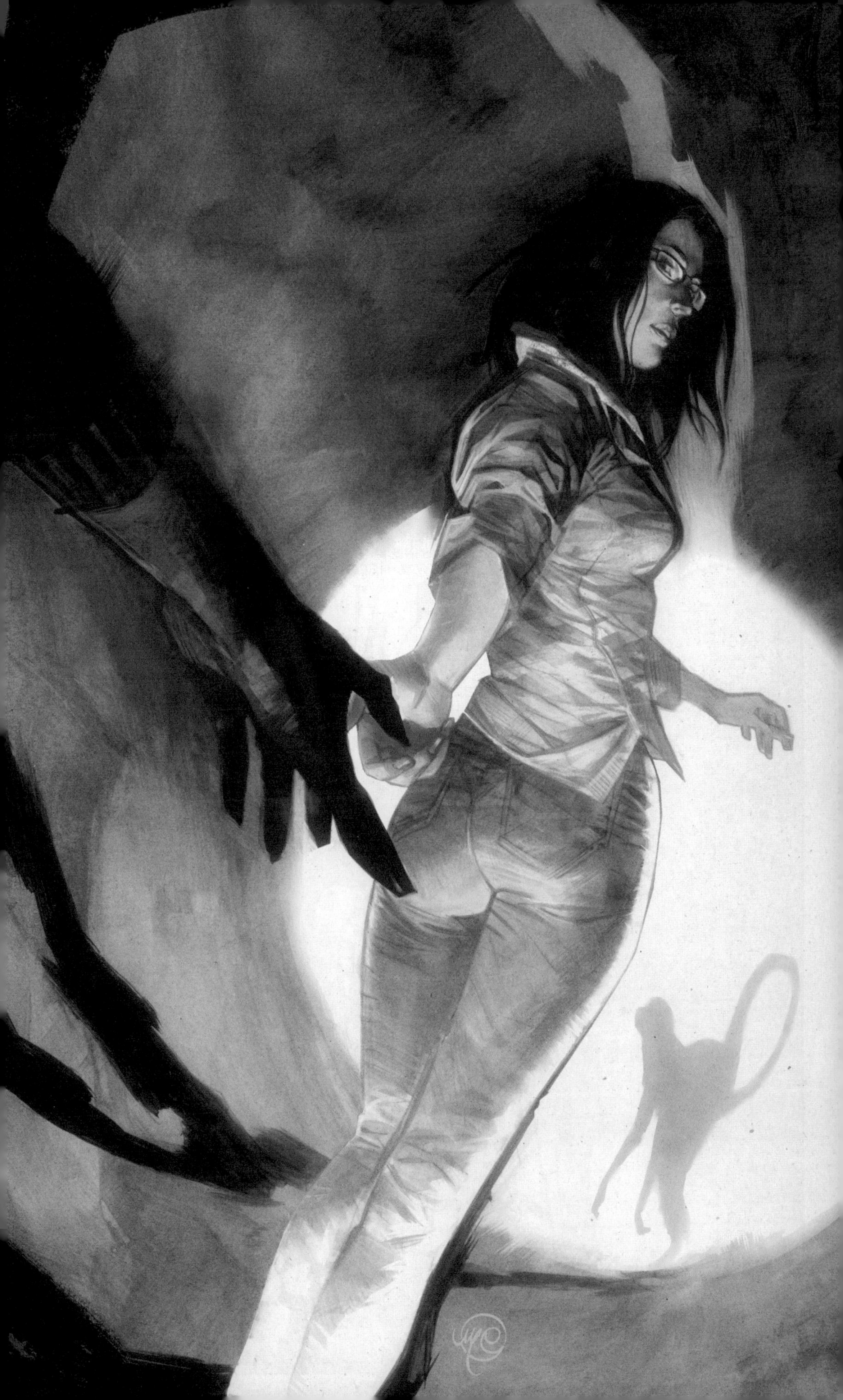

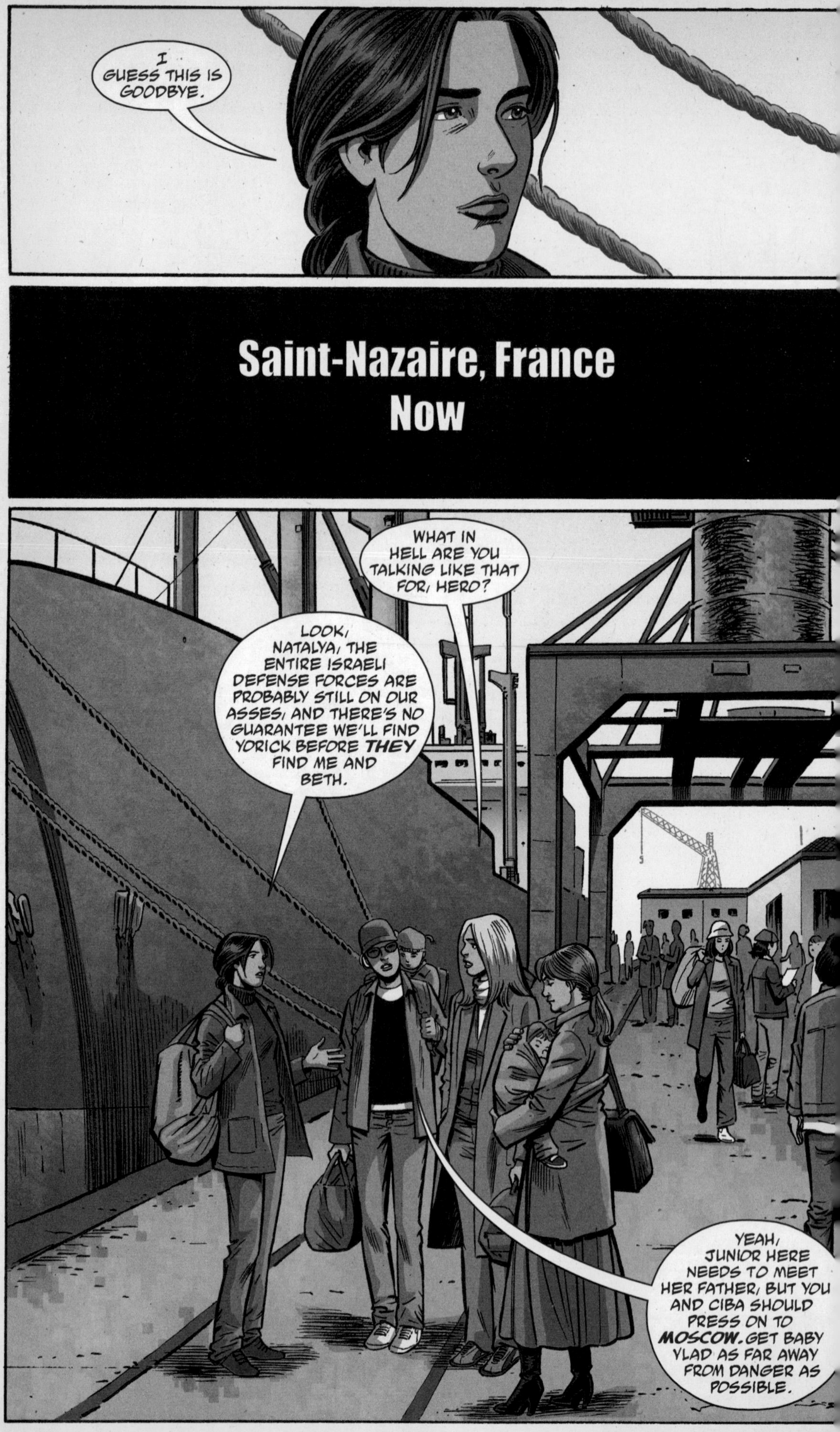

I GUESS THIS IS GOODBYE.
Saint-Nazaire, France
Now
WHAT IN HELL ARE YOU TALKING LIKE THAT FOR, HERO?
LOOK, NATALYA, THE ENTIRE ISRAELI DEFENSE FORCES ARE PROBABLY STILL ON OUR ASSES, AND THERE'S NO GUARANTEE WE'LL FIND YORICK BEFORE THEY FIND ME AND BETH.
YEAH, JUNIOR HERE NEEDS TO MEET HER FATHER, BUT YOU AND CIBA SHOULD PRESS ON TO MOSCOW. GET BABY VLAD AS FAR AWAY FROM DANGER AS POSSIBLE.

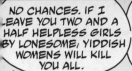

NO CHANCES. IF I LEAVE YOU TWO AND A HALF HELPLESS GIRLS BY LONESOME, YIDDISH WOMENS WILL KILL YOU ALL.

BESIDE, KREMLIN IS TOO HARSH FOR MAN-CHILDREN AT THIS TIME OF YEAR, EVEN FOR SON OF COSMONAUT.

I HAVE NO IDEA WHAT SHE JUST SAID, BUT I KNOW I WOULDN'T LAST AN HOUR WITH NAT AS MY ONLY CONVERSATION PARTNER.

HER ENGLISH ISN'T BROKEN, IT'S ANNIHILATED.

〈A MILLION TIMES BETTER THAN YOUR RUSSIAN, SWEETHEART.〉

I'M SORRY, I HATE TO BREAK UP THE YA-YA SISTERHOOD--

HEY, THAT WAS THE LAST MOVIE I SAW RIGHT BEFORE THE PLAGUE HIT. I WONDER IF IT KILLED ALL THE MEN ON IMPACT? DEATH BY CHICK FLICK.

--BUT THIS IS SERIOUS. OUR LITTLE CAT AND MOUSE GAME IS ONLY GOING TO GET MORE DANGEROUS ONCE WE'RE LANDLOCKED. ASSUMING YORICK AND HIS OTHER BETH ARE EVEN HERE YET, I CAN'T GUARANTEE WE'LL ALL, YOU KNOW, SURVIVE THE REUNION.

THANKS, HERO, BUT WE'RE NOT ABANDONING YOU GUYS.

I DON'T WANT A LIFE FOR VLADIMIR WITHOUT YOUR BROTHER IN IT. I KNOW IT'S OLD-FASHIONED...

...BUT I REALLY THINK BOYS NEED A STRONG MALE INFLUENCE.

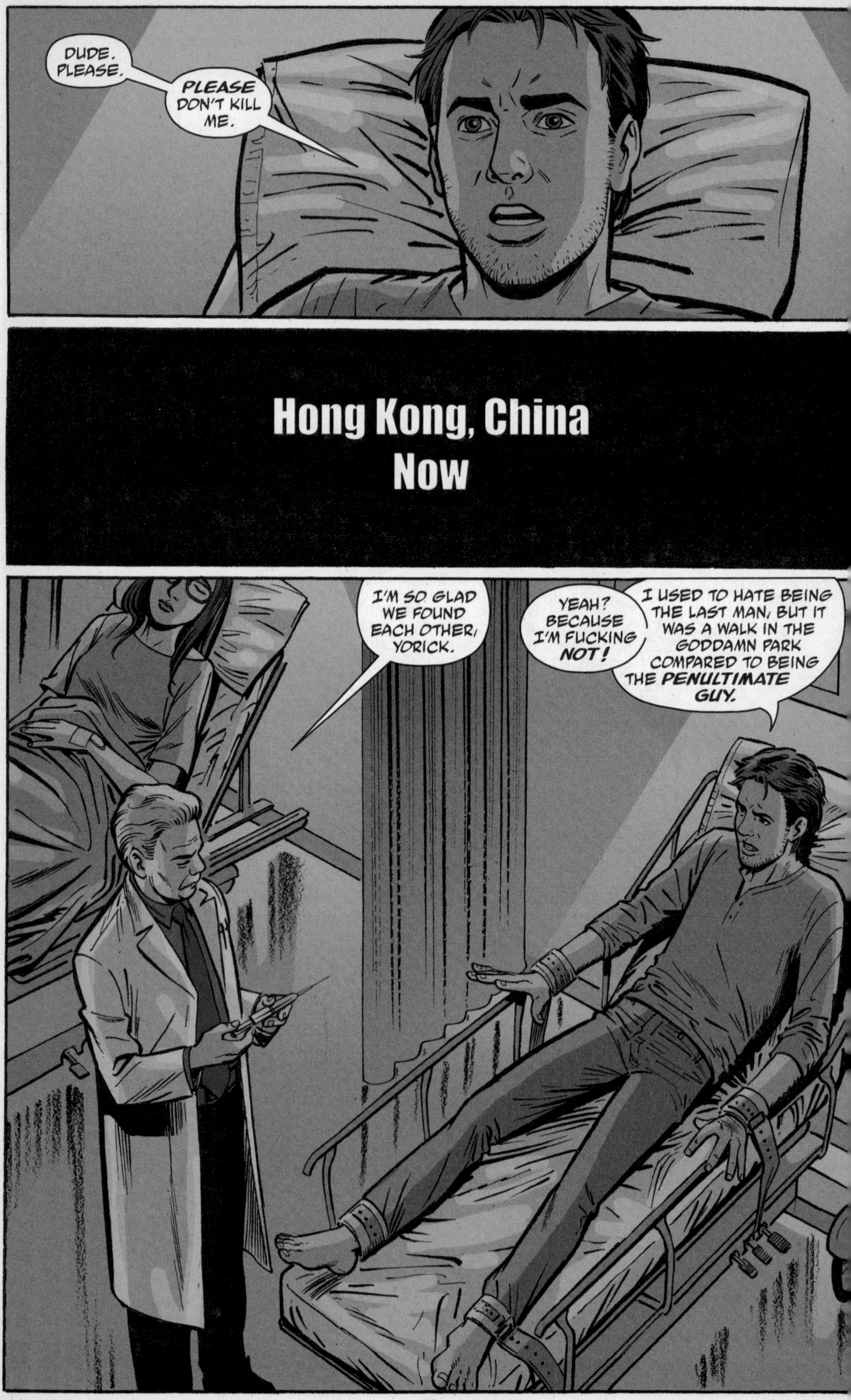
DUDE. PLEASE.
PLEASE DON'T KILL ME.
Hong Kong, China
Now
I'M SO GLAD WE FOUND EACH OTHER, YORICK.
YEAH? BECAUSE I'M FUCKING NOT!
I USED TO HATE BEING THE LAST MAN, BUT IT WAS A WALK IN THE GODDAMN PARK COMPARED TO BEING THE PENULTIMATE GUY.

EVER SINCE I WAS A LITTLE BOY, WOMEN HAVE TERRIFIED ME. I SUSPECT THIS IS WHY MY MALE COLLEAGUES AND I *MARGINALIZED* SO MANY LATER IN LIFE.

OUR SEXES MAY BE EQUAL, BUT THEY ARE NOT THE SAME.

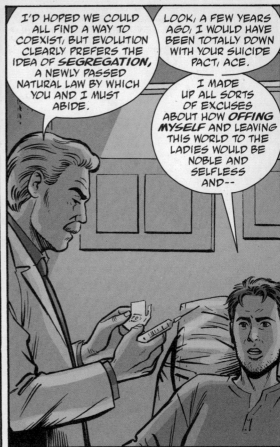

I'D HOPED WE COULD ALL FIND A WAY TO COEXIST, BUT EVOLUTION CLEARLY PREFERS THE IDEA OF *SEGREGATION,* A NEWLY PASSED NATURAL LAW BY WHICH YOU AND I MUST ABIDE.

LOOK, A FEW YEARS AGO, I WOULD HAVE BEEN TOTALLY DOWN WITH YOUR SUICIDE PACT, ACE.

I MADE UP ALL SORTS OF EXCUSES ABOUT HOW *OFFING MYSELF* AND LEAVING THIS WORLD TO THE LADIES WOULD BE NOBLE AND SELFLESS AND--

I'M SORRY, BUT THIS GRAND EXPERIMENT ISN'T OPEN TO PEER REVIEW.

JUST SHUT UP AND LISTEN TO ME, MATSUMORI! EVERY GUY GOES THROUGH A PERIOD WHERE HE'S...HE'S SCARED SHITLESS AND COMPLETELY BAFFLED BY GIRLS, RIGHT?

BUT THEN WE'RE SUPPOSED TO *GROW UP,* FIGURE OUT THAT THE BEST PLACE FOR ALL THE GREAT WOMEN PROBABLY ISN'T *BEHIND* EVERY GREAT MAN.

THE TWO SIDES ARE ONLY GONNA GET THROUGH THIS TOGETHER...SO WHY DON'T YOU STOP BEING SUCH A *PUSSY* AND MAN THE *FUCK* UP?

79

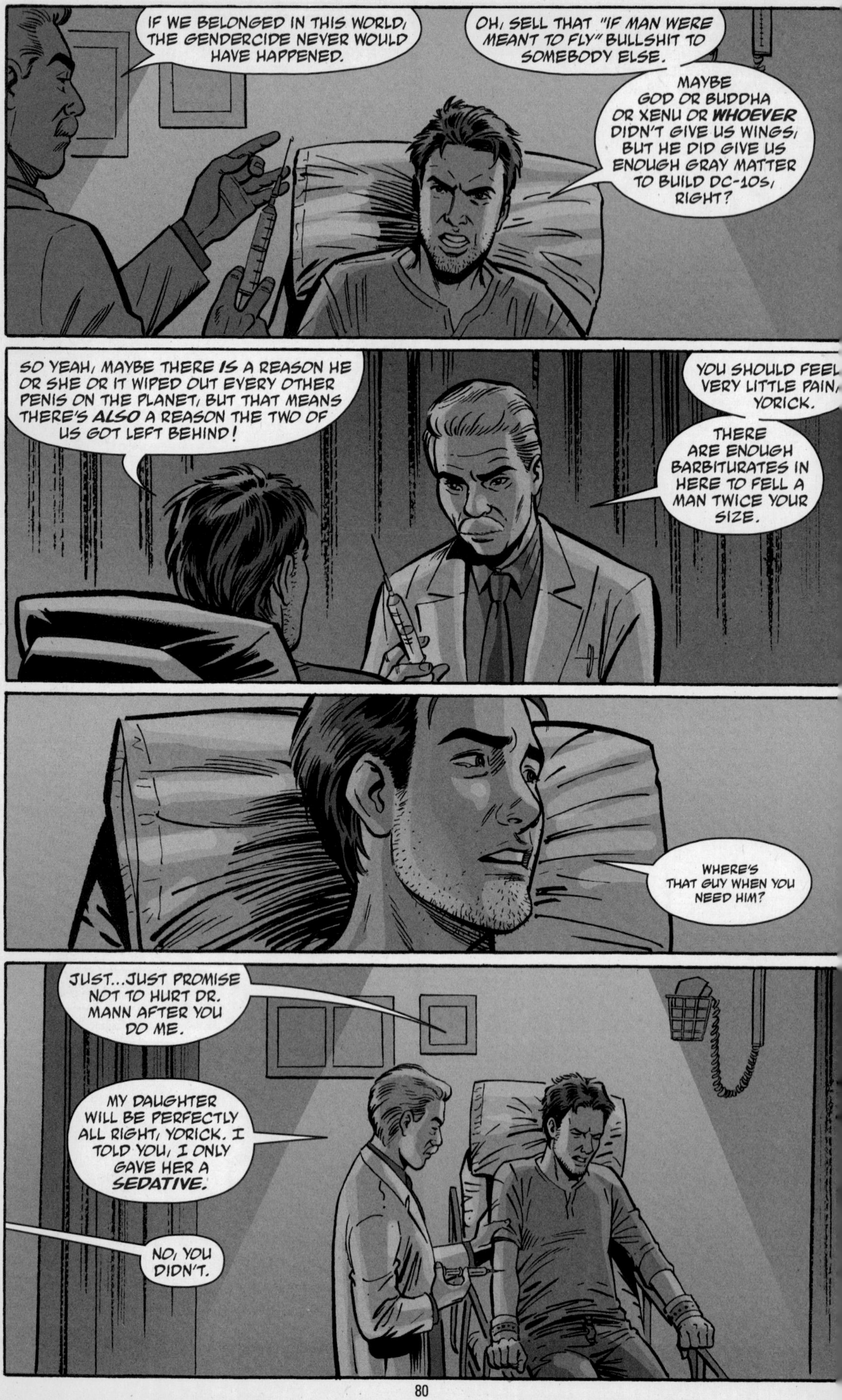
IF WE BELONGED IN THIS WORLD, THE GENDERCIDE NEVER WOULD HAVE HAPPENED.
OH, SELL THAT "IF MAN WERE MEANT TO FLY" BULLSHIT TO SOMEBODY ELSE.
MAYBE GOD OR BUDDHA OR XENU OR WHOEVER DIDN'T GIVE US WINGS, BUT HE DID GIVE US ENOUGH GRAY MATTER TO BUILD DC-10s, RIGHT?
SO YEAH, MAYBE THERE IS A REASON HE OR SHE OR IT WIPED OUT EVERY OTHER PENIS ON THE PLANET, BUT THAT MEANS THERE'S ALSO A REASON THE TWO OF US GOT LEFT BEHIND!
YOU SHOULD FEEL VERY LITTLE PAIN, YORICK.
THERE ARE ENOUGH BARBITURATES IN HERE TO FELL A MAN TWICE YOUR SIZE.
WHERE'S THAT GUY WHEN YOU NEED HIM?
JUST...JUST PROMISE NOT TO HURT DR. MANN AFTER YOU DO ME.
MY DAUGHTER WILL BE PERFECTLY ALL RIGHT, YORICK. I TOLD YOU, I ONLY GAVE HER A SEDATIVE.
NO, YOU DIDN'T.

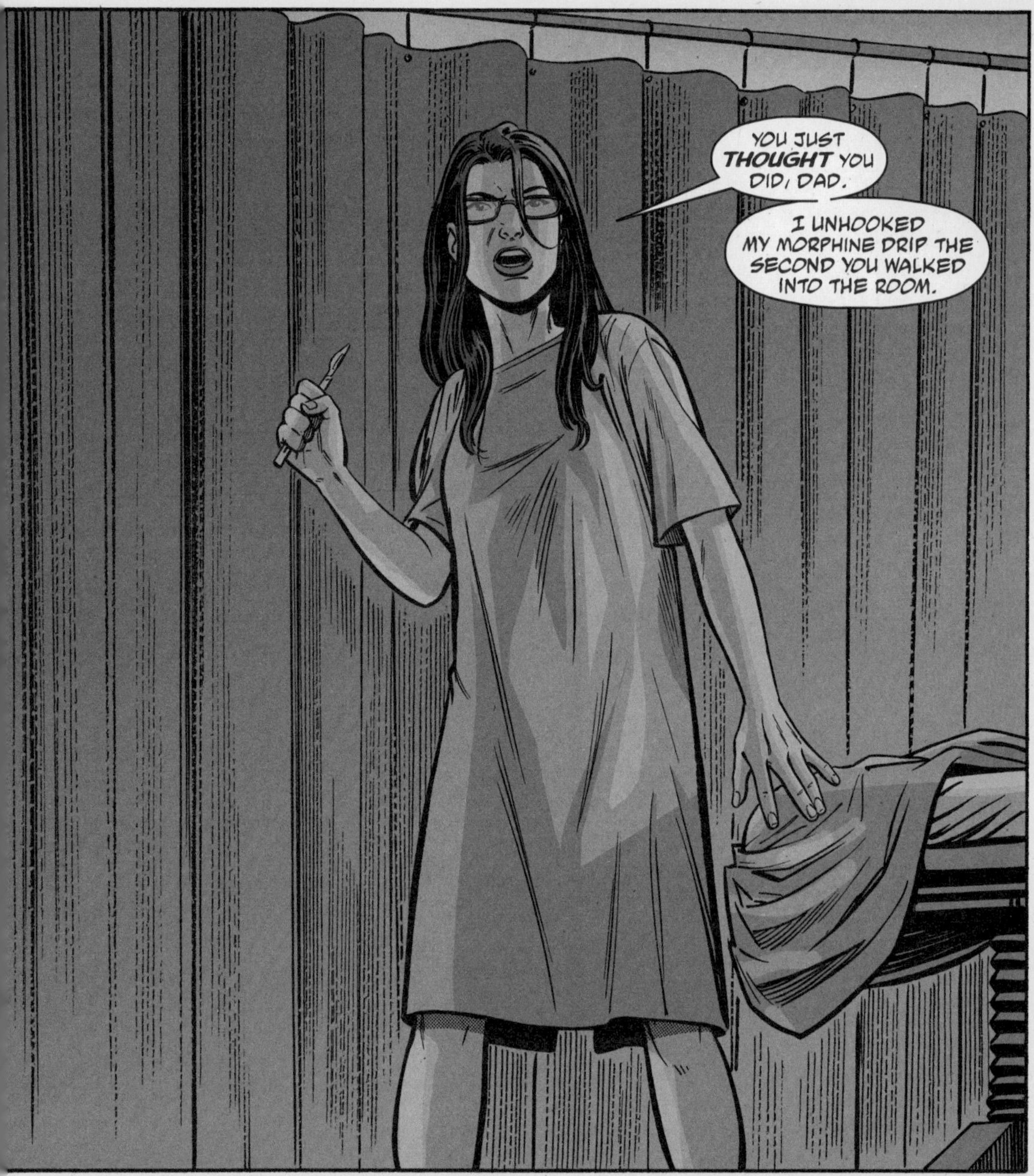
YOU JUST THOUGHT YOU DID, DAD.
I UNHOOKED MY MORPHINE DRIP THE SECOND YOU WALKED INTO THE ROOM.
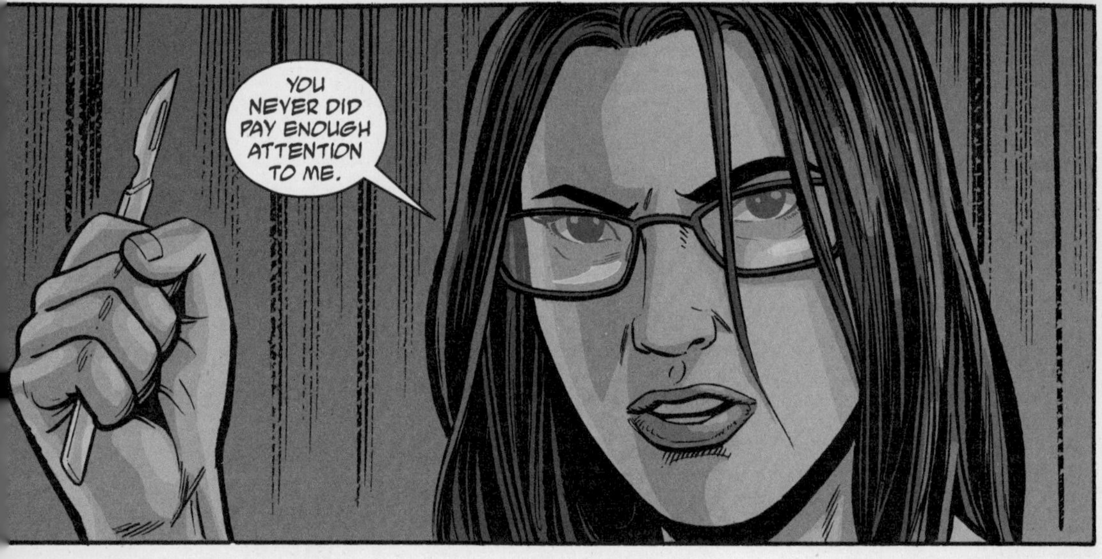
YOU NEVER DID PAY ENOUGH ATTENTION TO ME.

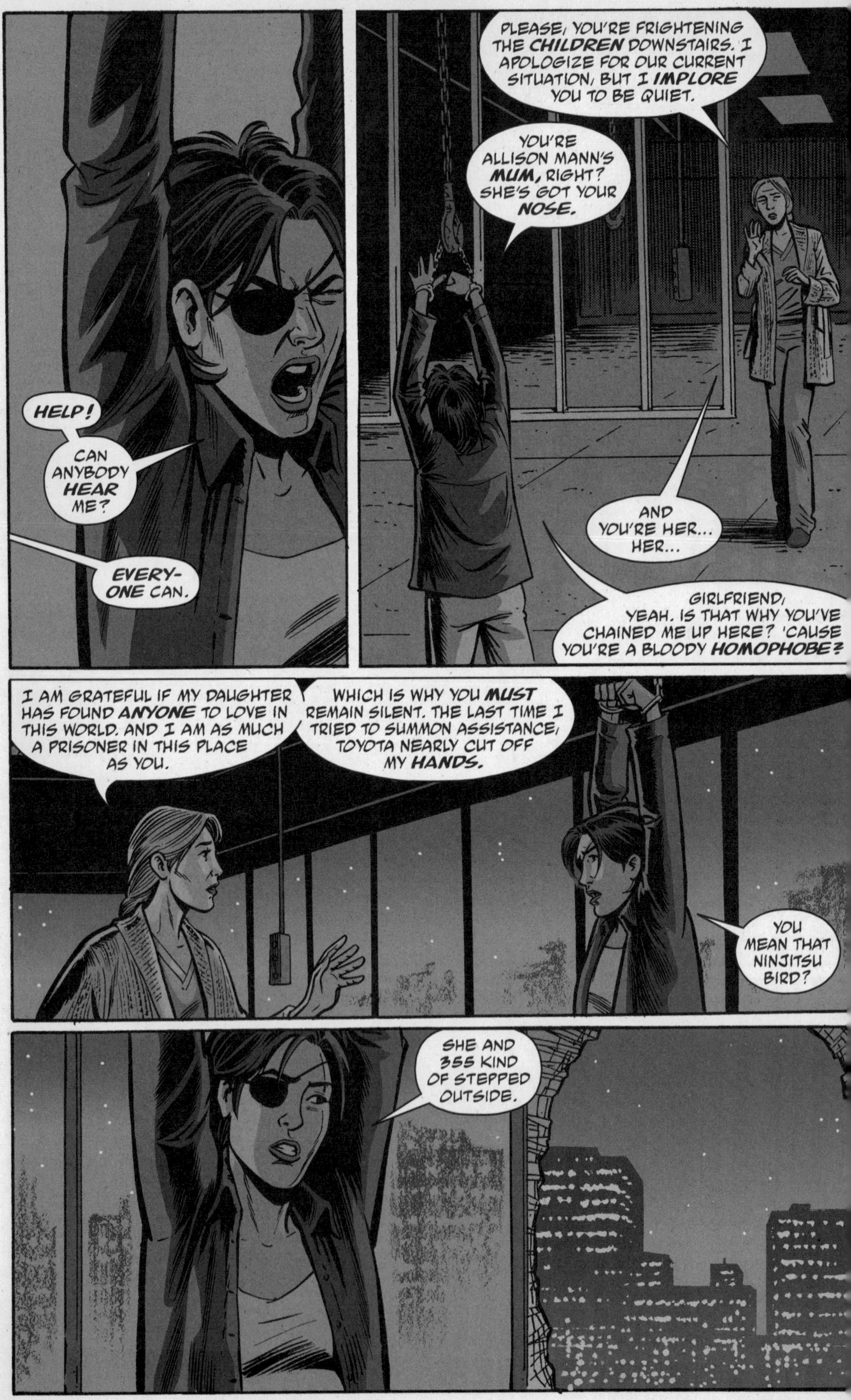
HELP!
CAN ANYBODY HEAR ME?
EVERY-ONE CAN.
PLEASE, YOU'RE FRIGHTENING THE CHILDREN DOWNSTAIRS. I APOLOGIZE FOR OUR CURRENT SITUATION, BUT I IMPLORE YOU TO BE QUIET.
YOU'RE ALLISON MANN'S MUM, RIGHT? SHE'S GOT YOUR NOSE.
AND YOU'RE HER... HER...
GIRLFRIEND, YEAH. IS THAT WHY YOU'VE CHAINED ME UP HERE? 'CAUSE YOU'RE A BLOODY HOMOPHOBE?
I AM GRATEFUL IF MY DAUGHTER HAS FOUND ANYONE TO LOVE IN THIS WORLD. AND I AM AS MUCH A PRISONER IN THIS PLACE AS YOU.
WHICH IS WHY YOU MUST REMAIN SILENT. THE LAST TIME I TRIED TO SUMMON ASSISTANCE, TOYOTA NEARLY CUT OFF MY HANDS.
YOU MEAN THAT NINJITSU BIRD?
SHE AND 355 KIND OF STEPPED OUTSIDE.

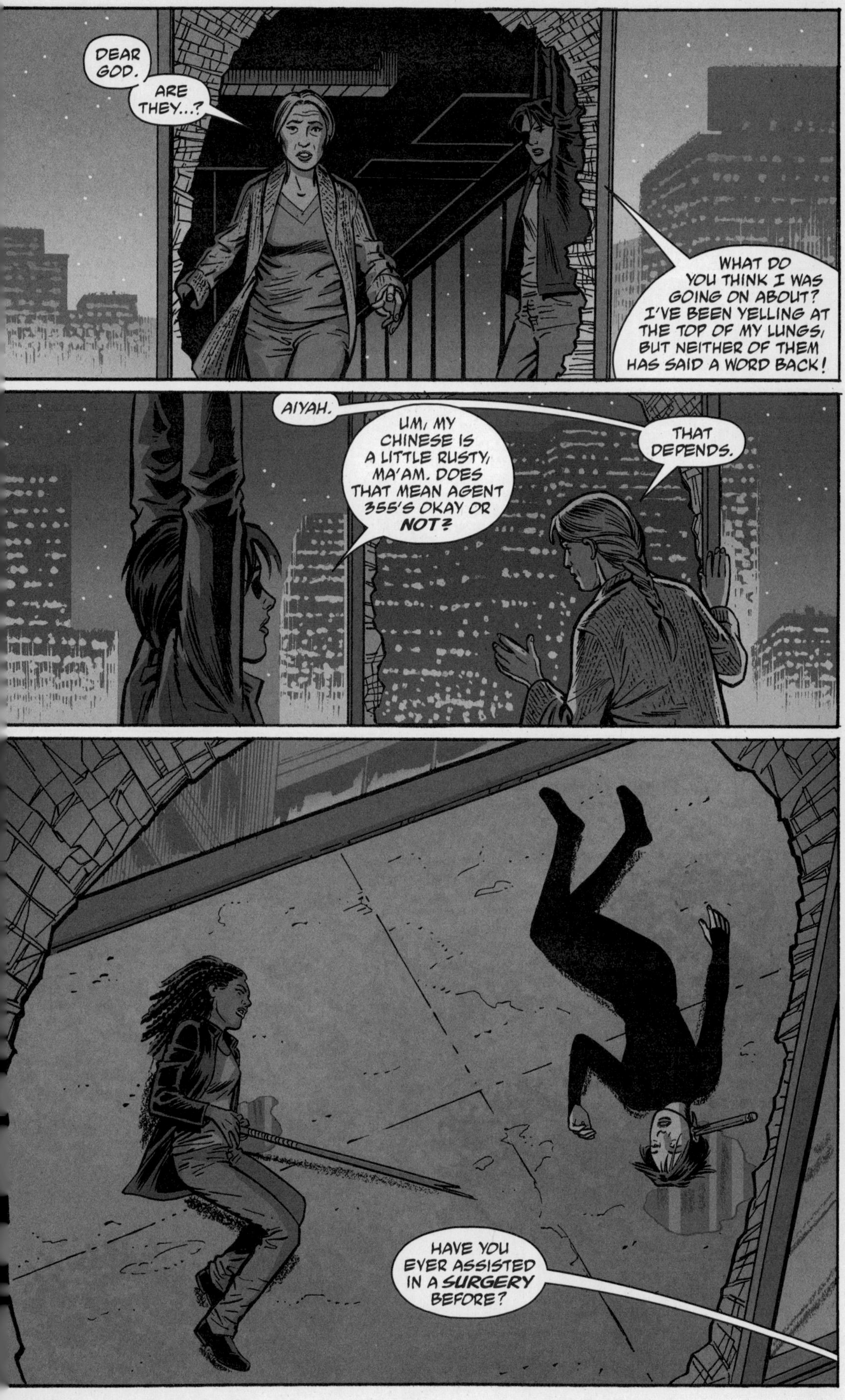
DEAR GOD.
ARE THEY...?
WHAT DO YOU THINK I WAS GOING ON ABOUT? I'VE BEEN YELLING AT THE TOP OF MY LUNGS, BUT NEITHER OF THEM HAS SAID A WORD BACK!
AIYAH.
THAT DEPENDS.
UM, MY CHINESE IS A LITTLE RUSTY, MA'AM. DOES THAT MEAN AGENT 355'S OKAY OR NOT?
HAVE YOU EVER ASSISTED IN A SURGERY BEFORE?

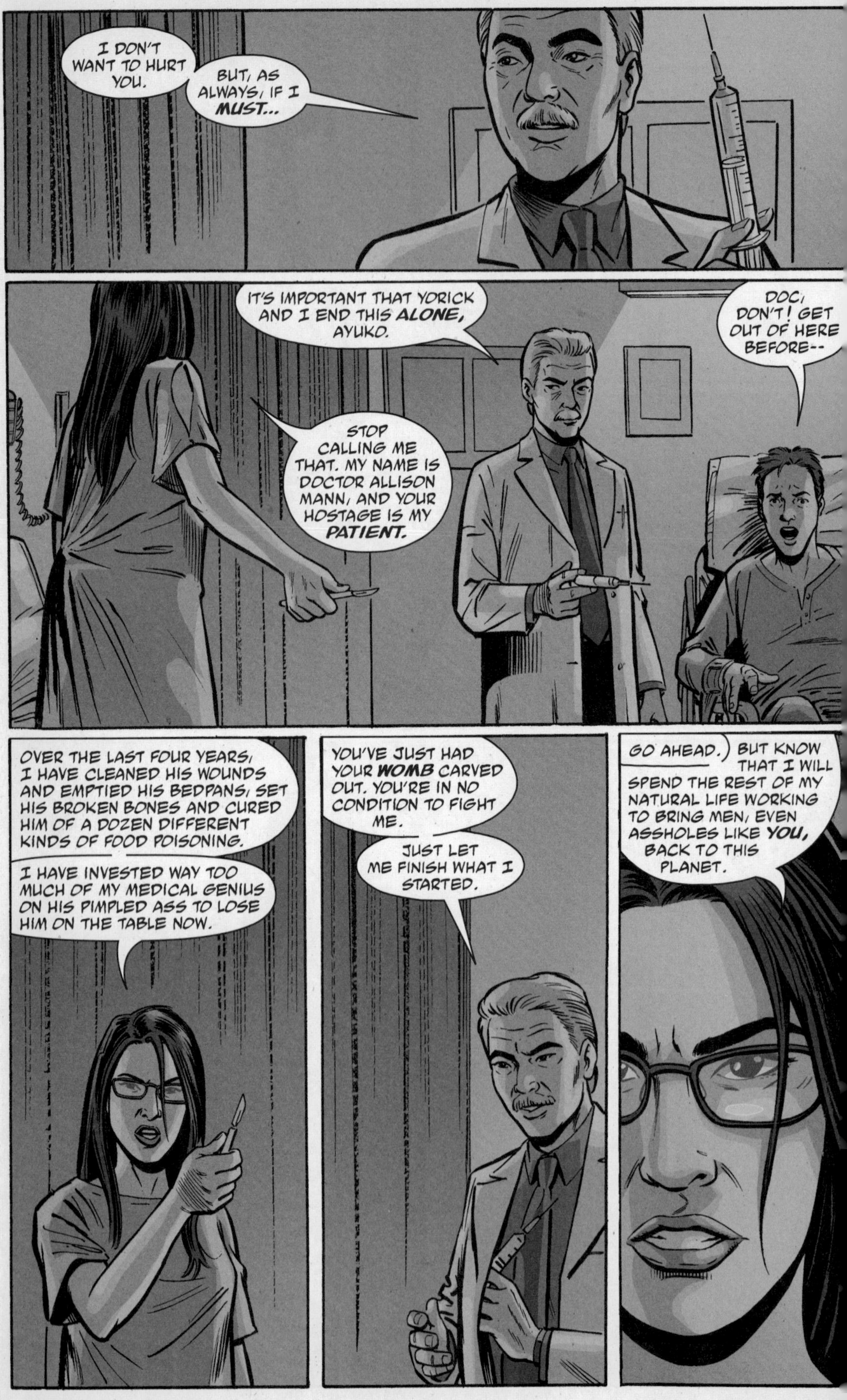

I DON'T WANT TO HURT YOU.
BUT, AS ALWAYS, IF I ***MUST...***
IT'S IMPORTANT THAT YORICK AND I END THIS ***ALONE,*** AYUKO.
DOC, DON'T! GET OUT OF HERE BEFORE--
STOP CALLING ME THAT. MY NAME IS DOCTOR ALLISON MANN, AND YOUR HOSTAGE IS MY ***PATIENT.***
OVER THE LAST FOUR YEARS, I HAVE CLEANED HIS WOUNDS AND EMPTIED HIS BEDPANS, SET HIS BROKEN BONES AND CURED HIM OF A DOZEN DIFFERENT KINDS OF FOOD POISONING.
I HAVE INVESTED WAY TOO MUCH OF MY MEDICAL GENIUS ON HIS PIMPLED ASS TO LOSE HIM ON THE TABLE NOW.
YOU'VE JUST HAD YOUR ***WOMB*** CARVED OUT. YOU'RE IN NO CONDITION TO FIGHT ME.
JUST LET ME FINISH WHAT I STARTED.
GO AHEAD.
BUT KNOW THAT I WILL SPEND THE REST OF MY NATURAL LIFE WORKING TO BRING MEN, EVEN ASSHOLES LIKE ***YOU,*** BACK TO THIS PLANET.

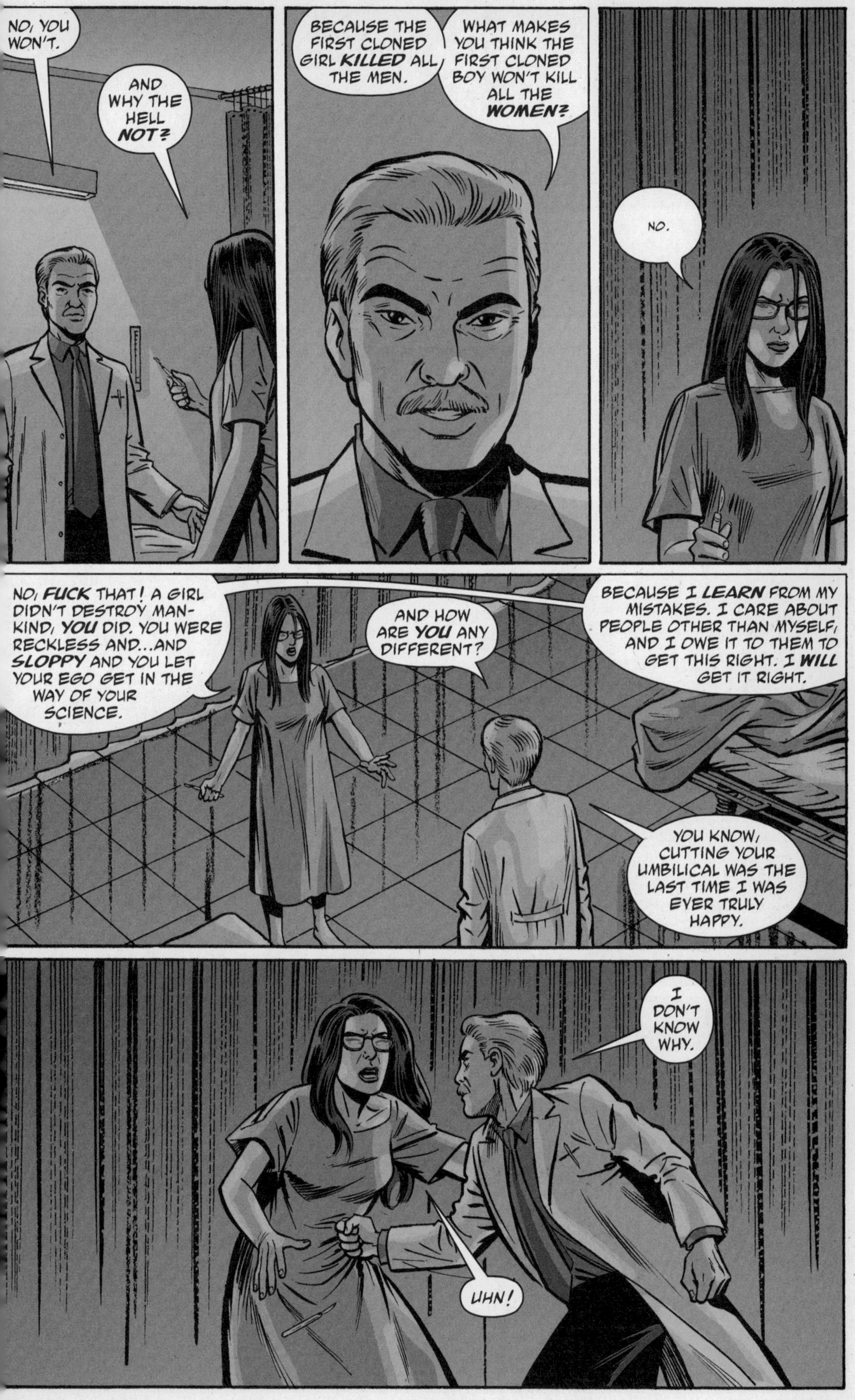
NO, YOU WON'T.
AND WHY THE HELL NOT?
BECAUSE THE FIRST CLONED GIRL KILLED ALL THE MEN.
WHAT MAKES YOU THINK THE FIRST CLONED BOY WON'T KILL ALL THE WOMEN?
NO.
NO, FUCK THAT! A GIRL DIDN'T DESTROY MAN-KIND, YOU DID. YOU WERE RECKLESS AND...AND SLOPPY AND YOU LET YOUR EGO GET IN THE WAY OF YOUR SCIENCE.
AND HOW ARE YOU ANY DIFFERENT?
BECAUSE I LEARN FROM MY MISTAKES. I CARE ABOUT PEOPLE OTHER THAN MYSELF, AND I OWE IT TO THEM TO GET THIS RIGHT. I WILL GET IT RIGHT.
YOU KNOW, CUTTING YOUR UMBILICAL WAS THE LAST TIME I WAS EVER TRULY HAPPY.
I DON'T KNOW WHY.
UHN!

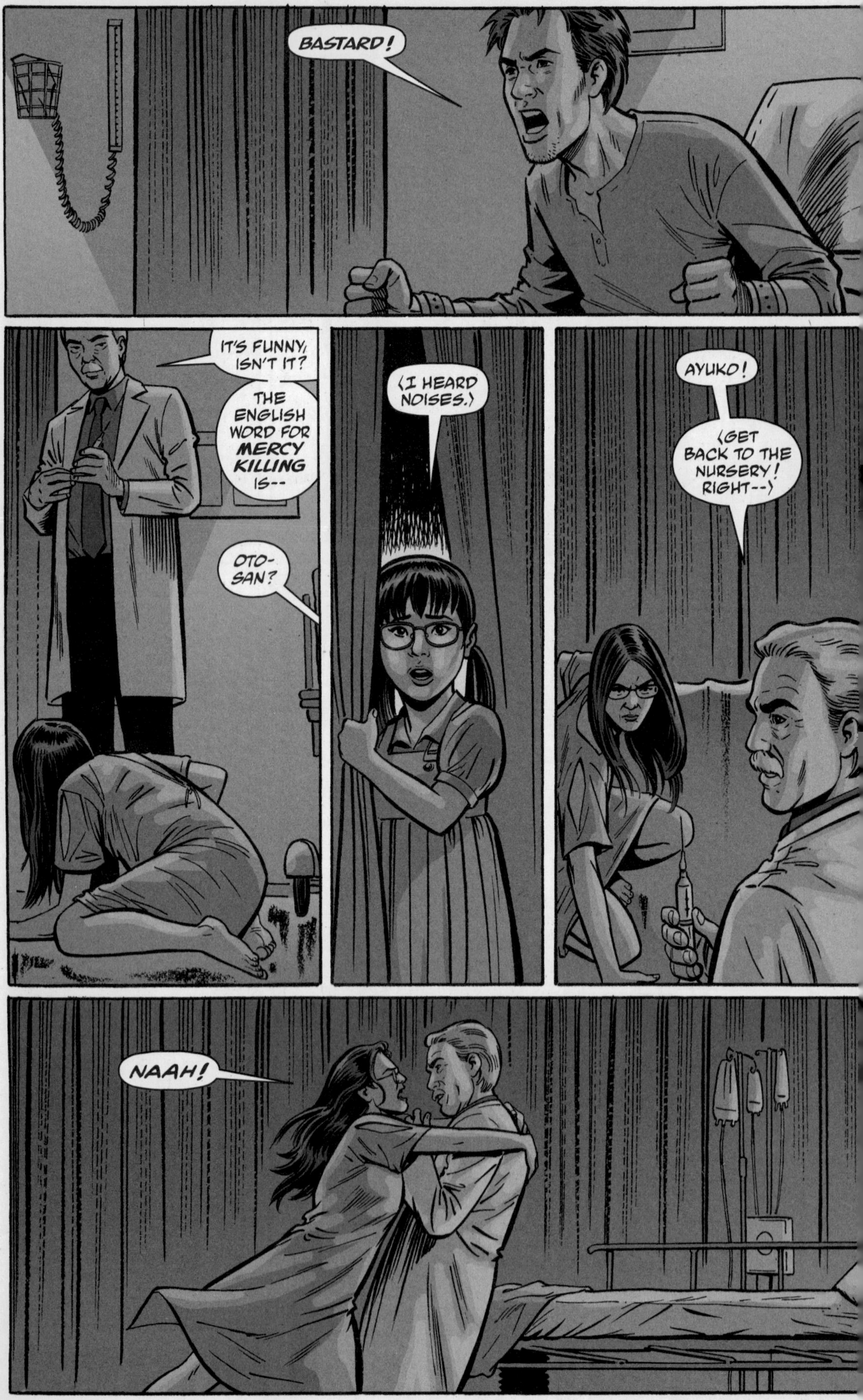
BASTARD!
IT'S FUNNY, ISN'T IT?
THE ENGLISH WORD FOR MERCY KILLING IS--
OTO-SAN?
⟨I HEARD NOISES.⟩
AYUKO!
⟨GET BACK TO THE NURSERY! RIGHT--⟩
NAAH!

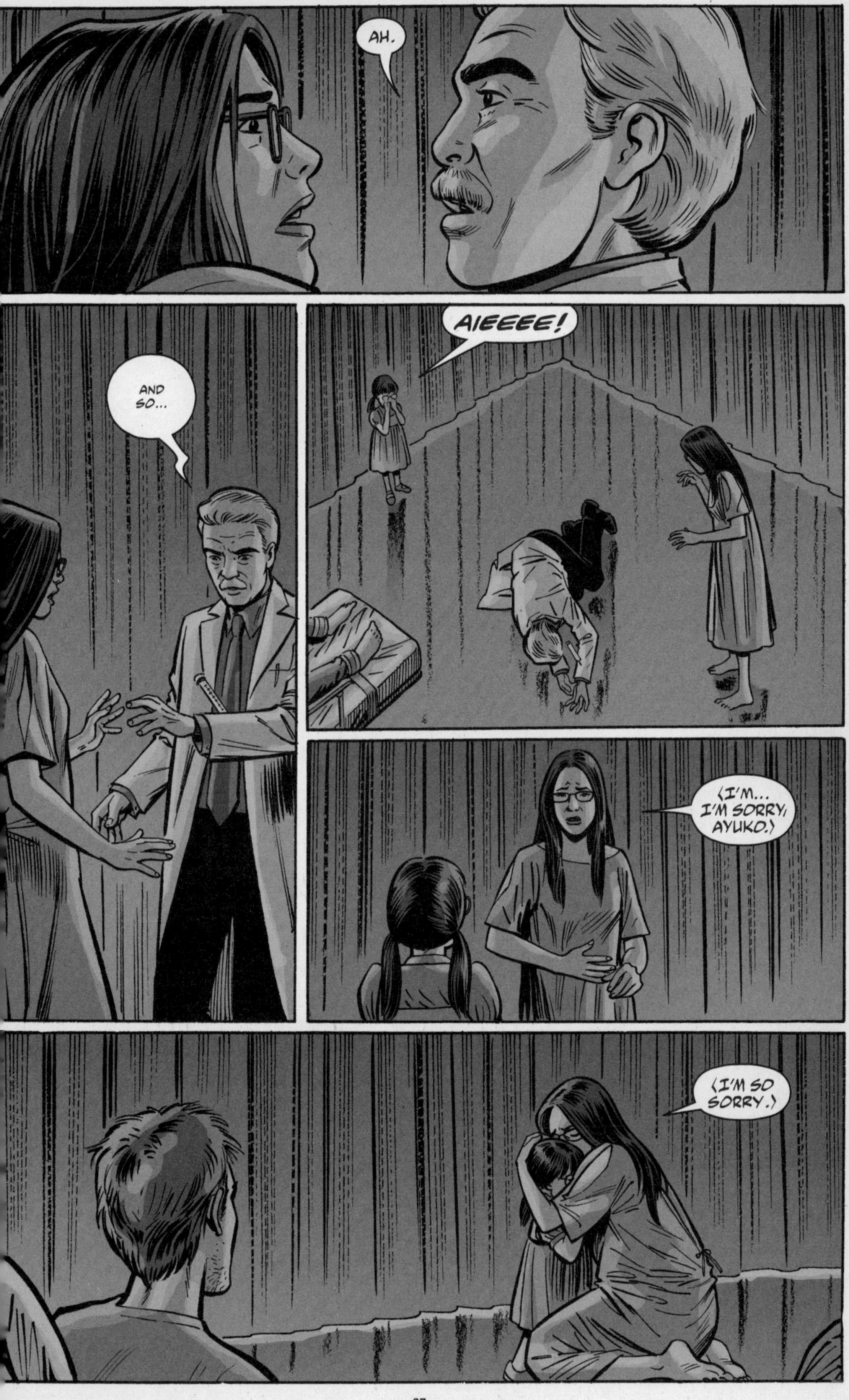
AH.
AND SO...
AIEEEE!
⟨I'M... I'M SORRY, AYUKO.⟩
⟨I'M SO SORRY.⟩

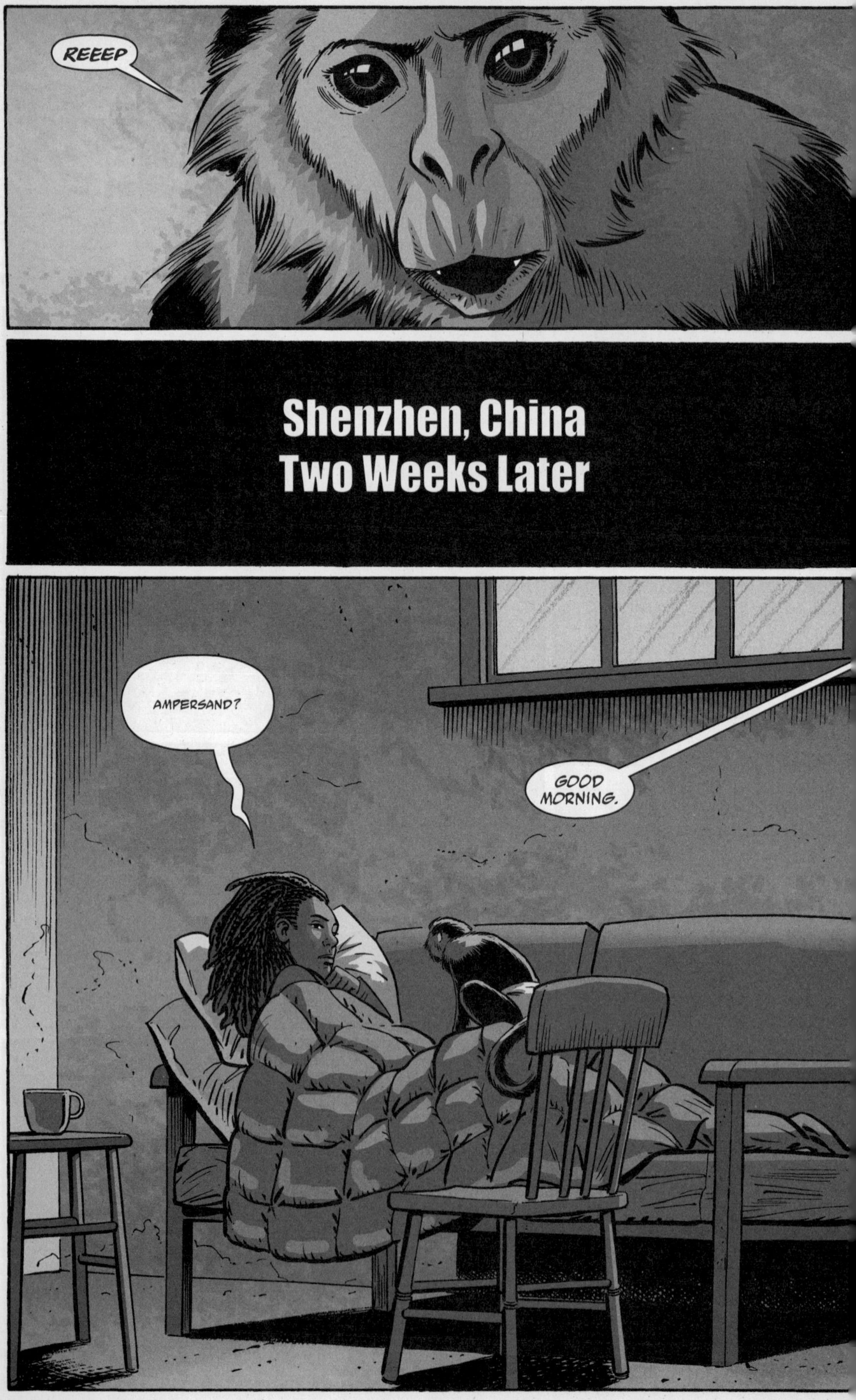
REEEP
Shenzhen, China
Two Weeks Later
AMPERSAND?
GOOD MORNING.

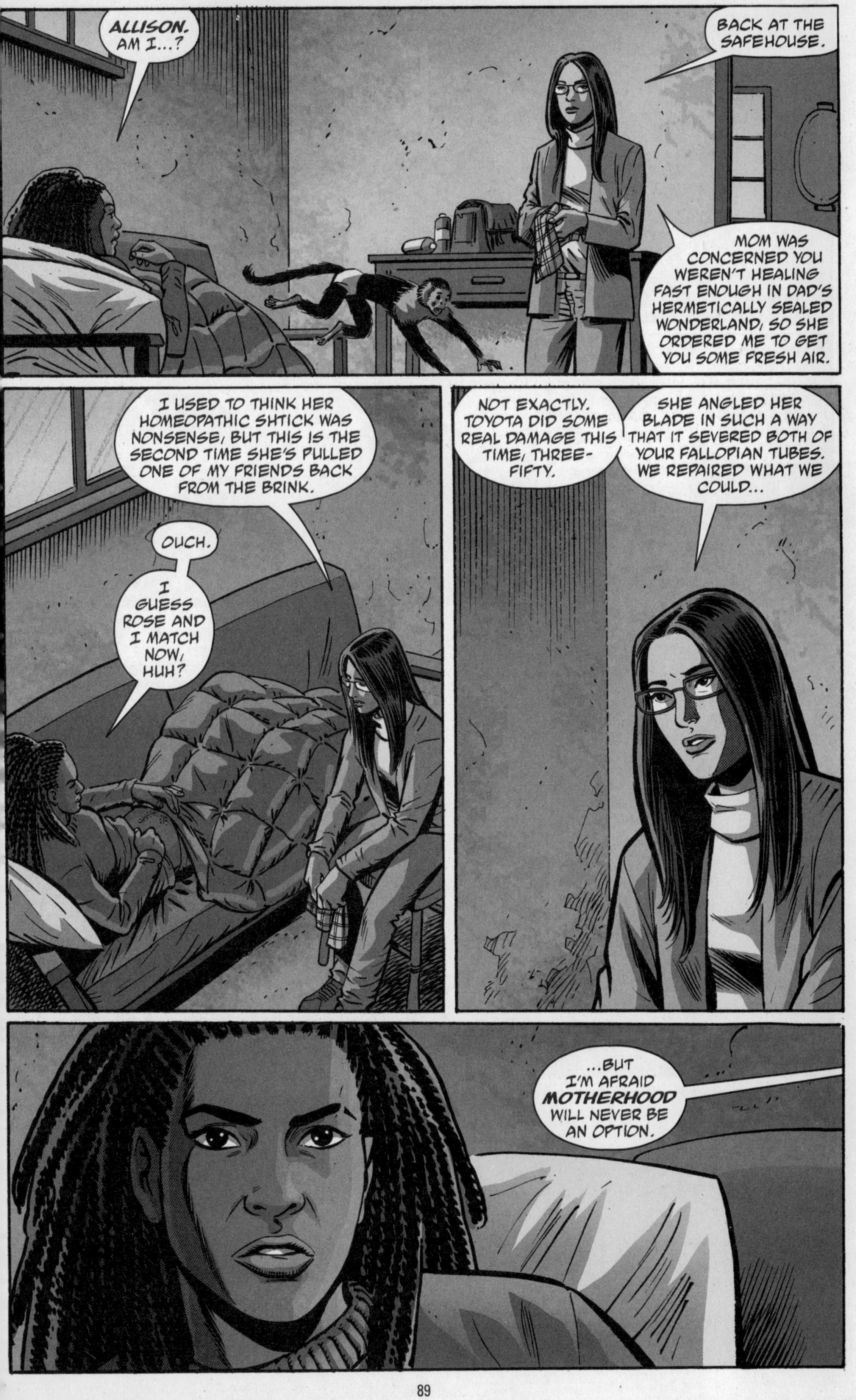
ALLISON. AM I...?
BACK AT THE SAFEHOUSE.
MOM WAS CONCERNED YOU WEREN'T HEALING FAST ENOUGH IN DAD'S HERMETICALLY SEALED WONDERLAND, SO SHE ORDERED ME TO GET YOU SOME FRESH AIR.
I USED TO THINK HER HOMEOPATHIC SHTICK WAS NONSENSE, BUT THIS IS THE SECOND TIME SHE'S PULLED ONE OF MY FRIENDS BACK FROM THE BRINK.
OUCH.
I GUESS ROSE AND I MATCH NOW, HUH?
NOT EXACTLY. TOYOTA DID SOME REAL DAMAGE THIS TIME, THREE-FIFTY.
SHE ANGLED HER BLADE IN SUCH A WAY THAT IT SEVERED BOTH OF YOUR FALLOPIAN TUBES. WE REPAIRED WHAT WE COULD...
...BUT I'M AFRAID MOTHERHOOD WILL NEVER BE AN OPTION.

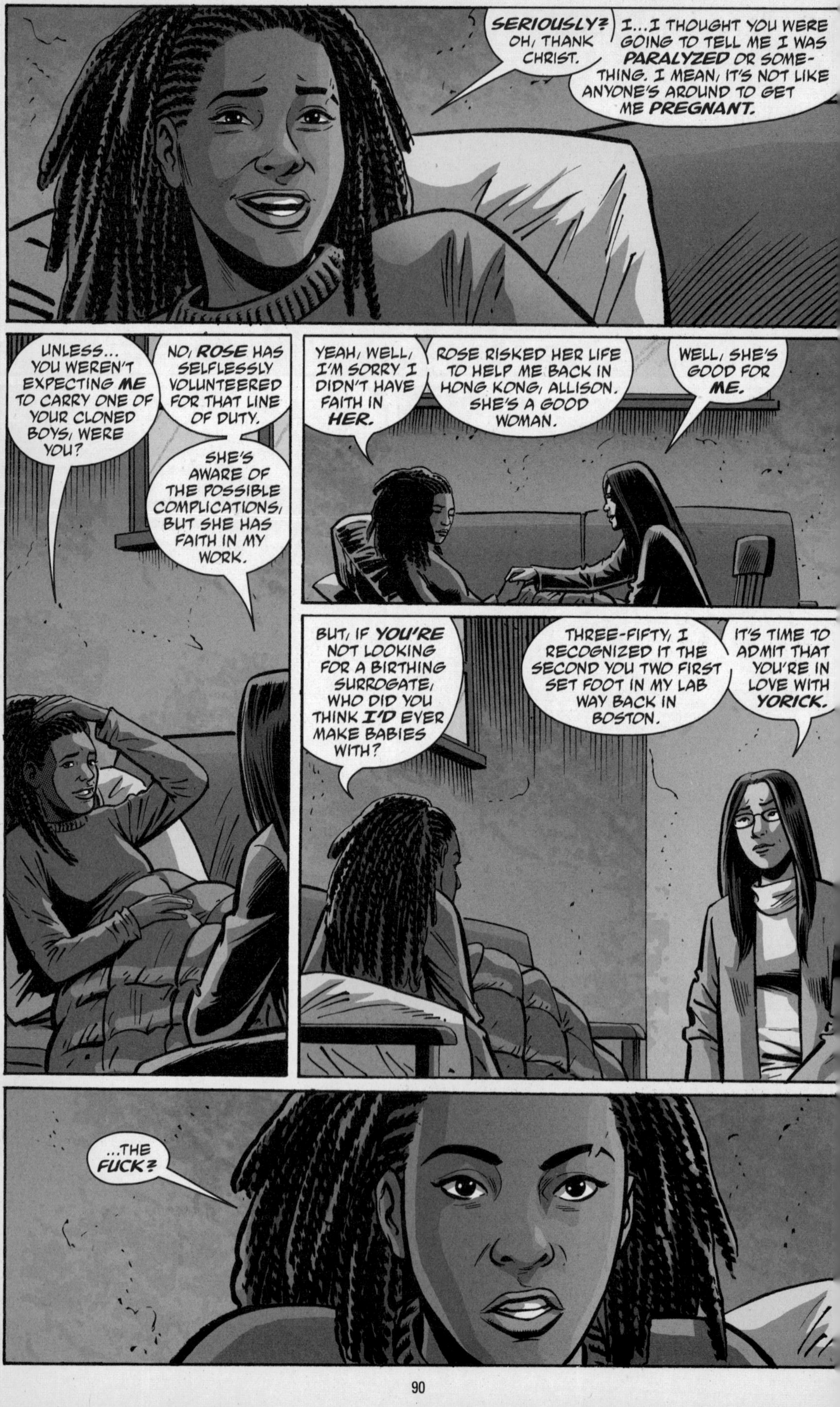
SERIOUSLY? OH, THANK CHRIST.
I...I THOUGHT YOU WERE GOING TO TELL ME I WAS PARALYZED OR SOMETHING. I MEAN, IT'S NOT LIKE ANYONE'S AROUND TO GET ME PREGNANT.
UNLESS... YOU WEREN'T EXPECTING ME TO CARRY ONE OF YOUR CLONED BOYS, WERE YOU?
NO, ROSE HAS SELFLESSLY VOLUNTEERED FOR THAT LINE OF DUTY.
SHE'S AWARE OF THE POSSIBLE COMPLICATIONS, BUT SHE HAS FAITH IN MY WORK.
YEAH, WELL, I'M SORRY I DIDN'T HAVE FAITH IN HER.
ROSE RISKED HER LIFE TO HELP ME BACK IN HONG KONG, ALLISON. SHE'S A GOOD WOMAN.
WELL, SHE'S GOOD FOR ME.
BUT, IF YOU'RE NOT LOOKING FOR A BIRTHING SURROGATE, WHO DID YOU THINK I'D EVER MAKE BABIES WITH?
THREE-FIFTY, I RECOGNIZED IT THE SECOND YOU TWO FIRST SET FOOT IN MY LAB WAY BACK IN BOSTON.
IT'S TIME TO ADMIT THAT YOU'RE IN LOVE WITH YORICK.
...THE FUCK?

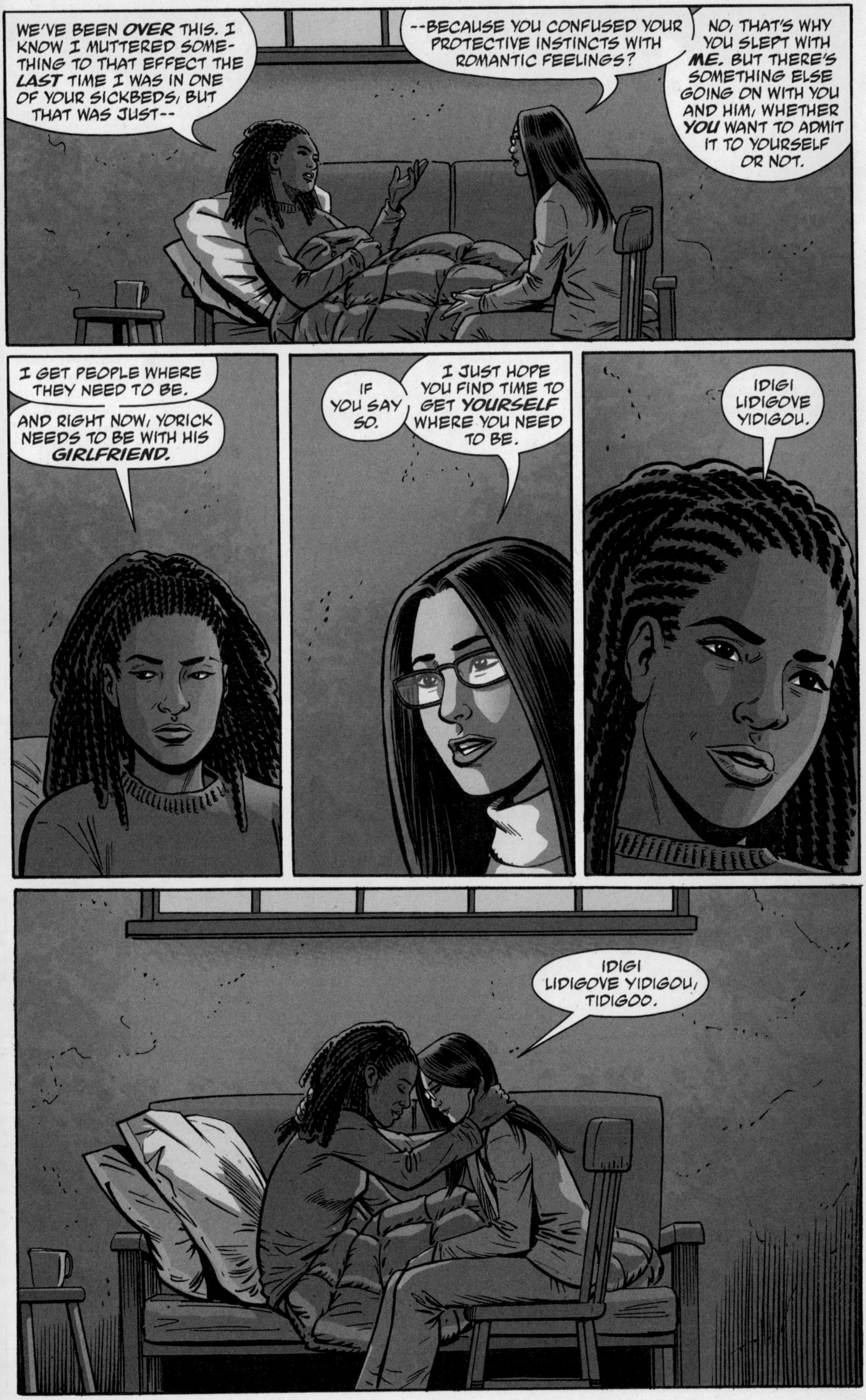
WE'VE BEEN OVER THIS. I KNOW I MUTTERED SOMETHING TO THAT EFFECT THE LAST TIME I WAS IN ONE OF YOUR SICKBEDS, BUT THAT WAS JUST--
--BECAUSE YOU CONFUSED YOUR PROTECTIVE INSTINCTS WITH ROMANTIC FEELINGS?
NO, THAT'S WHY YOU SLEPT WITH ME. BUT THERE'S SOMETHING ELSE GOING ON WITH YOU AND HIM, WHETHER YOU WANT TO ADMIT IT TO YOURSELF OR NOT.
I GET PEOPLE WHERE THEY NEED TO BE.
AND RIGHT NOW, YORICK NEEDS TO BE WITH HIS GIRLFRIEND.
IF YOU SAY SO.
I JUST HOPE YOU FIND TIME TO GET YOURSELF WHERE YOU NEED TO BE.
IDIGI LIDIGOVE YIDIGOU.
IDIGI LIDIGOVE YIDIGOU, TIDIGOO.

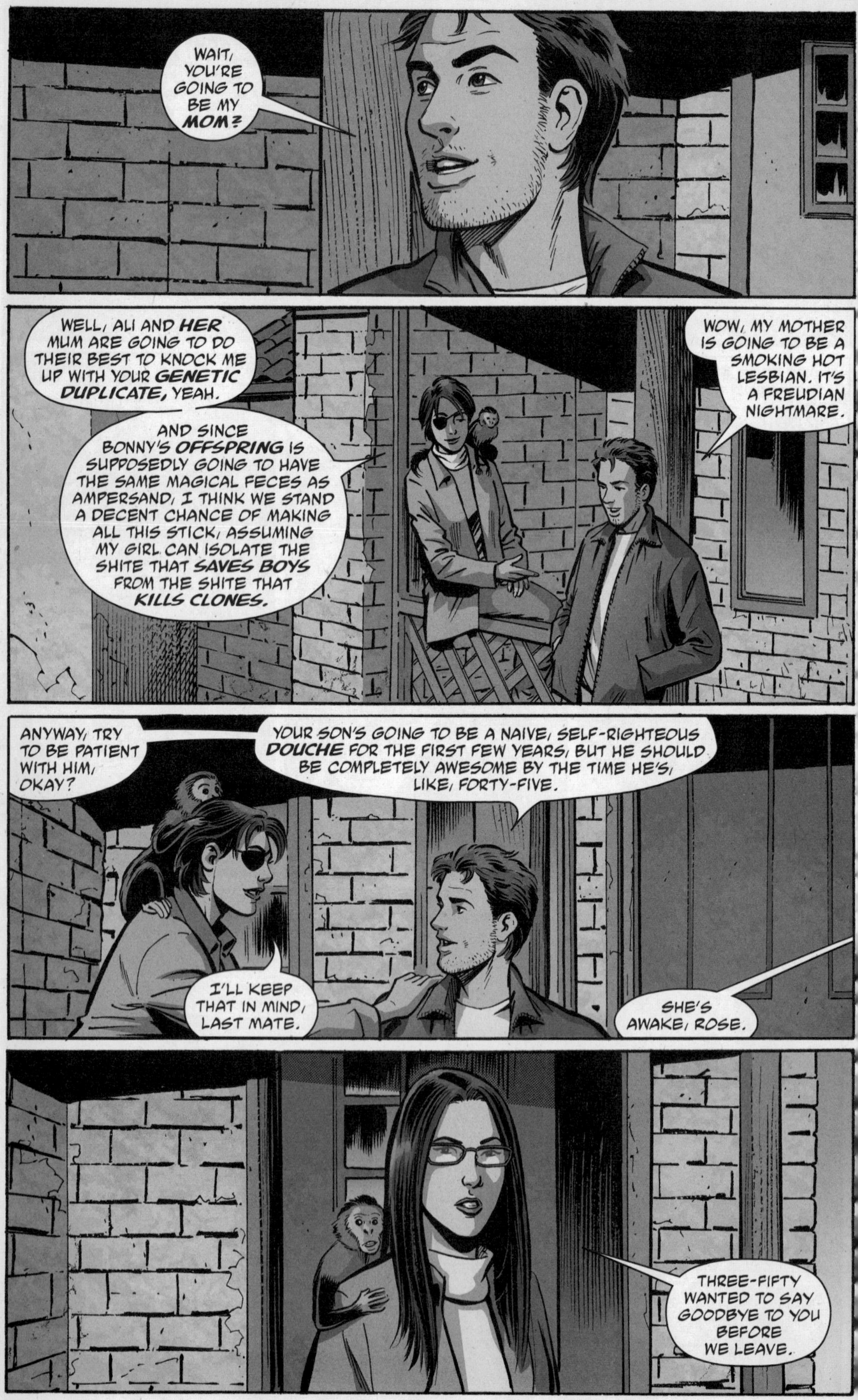

WAIT, YOU'RE GOING TO BE MY MOM?
WELL, ALI AND HER MUM ARE GOING TO DO THEIR BEST TO KNOCK ME UP WITH YOUR GENETIC DUPLICATE, YEAH.
AND SINCE BONNY'S OFFSPRING IS SUPPOSEDLY GOING TO HAVE THE SAME MAGICAL FECES AS AMPERSAND, I THINK WE STAND A DECENT CHANCE OF MAKING ALL THIS STICK, ASSUMING MY GIRL CAN ISOLATE THE SHITE THAT SAVES BOYS FROM THE SHITE THAT KILLS CLONES.
WOW, MY MOTHER IS GOING TO BE A SMOKING HOT LESBIAN. IT'S A FREUDIAN NIGHTMARE.
ANYWAY, TRY TO BE PATIENT WITH HIM, OKAY?
YOUR SON'S GOING TO BE A NAIVE, SELF-RIGHTEOUS DOUCHE FOR THE FIRST FEW YEARS, BUT HE SHOULD BE COMPLETELY AWESOME BY THE TIME HE'S, LIKE, FORTY-FIVE.
I'LL KEEP THAT IN MIND, LAST MATE.
SHE'S AWAKE, ROSE.
THREE-FIFTY WANTED TO SAY GOODBYE TO YOU BEFORE WE LEAVE.

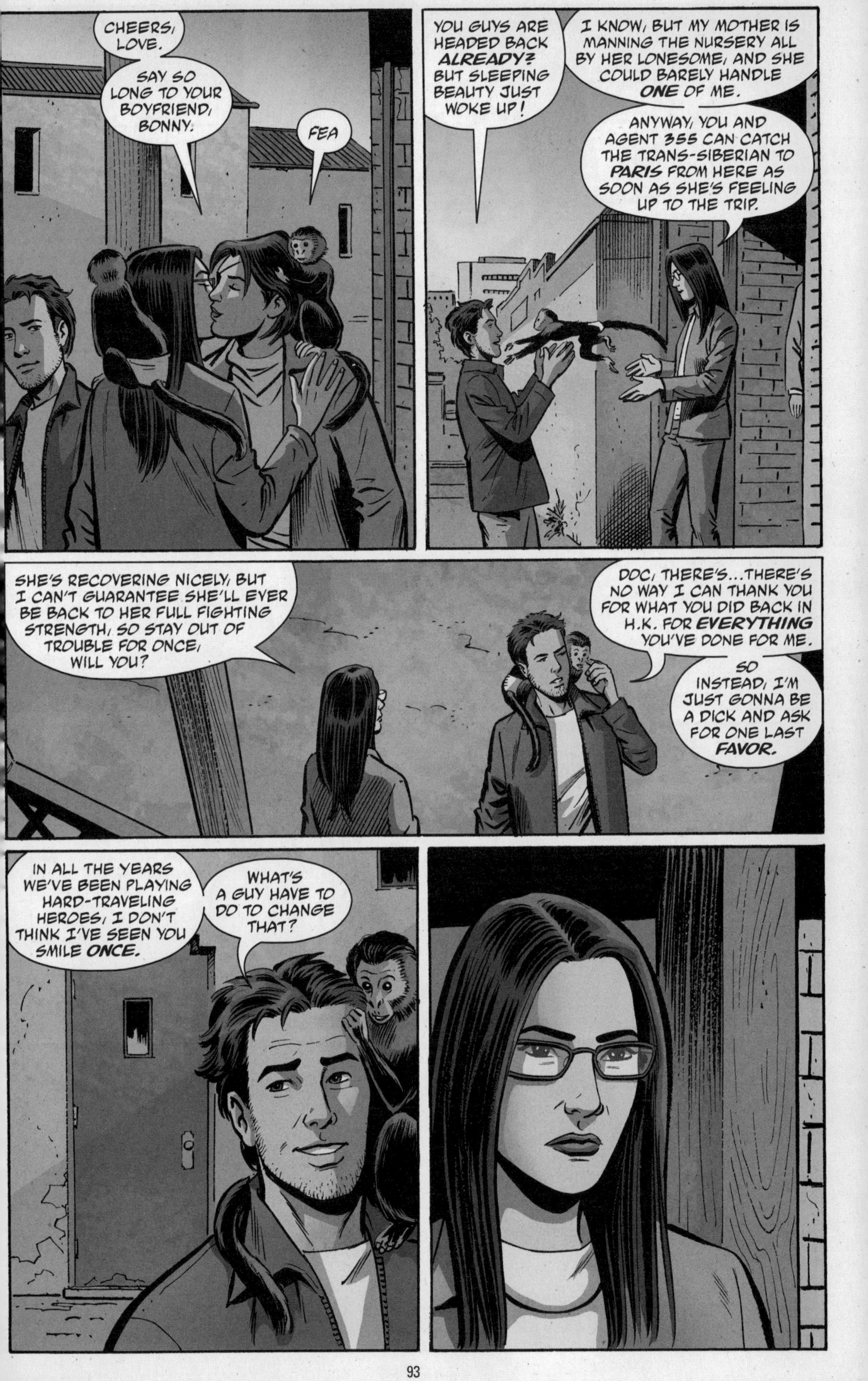
CHEERS, LOVE.
SAY SO LONG TO YOUR BOYFRIEND, BONNY.
FEA
YOU GUYS ARE HEADED BACK ALREADY? BUT SLEEPING BEAUTY JUST WOKE UP!
I KNOW, BUT MY MOTHER IS MANNING THE NURSERY ALL BY HER LONESOME, AND SHE COULD BARELY HANDLE ONE OF ME.
ANYWAY, YOU AND AGENT 355 CAN CATCH THE TRANS-SIBERIAN TO PARIS FROM HERE AS SOON AS SHE'S FEELING UP TO THE TRIP.
SHE'S RECOVERING NICELY, BUT I CAN'T GUARANTEE SHE'LL EVER BE BACK TO HER FULL FIGHTING STRENGTH, SO STAY OUT OF TROUBLE FOR ONCE, WILL YOU?
DOC, THERE'S...THERE'S NO WAY I CAN THANK YOU FOR WHAT YOU DID BACK IN H.K. FOR EVERYTHING YOU'VE DONE FOR ME.
SO INSTEAD, I'M JUST GONNA BE A DICK AND ASK FOR ONE LAST FAVOR.
IN ALL THE YEARS WE'VE BEEN PLAYING HARD-TRAVELING HEROES, I DON'T THINK I'VE SEEN YOU SMILE ONCE.
WHAT'S A GUY HAVE TO DO TO CHANGE THAT?

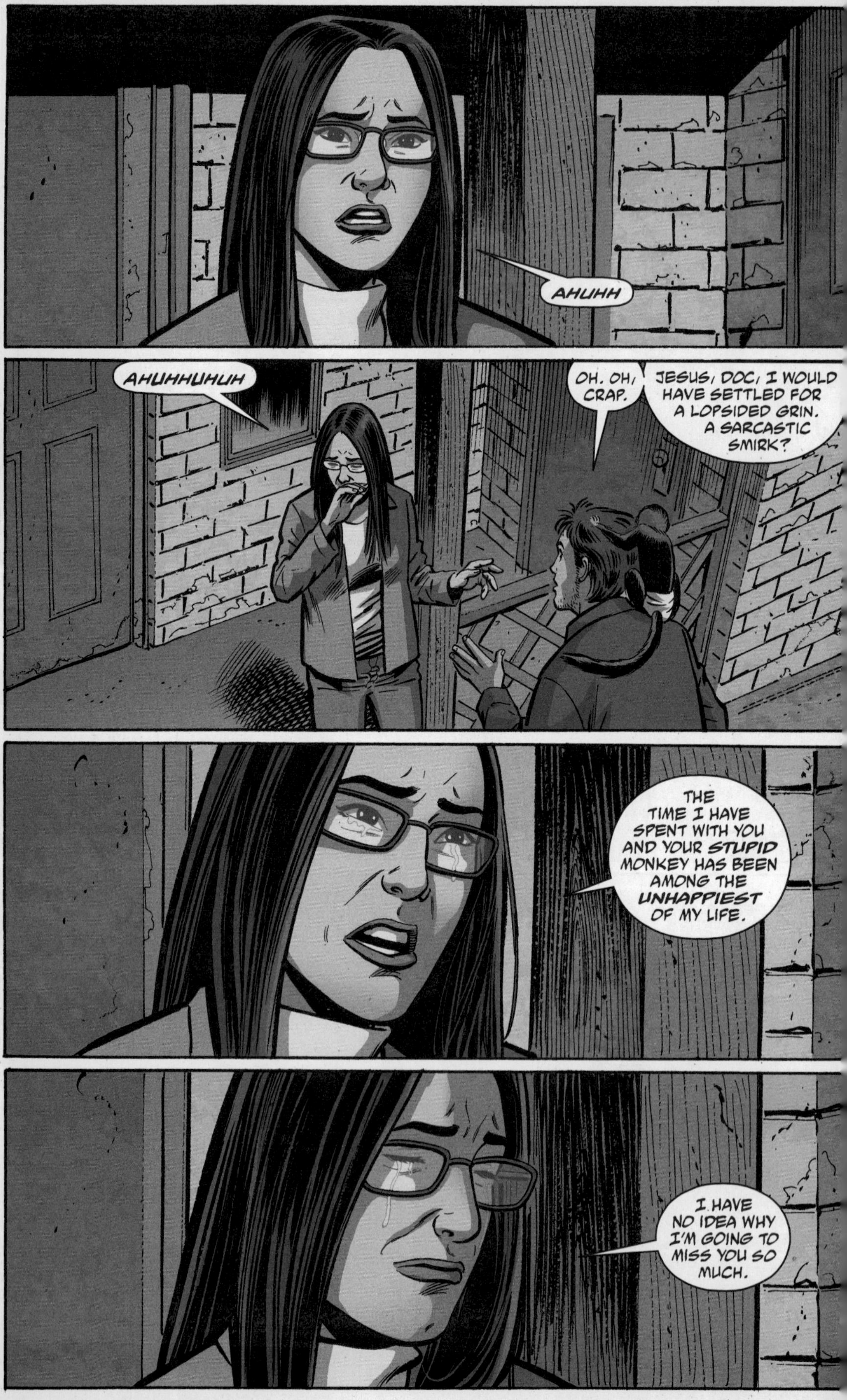
AHUHH
AHUHHUHUH
OH. OH, CRAP.
JESUS, DOC, I WOULD HAVE SETTLED FOR A LOPSIDED GRIN. A SARCASTIC SMIRK?
THE TIME I HAVE SPENT WITH YOU AND YOUR STUPID MONKEY HAS BEEN AMONG THE UNHAPPIEST OF MY LIFE.
I HAVE NO IDEA WHY I'M GOING TO MISS YOU SO MUCH.

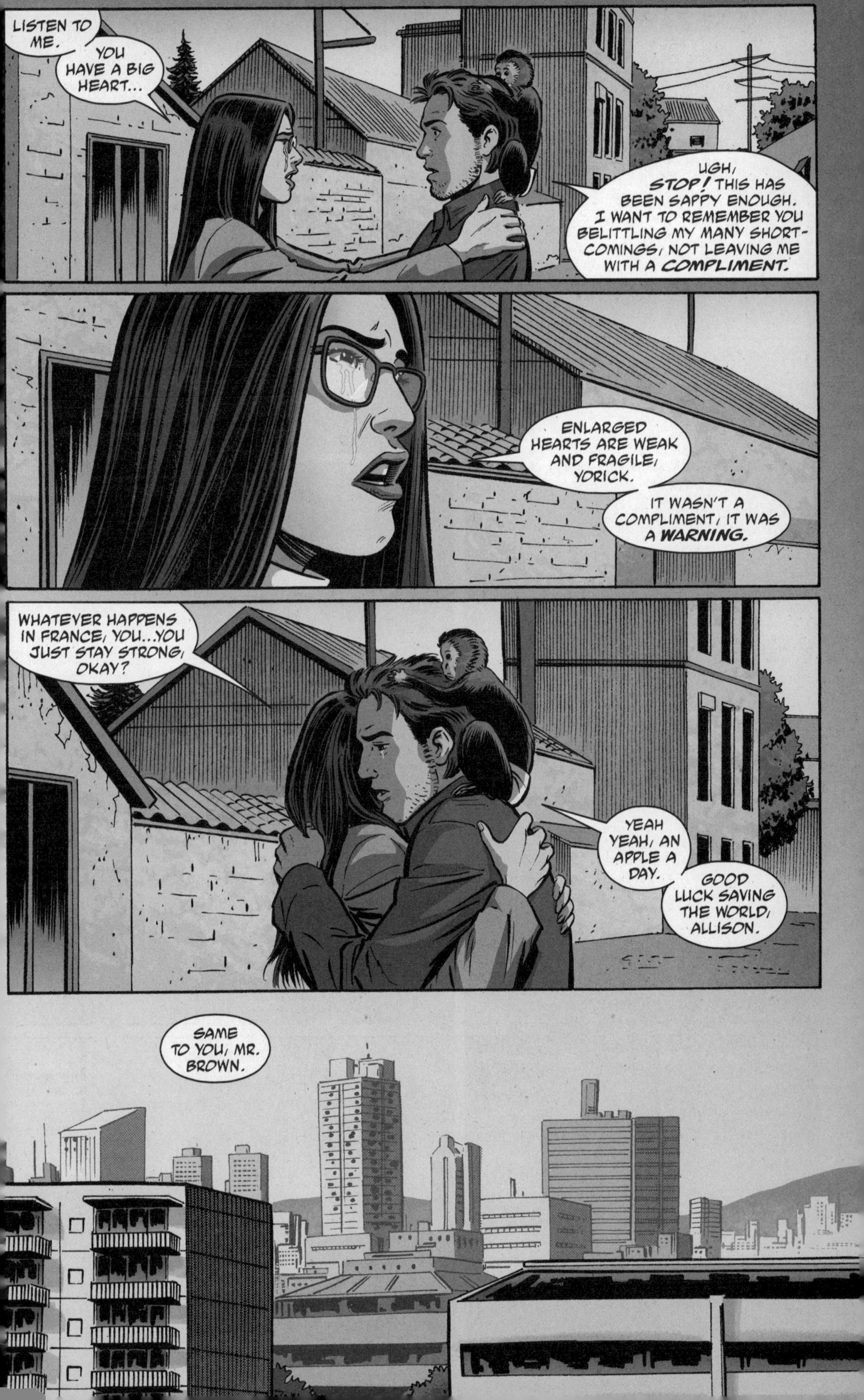

LISTEN TO ME.
YOU HAVE A BIG HEART...
UGH, STOP! THIS HAS BEEN SAPPY ENOUGH. I WANT TO REMEMBER YOU BELITTLING MY MANY SHORT-COMINGS, NOT LEAVING ME WITH A COMPLIMENT.
ENLARGED HEARTS ARE WEAK AND FRAGILE, YORICK.
IT WASN'T A COMPLIMENT, IT WAS A WARNING.
WHATEVER HAPPENS IN FRANCE, YOU...YOU JUST STAY STRONG, OKAY?
YEAH YEAH, AN APPLE A DAY.
GOOD LUCK SAVING THE WORLD, ALLISON.
SAME TO YOU, MR. BROWN.

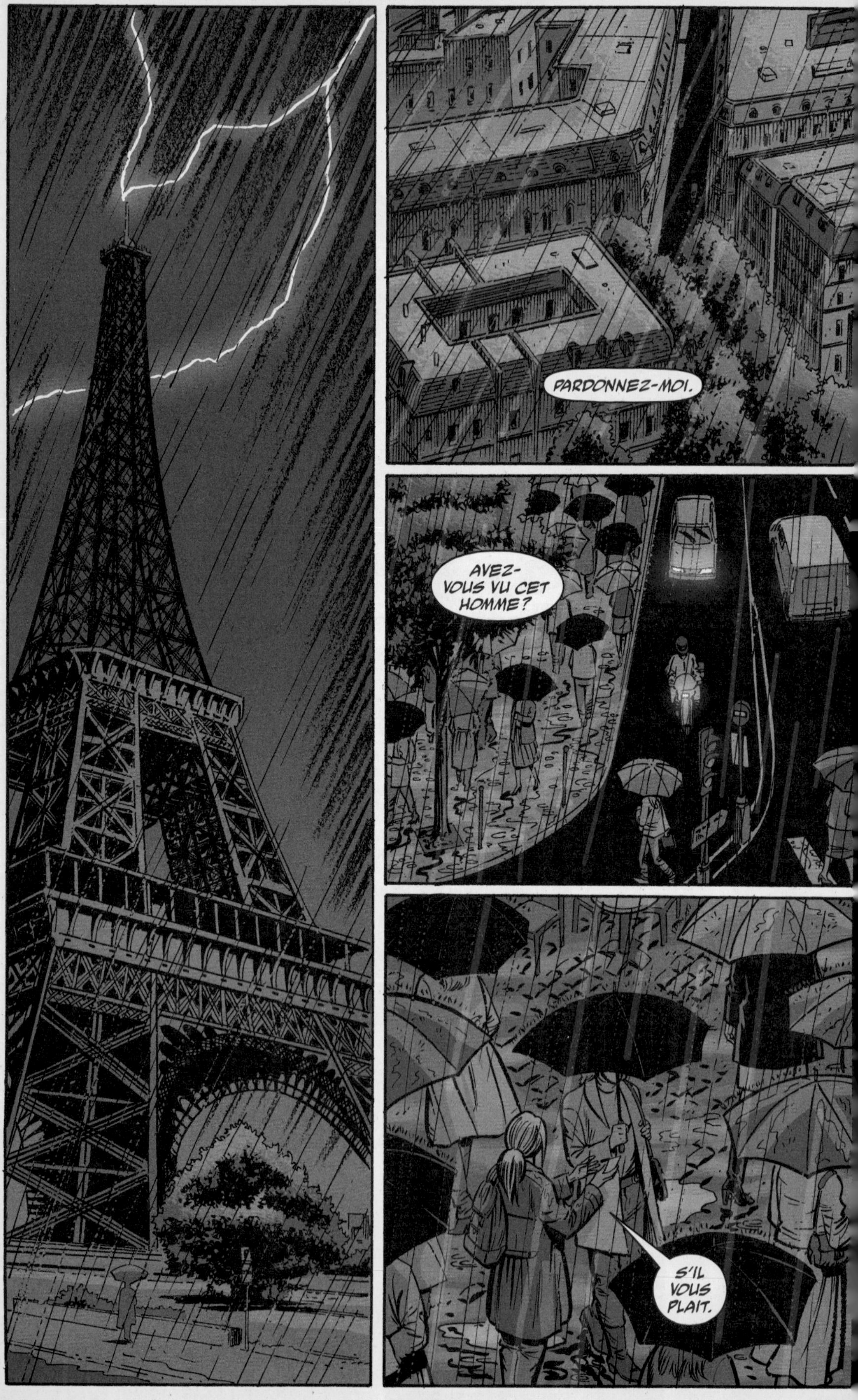
PARDONNEZ-MOI.
AVEZ-VOUS VU CET HOMME?
S'IL VOUS PLAIT.

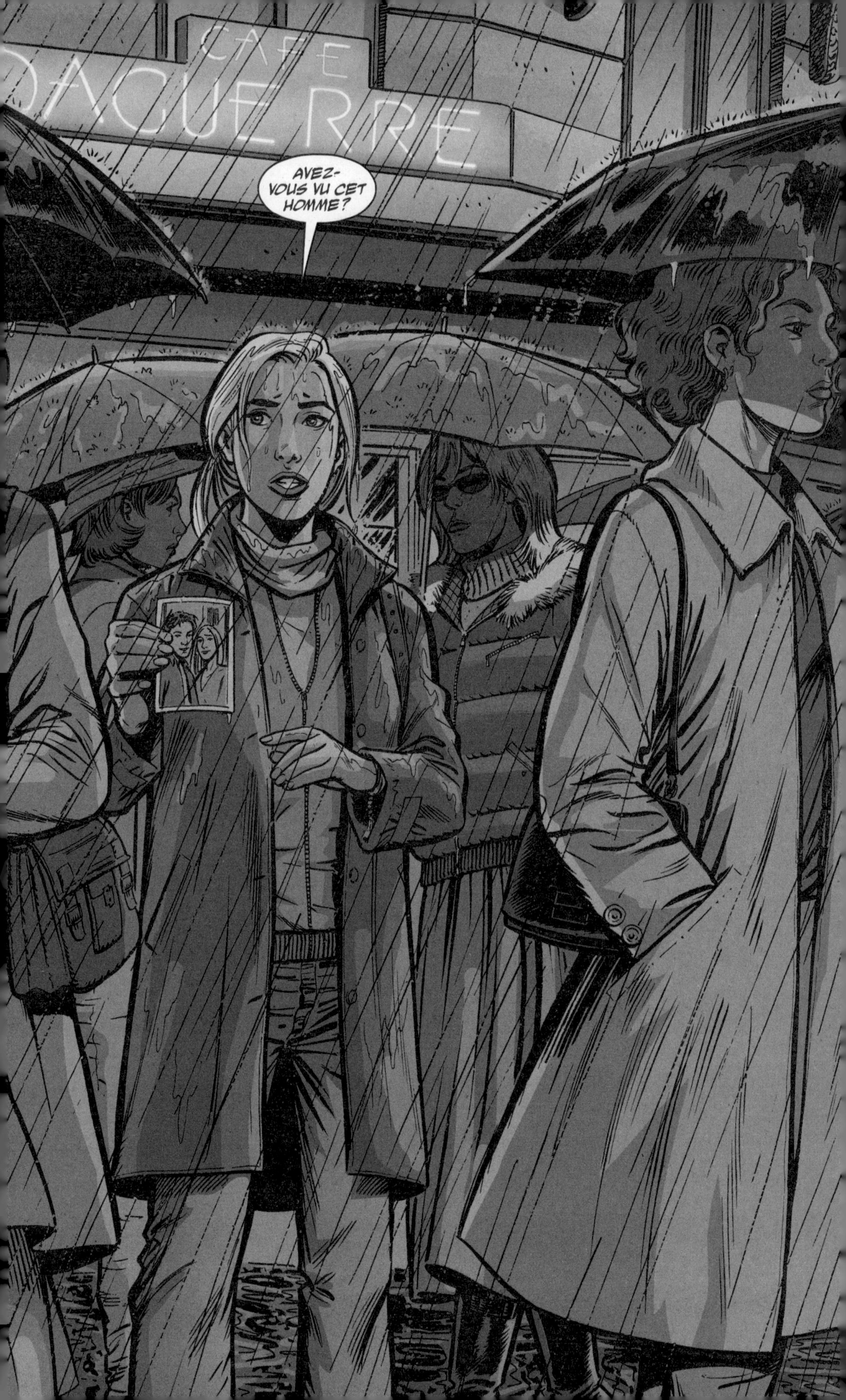
CAFE
DAGUERRE
AVEZ-VOUS VU CET HOMME?

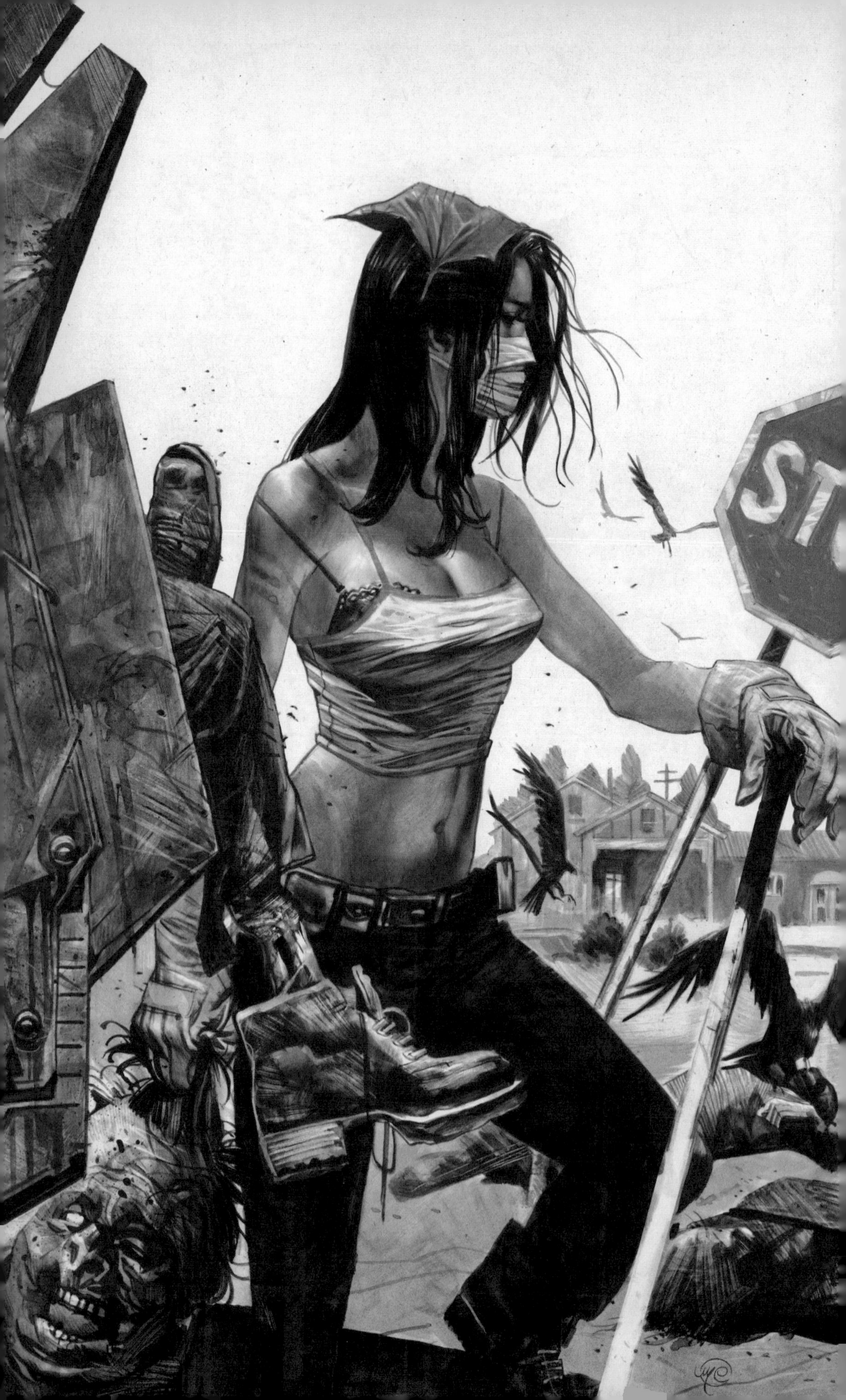
ST

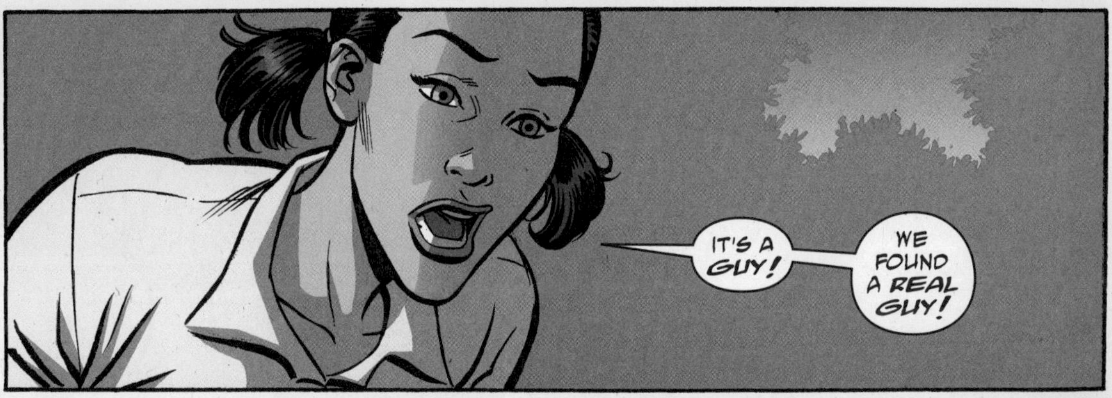
IT'S A GUY!
WE FOUND A REAL GUY!

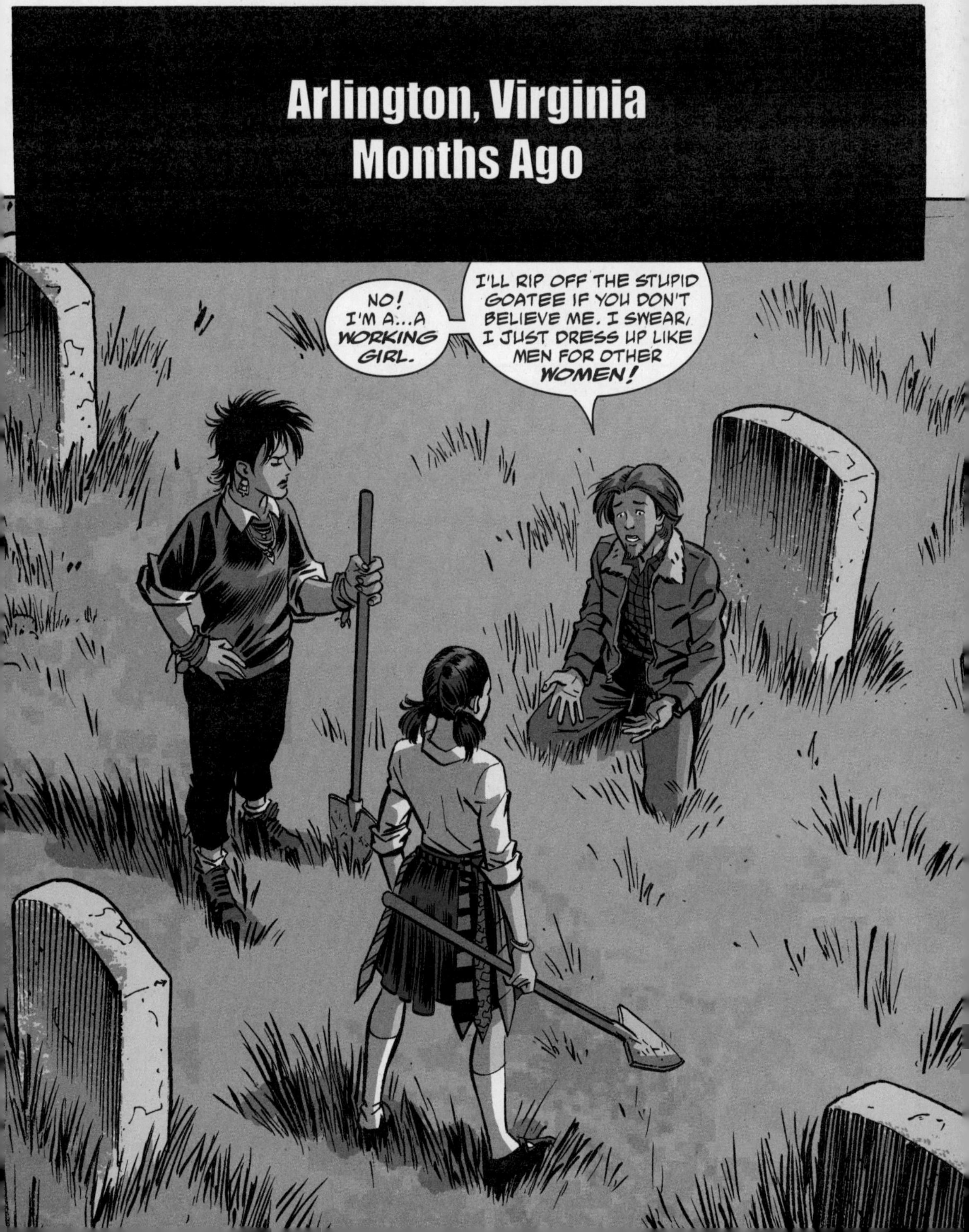
Arlington, Virginia
Months Ago
NO! I'M A...A WORKING GIRL.
I'LL RIP OFF THE STUPID GOATEE IF YOU DON'T BELIEVE ME. I SWEAR, I JUST DRESS UP LIKE MEN FOR OTHER WOMEN!

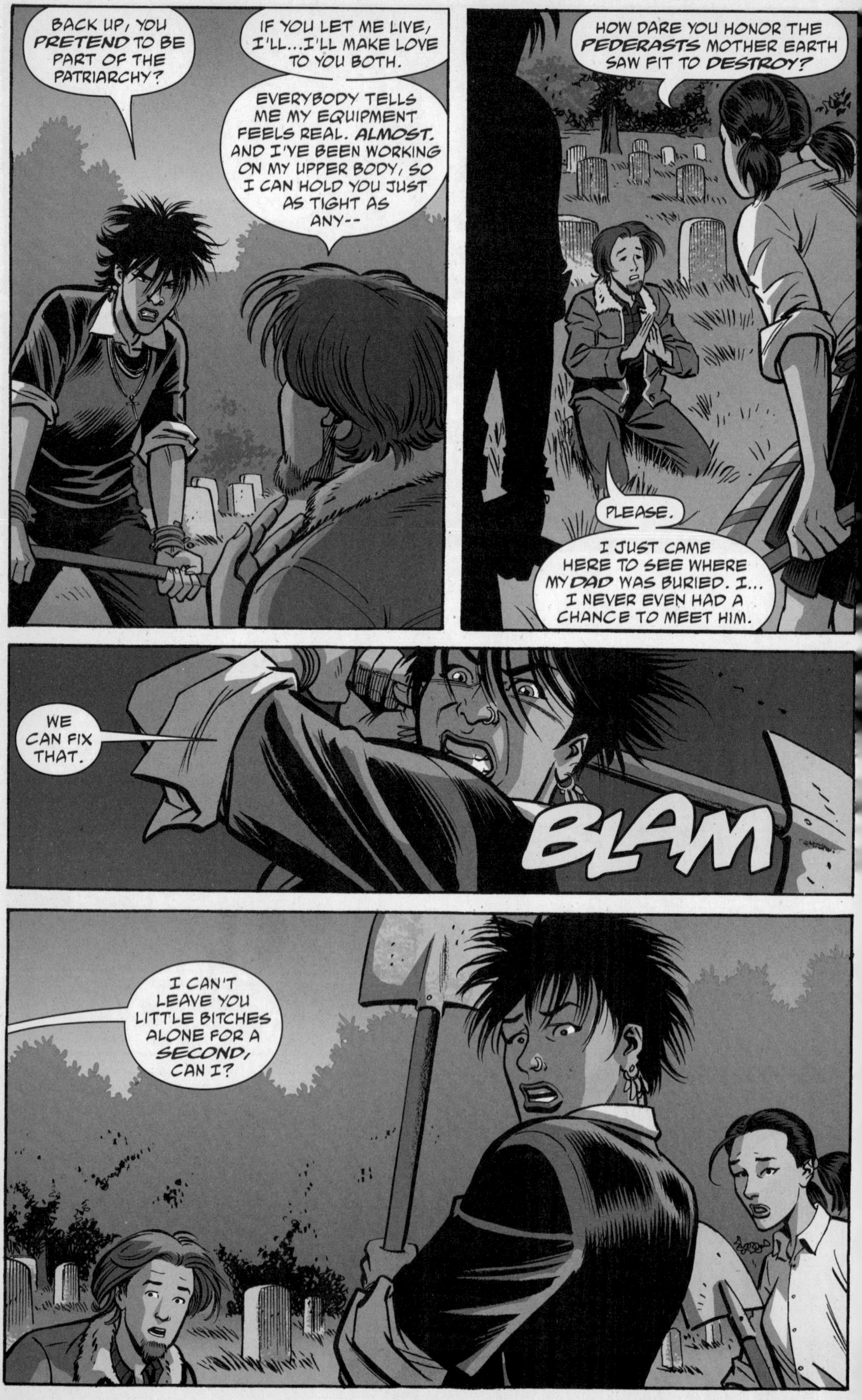
BACK UP, YOU PRETEND TO BE PART OF THE PATRIARCHY?
IF YOU LET ME LIVE, I'LL...I'LL MAKE LOVE TO YOU BOTH.
EVERYBODY TELLS ME MY EQUIPMENT FEELS REAL. ALMOST. AND I'VE BEEN WORKING ON MY UPPER BODY, SO I CAN HOLD YOU JUST AS TIGHT AS ANY--
HOW DARE YOU HONOR THE PEDERASTS MOTHER EARTH SAW FIT TO DESTROY?
PLEASE.
I JUST CAME HERE TO SEE WHERE MY DAD WAS BURIED. I... I NEVER EVEN HAD A CHANCE TO MEET HIM.
WE CAN FIX THAT.
BLAM
I CAN'T LEAVE YOU LITTLE BITCHES ALONE FOR A SECOND, CAN I?

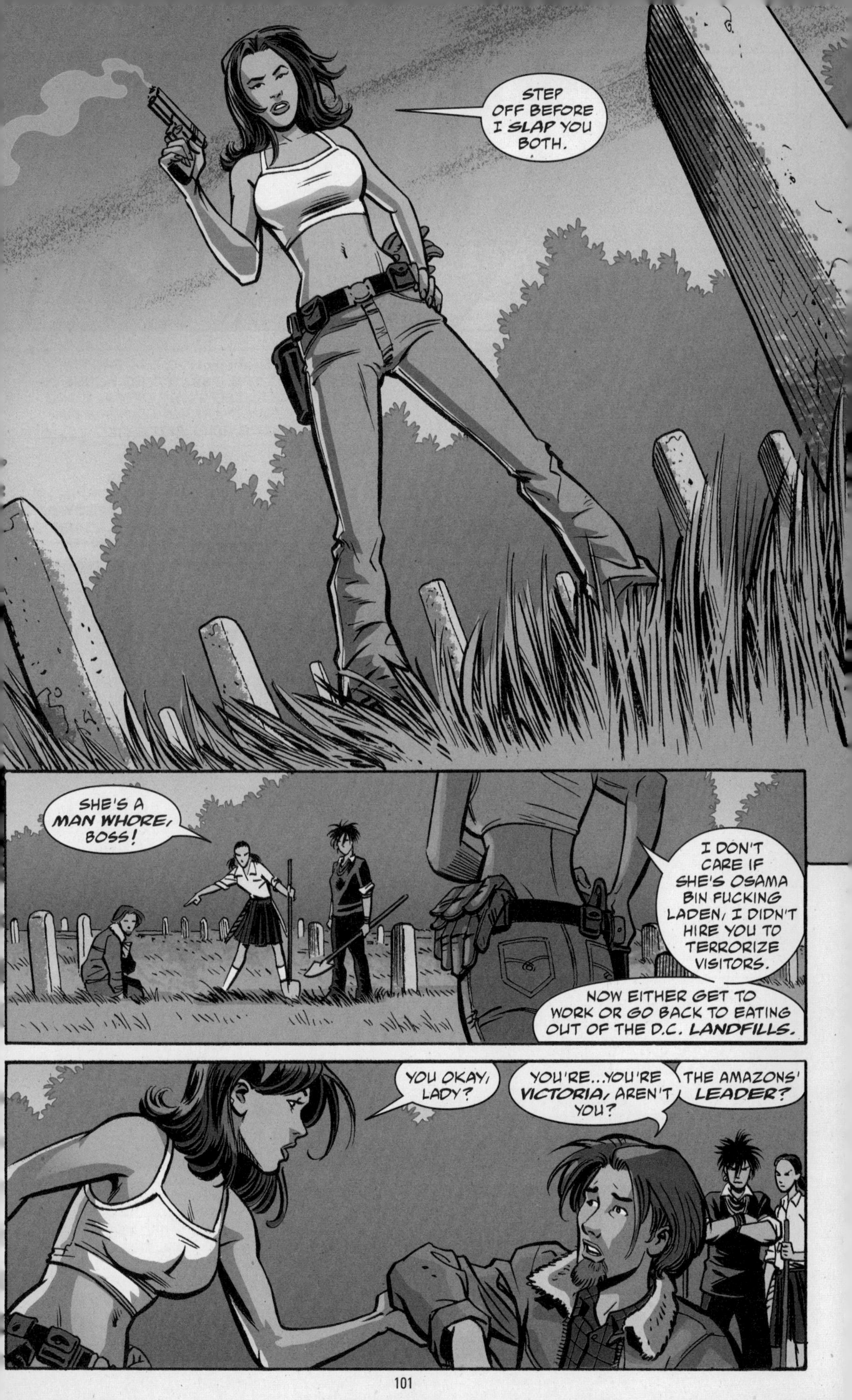
STEP OFF BEFORE I SLAP YOU BOTH.
SHE'S A MAN WHORE, BOSS!
I DON'T CARE IF SHE'S OSAMA BIN FUCKING LADEN, I DIDN'T HIRE YOU TO TERRORIZE VISITORS.
NOW EITHER GET TO WORK OR GO BACK TO EATING OUT OF THE D.C. LANDFILLS.
YOU OKAY, LADY?
YOU'RE...YOU'RE VICTORIA, AREN'T YOU?
THE AMAZONS' LEADER?

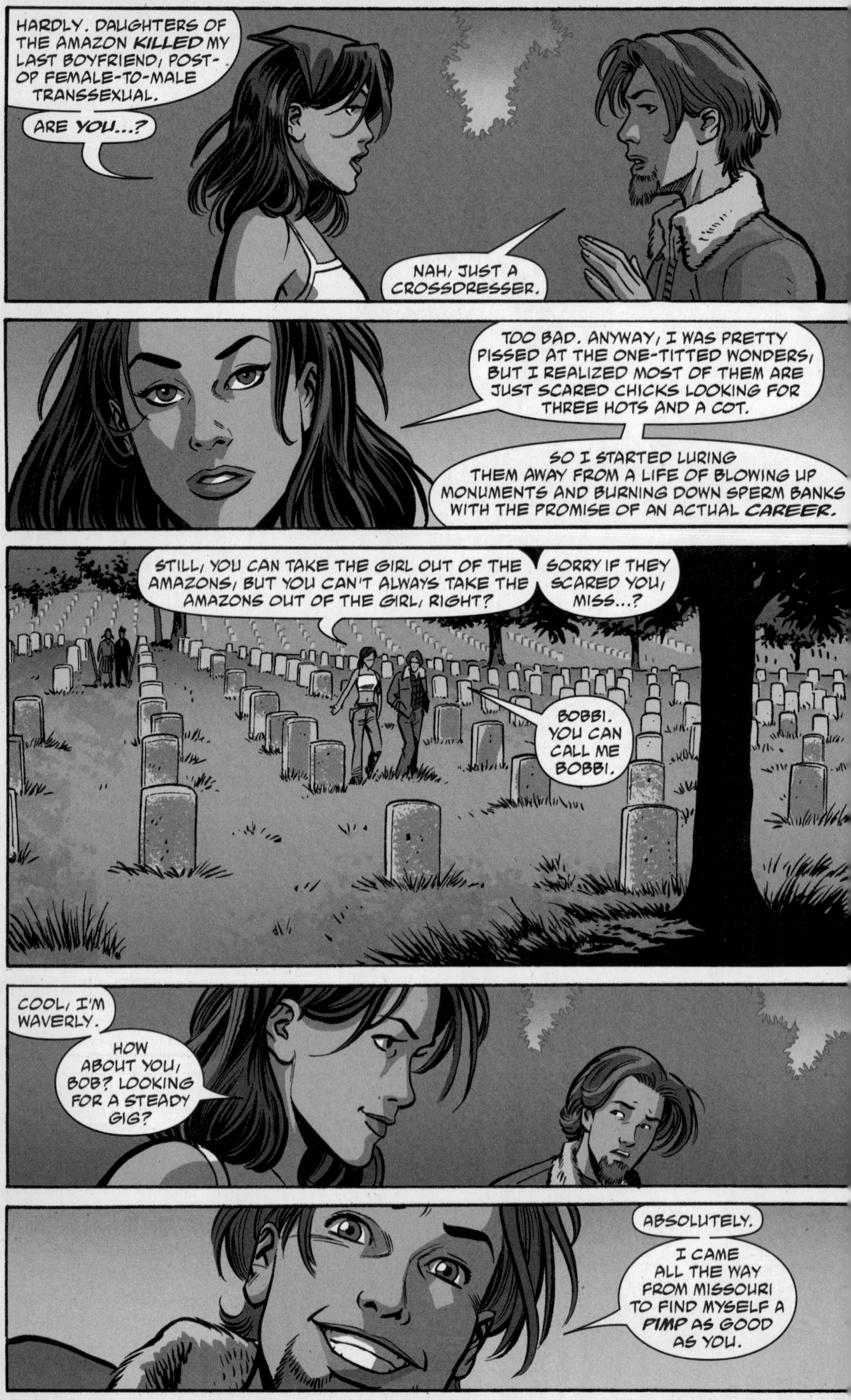
HARDLY. DAUGHTERS OF THE AMAZON KILLED MY LAST BOYFRIEND, POST-OP FEMALE-TO-MALE TRANSSEXUAL.
ARE YOU...?
NAH, JUST A CROSSDRESSER.
TOO BAD. ANYWAY, I WAS PRETTY PISSED AT THE ONE-TITTED WONDERS, BUT I REALIZED MOST OF THEM ARE JUST SCARED CHICKS LOOKING FOR THREE HOTS AND A COT.
SO I STARTED LURING THEM AWAY FROM A LIFE OF BLOWING UP MONUMENTS AND BURNING DOWN SPERM BANKS WITH THE PROMISE OF AN ACTUAL CAREER.
STILL, YOU CAN TAKE THE GIRL OUT OF THE AMAZONS, BUT YOU CAN'T ALWAYS TAKE THE AMAZONS OUT OF THE GIRL, RIGHT?
SORRY IF THEY SCARED YOU, MISS...?
BOBBI. YOU CAN CALL ME BOBBI.
COOL, I'M WAVERLY.
HOW ABOUT YOU, BOB? LOOKING FOR A STEADY GIG?
ABSOLUTELY.
I CAME ALL THE WAY FROM MISSOURI TO FIND MYSELF A PIMP AS GOOD AS YOU.

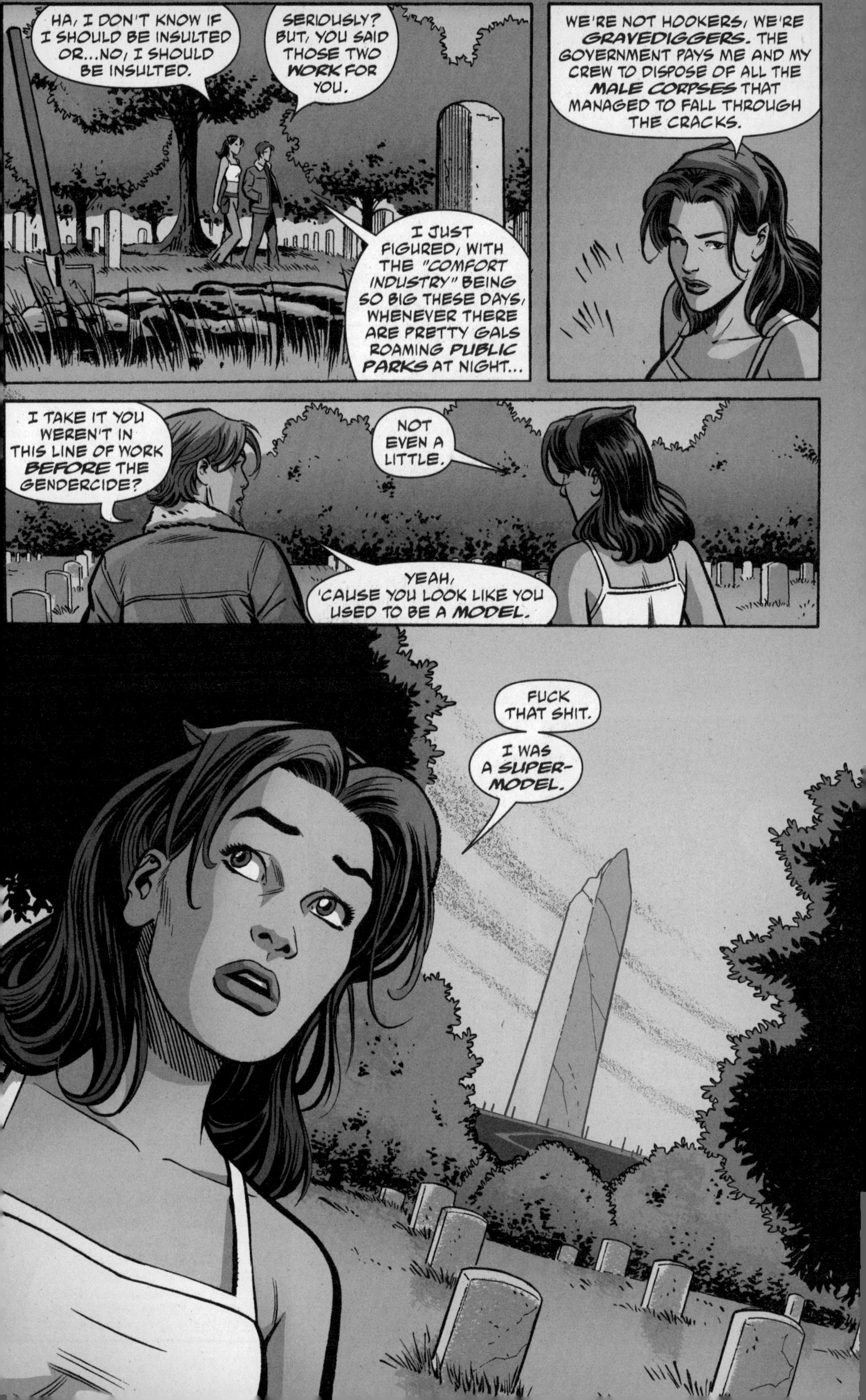
HA, I DON'T KNOW IF I SHOULD BE INSULTED OR...NO, I SHOULD BE INSULTED.
SERIOUSLY? BUT, YOU SAID THOSE TWO WORK FOR YOU.
I JUST FIGURED, WITH THE "COMFORT INDUSTRY" BEING SO BIG THESE DAYS, WHENEVER THERE ARE PRETTY GALS ROAMING PUBLIC PARKS AT NIGHT...
WE'RE NOT HOOKERS, WE'RE GRAVEDIGGERS. THE GOVERNMENT PAYS ME AND MY CREW TO DISPOSE OF ALL THE MALE CORPSES THAT MANAGED TO FALL THROUGH THE CRACKS.
I TAKE IT YOU WEREN'T IN THIS LINE OF WORK BEFORE THE GENDERCIDE?
NOT EVEN A LITTLE.
YEAH, 'CAUSE YOU LOOK LIKE YOU USED TO BE A MODEL.
FUCK THAT SHIT.
I WAS A SUPER-MODEL.

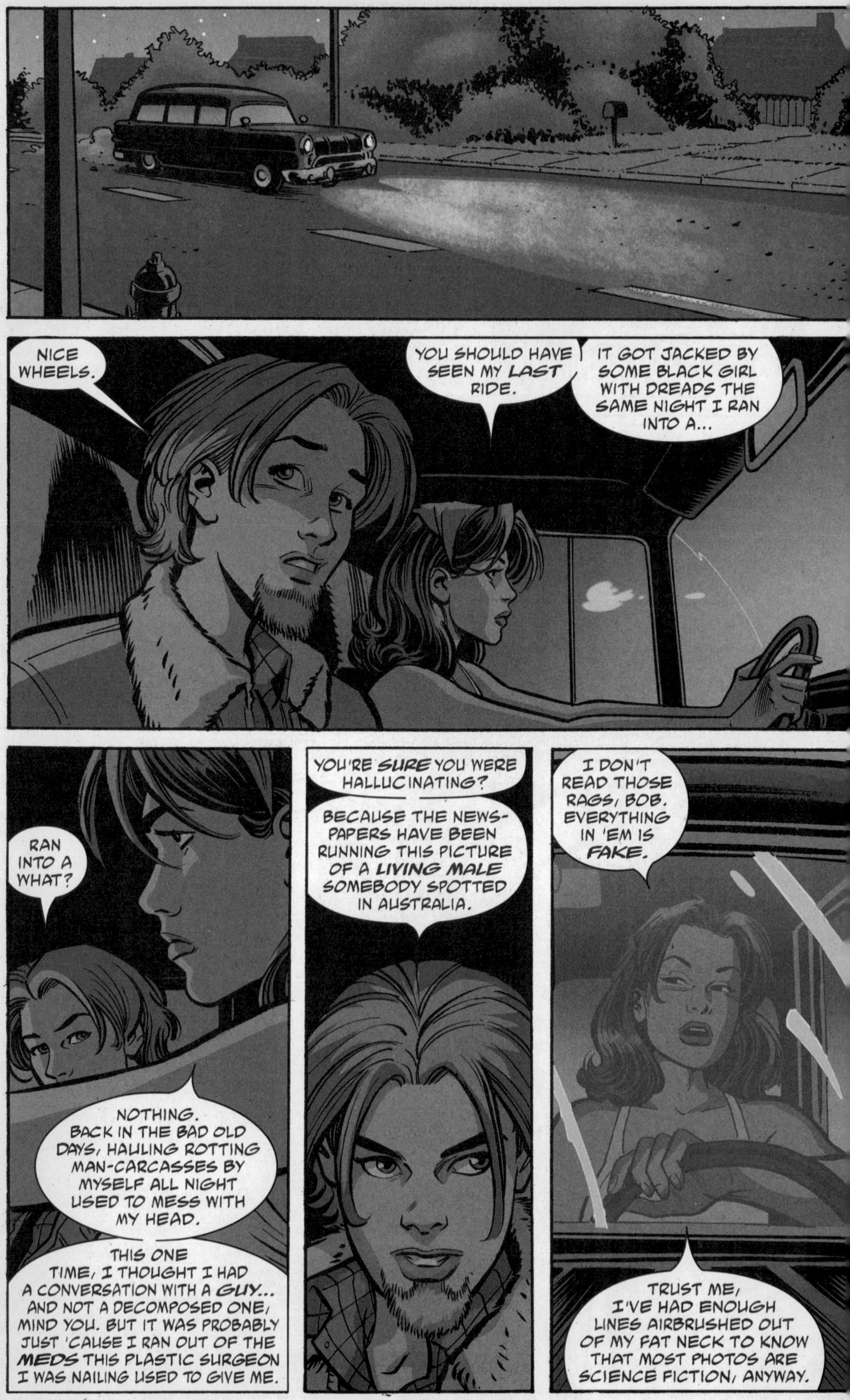
NICE WHEELS.
YOU SHOULD HAVE SEEN MY LAST RIDE.
IT GOT JACKED BY SOME BLACK GIRL WITH DREADS THE SAME NIGHT I RAN INTO A...
RAN INTO A WHAT?
NOTHING. BACK IN THE BAD OLD DAYS, HAULING ROTTING MAN-CARCASSES BY MYSELF ALL NIGHT USED TO MESS WITH MY HEAD.
THIS ONE TIME, I THOUGHT I HAD A CONVERSATION WITH A GUY... AND NOT A DECOMPOSED ONE, MIND YOU. BUT IT WAS PROBABLY JUST 'CAUSE I RAN OUT OF THE MEDS THIS PLASTIC SURGEON I WAS NAILING USED TO GIVE ME.
YOU'RE SURE YOU WERE HALLUCINATING?
BECAUSE THE NEWS-PAPERS HAVE BEEN RUNNING THIS PICTURE OF A LIVING MALE SOMEBODY SPOTTED IN AUSTRALIA.
I DON'T READ THOSE RAGS, BOB. EVERYTHING IN 'EM IS FAKE.
TRUST ME, I'VE HAD ENOUGH LINES AIRBRUSHED OUT OF MY FAT NECK TO KNOW THAT MOST PHOTOS ARE SCIENCE FICTION, ANYWAY.

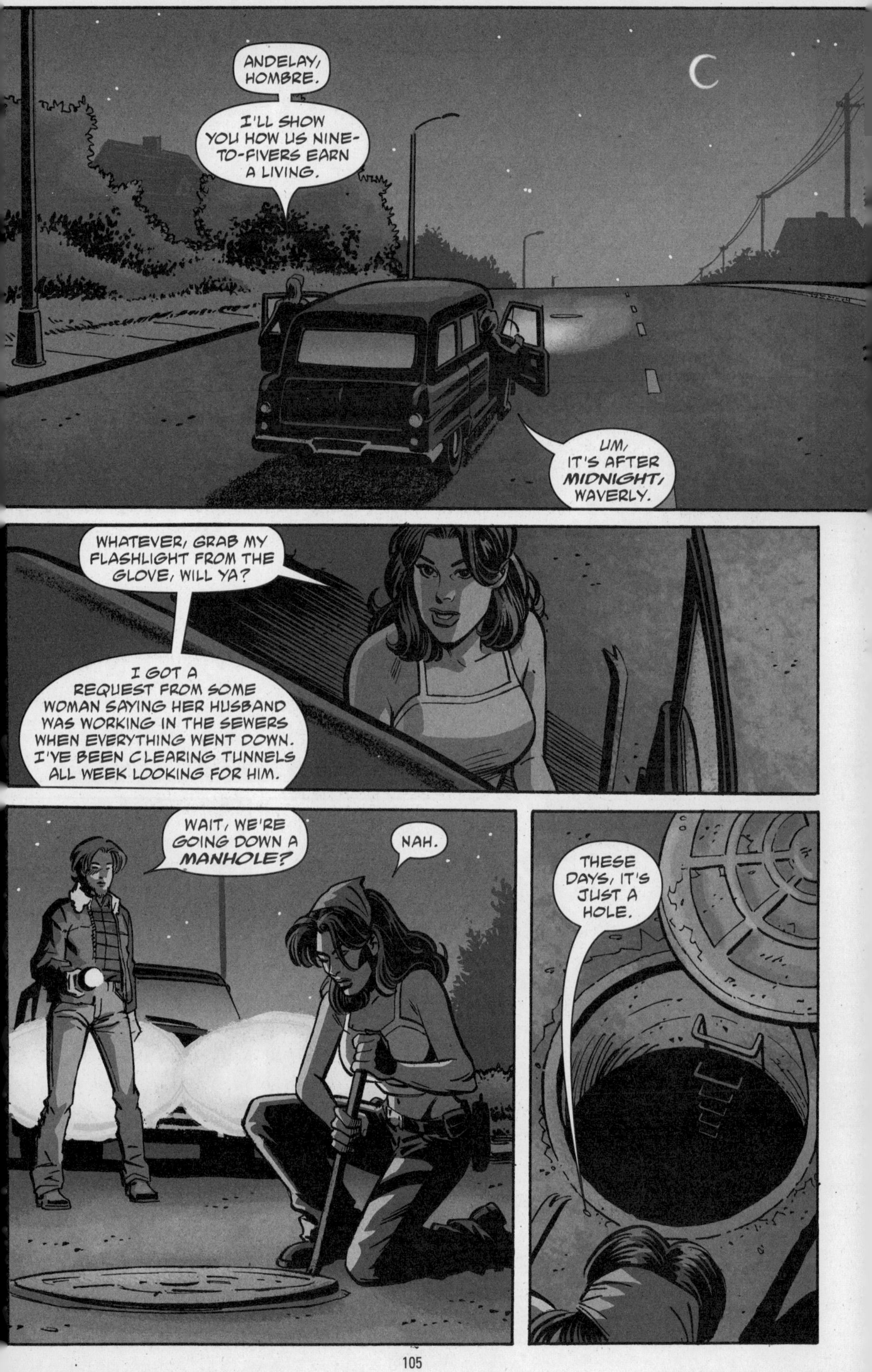

ANDELAY, HOMBRE.
I'LL SHOW YOU HOW US NINE-TO-FIVERS EARN A LIVING.
UM, IT'S AFTER MIDNIGHT, WAVERLY.
WHATEVER, GRAB MY FLASHLIGHT FROM THE GLOVE, WILL YA?
I GOT A REQUEST FROM SOME WOMAN SAYING HER HUSBAND WAS WORKING IN THE SEWERS WHEN EVERYTHING WENT DOWN. I'VE BEEN CLEARING TUNNELS ALL WEEK LOOKING FOR HIM.
WAIT, WE'RE GOING DOWN A MANHOLE?
NAH.
THESE DAYS, IT'S JUST A HOLE.

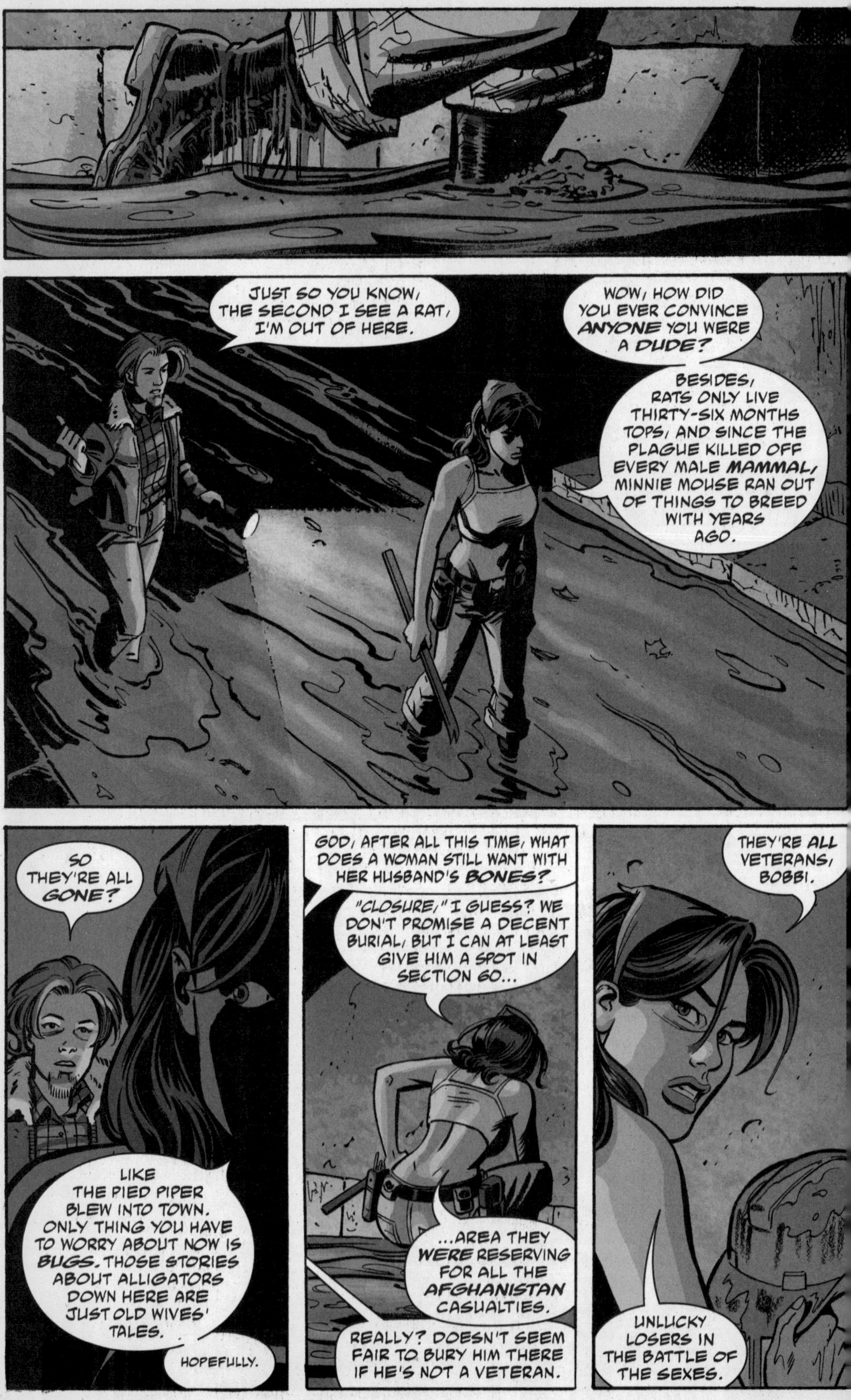
JUST SO YOU KNOW, THE SECOND I SEE A RAT, I'M OUT OF HERE.
WOW, HOW DID YOU EVER CONVINCE *ANYONE* YOU WERE A *DUDE?*
BESIDES, RATS ONLY LIVE THIRTY-SIX MONTHS TOPS, AND SINCE THE PLAGUE KILLED OFF EVERY MALE *MAMMAL,* MINNIE MOUSE RAN OUT OF THINGS TO BREED WITH YEARS AGO.
SO THEY'RE ALL *GONE?*
LIKE THE PIED PIPER BLEW INTO TOWN. ONLY THING YOU HAVE TO WORRY ABOUT NOW IS *BUGS.* THOSE STORIES ABOUT ALLIGATORS DOWN HERE ARE JUST OLD WIVES' TALES.
HOPEFULLY.
GOD, AFTER ALL THIS TIME, WHAT DOES A WOMAN STILL WANT WITH HER HUSBAND'S *BONES?*
"CLOSURE," I GUESS? WE DON'T PROMISE A DECENT BURIAL, BUT I CAN AT LEAST GIVE HIM A SPOT IN SECTION 60...
...AREA THEY *WERE* RESERVING FOR ALL THE *AFGHANISTAN* CASUALTIES.
REALLY? DOESN'T SEEM FAIR TO BURY HIM THERE IF HE'S NOT A VETERAN.
THEY'RE *ALL* VETERANS, BOBBI.
UNLUCKY LOSERS IN THE BATTLE OF THE SEXES.

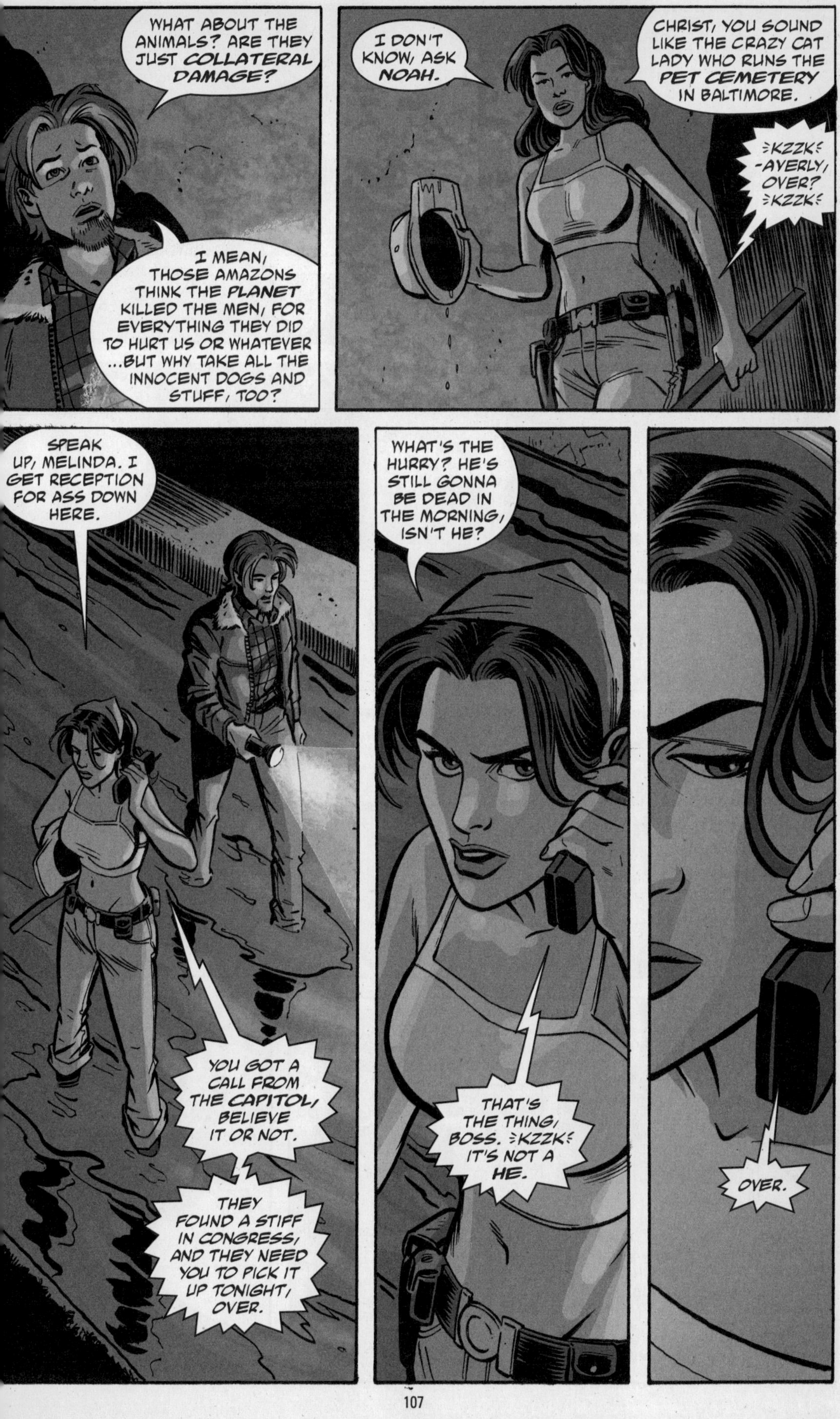
WHAT ABOUT THE ANIMALS? ARE THEY JUST COLLATERAL DAMAGE?
I MEAN, THOSE AMAZONS THINK THE PLANET KILLED THE MEN, FOR EVERYTHING THEY DID TO HURT US OR WHATEVER ...BUT WHY TAKE ALL THE INNOCENT DOGS AND STUFF, TOO?
I DON'T KNOW, ASK NOAH.
CHRIST, YOU SOUND LIKE THE CRAZY CAT LADY WHO RUNS THE PET CEMETERY IN BALTIMORE.
KZZK -AYERLY, OVER? KZZK
SPEAK UP, MELINDA. I GET RECEPTION FOR ASS DOWN HERE.
YOU GOT A CALL FROM THE CAPITOL, BELIEVE IT OR NOT.
THEY FOUND A STIFF IN CONGRESS, AND THEY NEED YOU TO PICK IT UP TONIGHT, OVER.
WHAT'S THE HURRY? HE'S STILL GONNA BE DEAD IN THE MORNING, ISN'T HE?
THAT'S THE THING, BOSS. KZZK IT'S NOT A HE.
OVER.

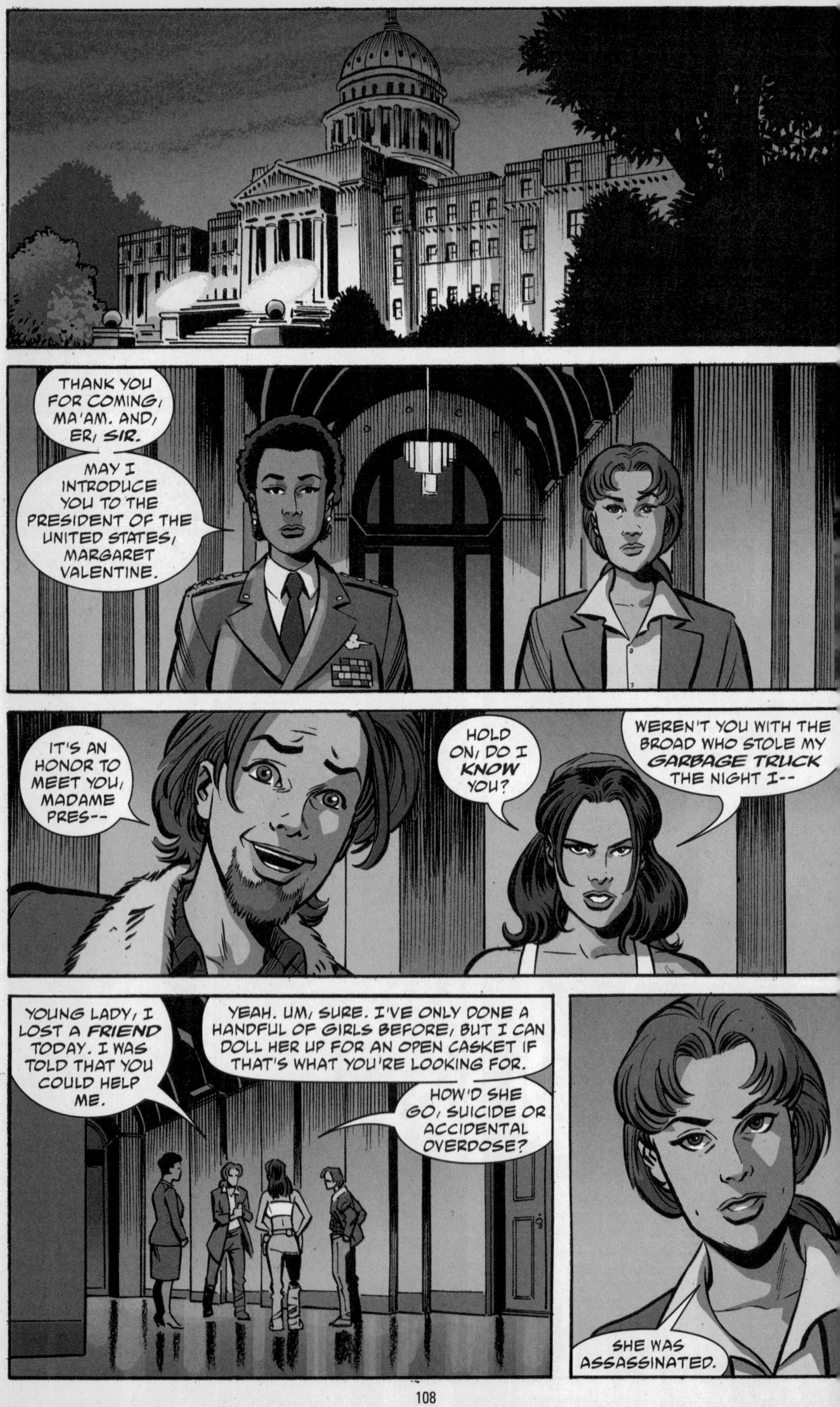

THANK YOU FOR COMING, MA'AM. AND, ER, SIR.
MAY I INTRODUCE YOU TO THE PRESIDENT OF THE UNITED STATES, MARGARET VALENTINE.
IT'S AN HONOR TO MEET YOU, MADAME PRES--
HOLD ON, DO I KNOW YOU?
WEREN'T YOU WITH THE BROAD WHO STOLE MY GARBAGE TRUCK THE NIGHT I--
YOUNG LADY, I LOST A FRIEND TODAY. I WAS TOLD THAT YOU COULD HELP ME.
YEAH. UM, SURE. I'VE ONLY DONE A HANDFUL OF GIRLS BEFORE, BUT I CAN DOLL HER UP FOR AN OPEN CASKET IF THAT'S WHAT YOU'RE LOOKING FOR.
HOW'D SHE GO, SUICIDE OR ACCIDENTAL OVERDOSE?
SHE WAS ASSASSINATED.

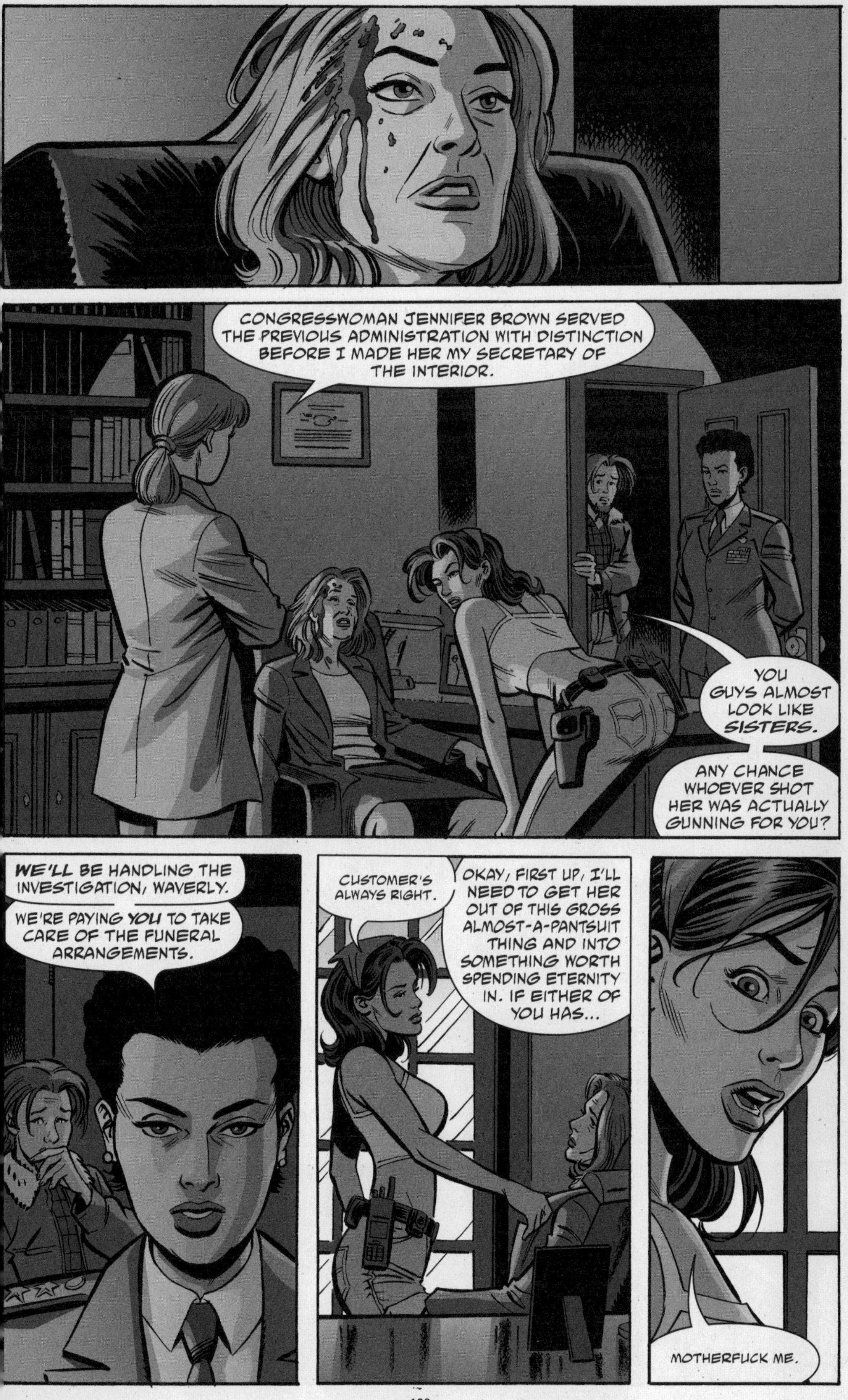
CONGRESSWOMAN JENNIFER BROWN SERVED THE PREVIOUS ADMINISTRATION WITH DISTINCTION BEFORE I MADE HER MY SECRETARY OF THE INTERIOR.
YOU GUYS ALMOST LOOK LIKE SISTERS.
ANY CHANCE WHOEVER SHOT HER WAS ACTUALLY GUNNING FOR YOU?
WE'LL BE HANDLING THE INVESTIGATION, WAVERLY.
WE'RE PAYING YOU TO TAKE CARE OF THE FUNERAL ARRANGEMENTS.
CUSTOMER'S ALWAYS RIGHT.
OKAY, FIRST UP, I'LL NEED TO GET HER OUT OF THIS GROSS ALMOST-A-PANTSUIT THING AND INTO SOMETHING WORTH SPENDING ETERNITY IN. IF EITHER OF YOU HAS...
MOTHERFUCK ME.

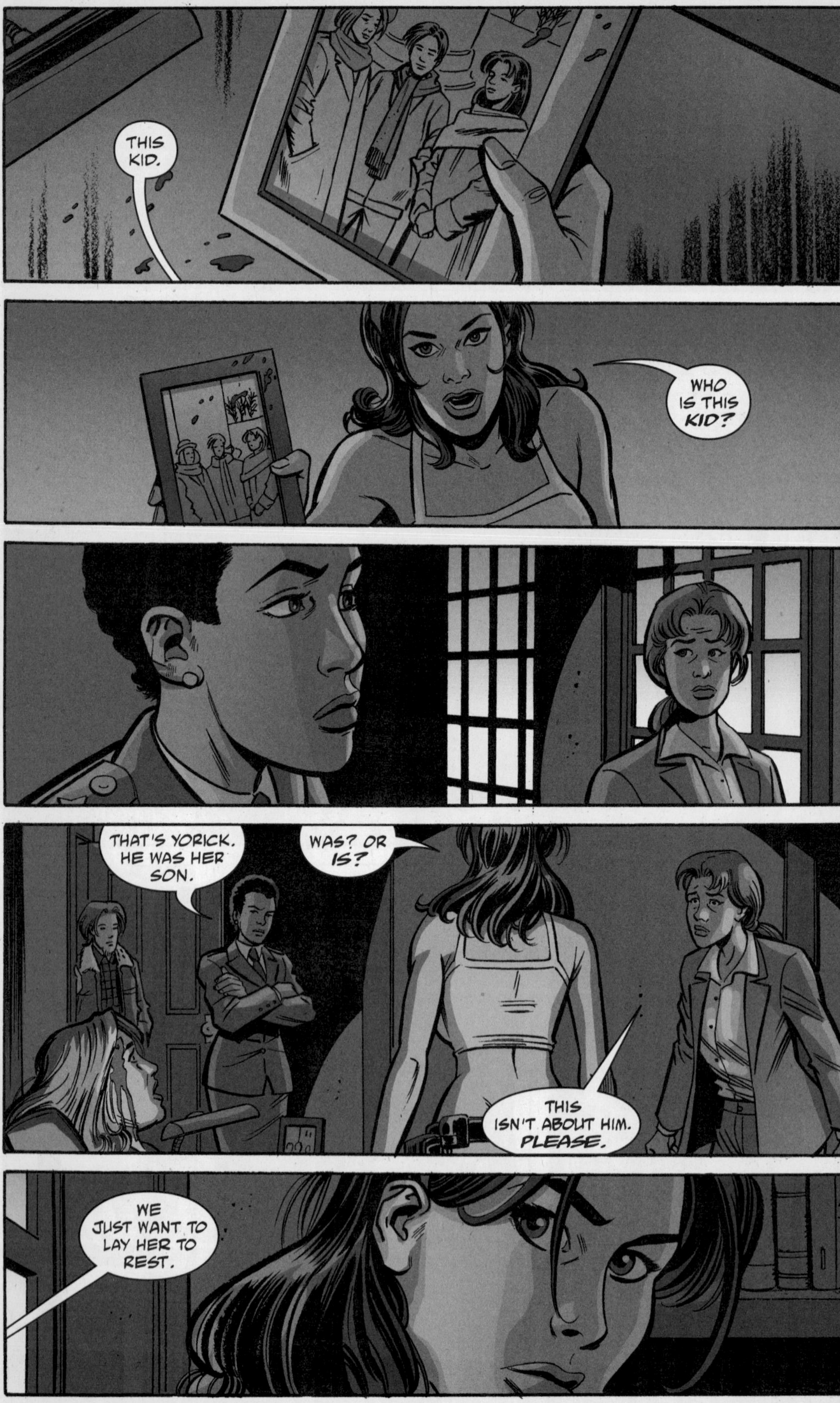
THIS KID.
WHO IS THIS KID?
THAT'S YORICK. HE WAS HER SON.
WAS? OR IS?
THIS ISN'T ABOUT HIM. PLEASE.
WE JUST WANT TO LAY HER TO REST.

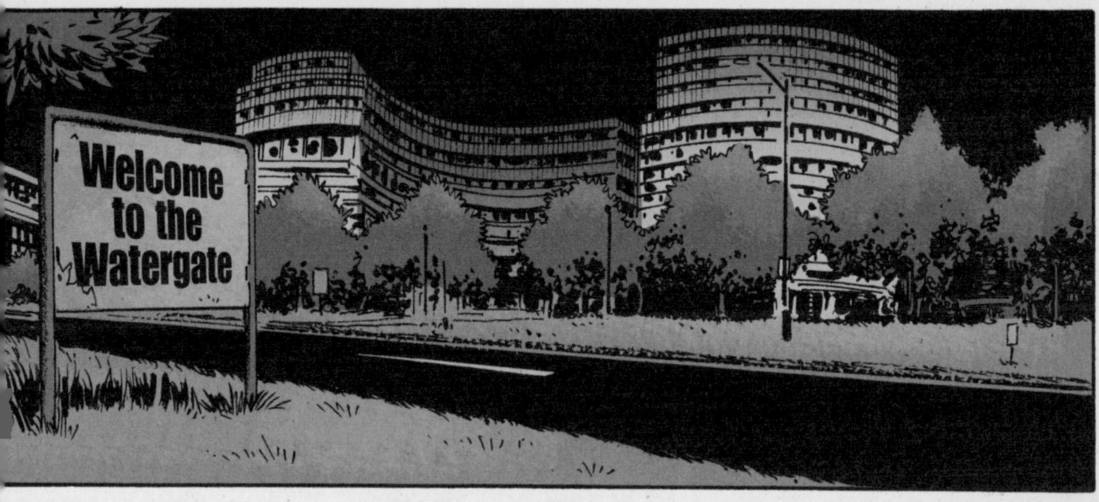
Welcome
to the
Watergate

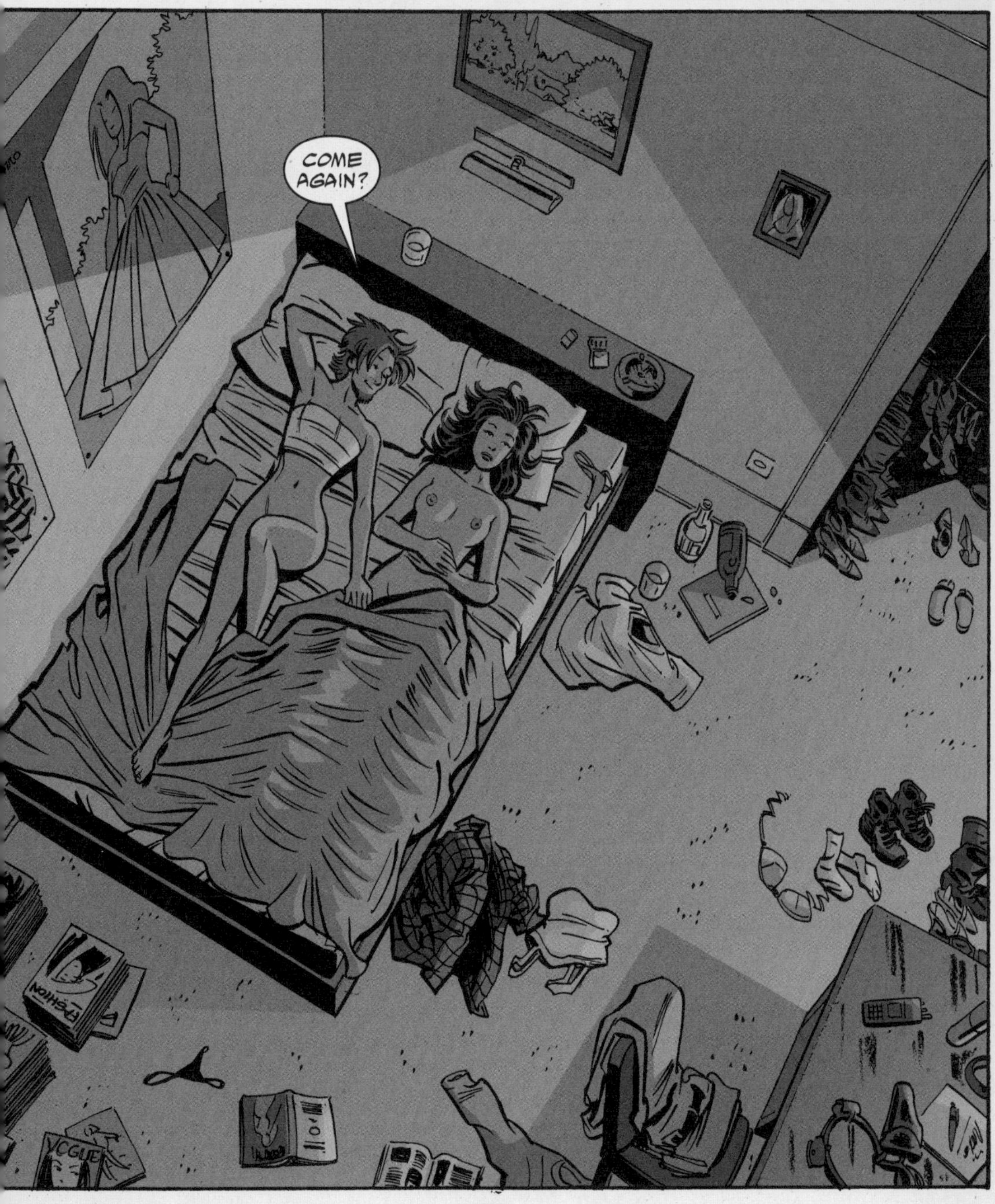
COME AGAIN?
FASHION
VOGUE

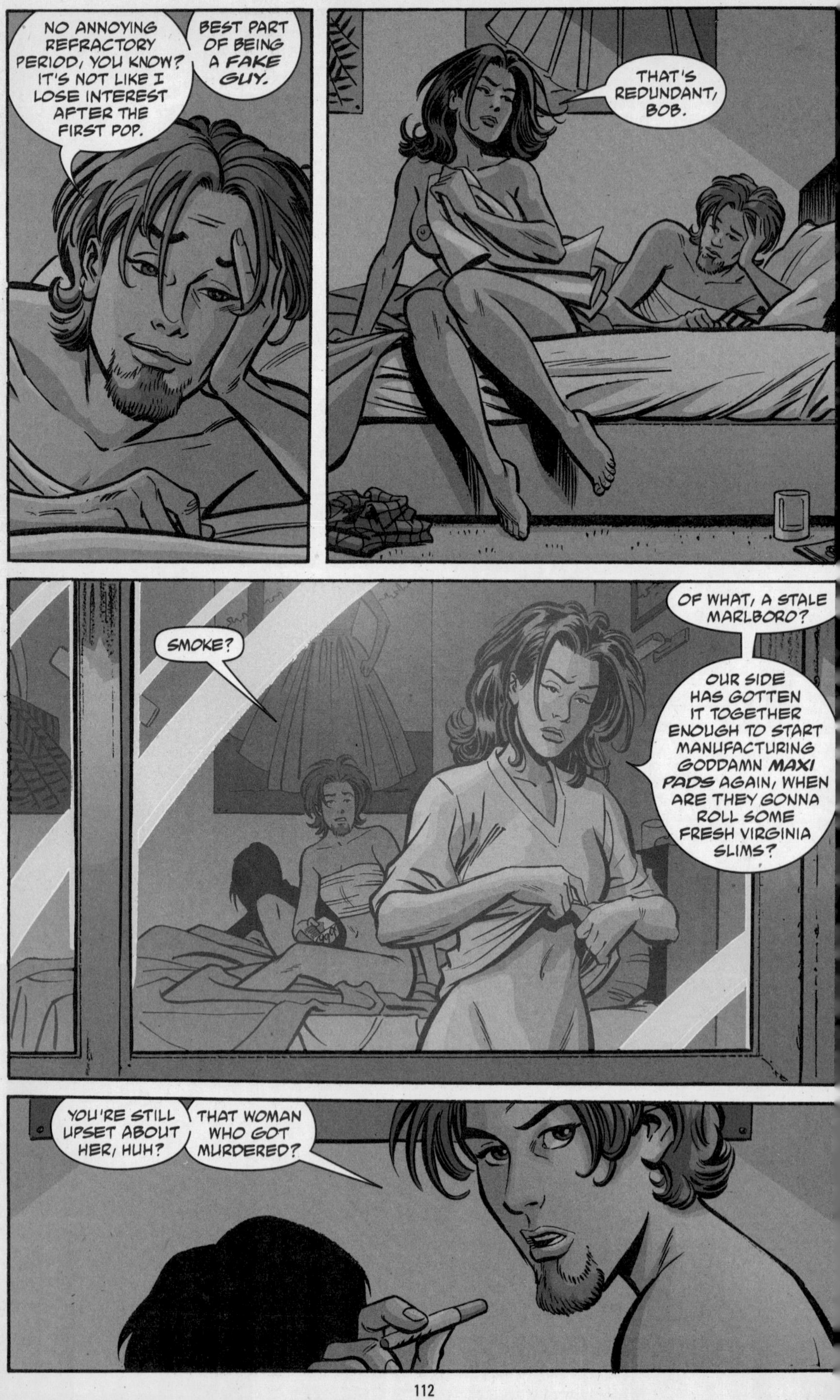
NO ANNOYING REFRACTORY PERIOD, YOU KNOW? IT'S NOT LIKE I LOSE INTEREST AFTER THE FIRST POP.
BEST PART OF BEING A *FAKE GUY.*
THAT'S REDUNDANT, BOB.
SMOKE?
OF WHAT, A STALE MARLBORO?
OUR SIDE HAS GOTTEN IT TOGETHER ENOUGH TO START MANUFACTURING GODDAMN *MAXI PADS* AGAIN, WHEN ARE THEY GONNA ROLL SOME FRESH VIRGINIA SLIMS?
YOU'RE STILL UPSET ABOUT HER, HUH?
THAT WOMAN WHO GOT MURDERED?

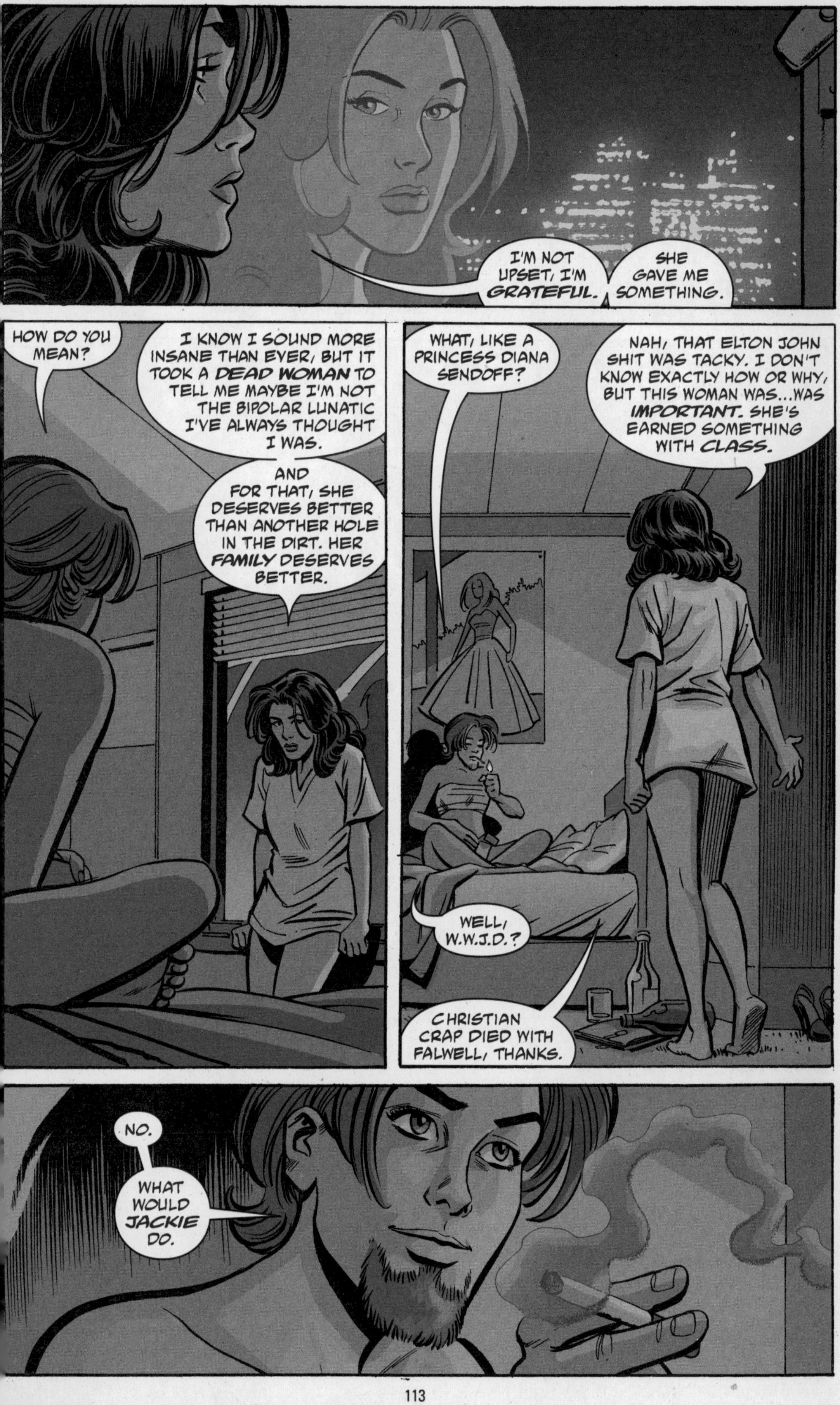
I'M NOT UPSET, I'M GRATEFUL.
SHE GAVE ME SOMETHING.
HOW DO YOU MEAN?
I KNOW I SOUND MORE INSANE THAN EVER, BUT IT TOOK A DEAD WOMAN TO TELL ME MAYBE I'M NOT THE BIPOLAR LUNATIC I'VE ALWAYS THOUGHT I WAS.
AND FOR THAT, SHE DESERVES BETTER THAN ANOTHER HOLE IN THE DIRT. HER FAMILY DESERVES BETTER.
WHAT, LIKE A PRINCESS DIANA SENDOFF?
NAH, THAT ELTON JOHN SHIT WAS TACKY. I DON'T KNOW EXACTLY HOW OR WHY, BUT THIS WOMAN WAS...WAS IMPORTANT. SHE'S EARNED SOMETHING WITH CLASS.
WELL, W.W.J.D.?
CHRISTIAN CRAP DIED WITH FALWELL, THANKS.
NO.
WHAT WOULD JACKIE DO.

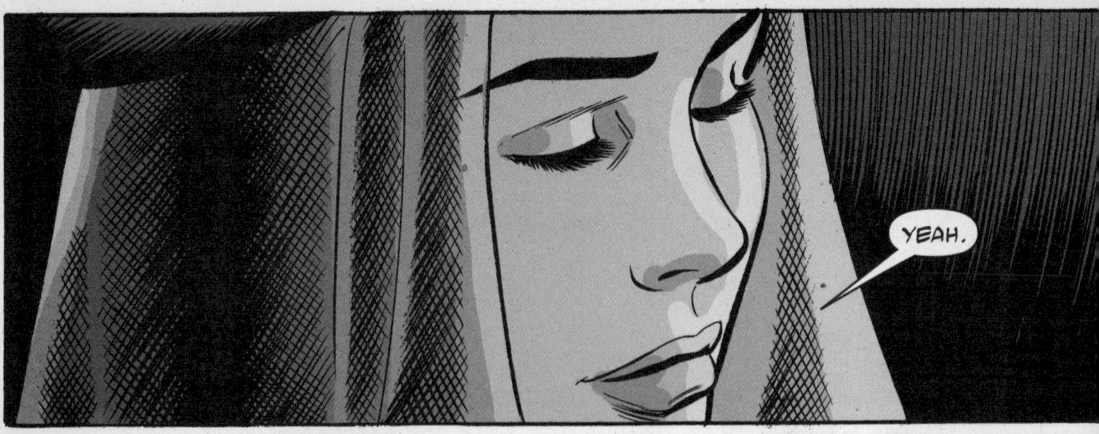
YEAH.

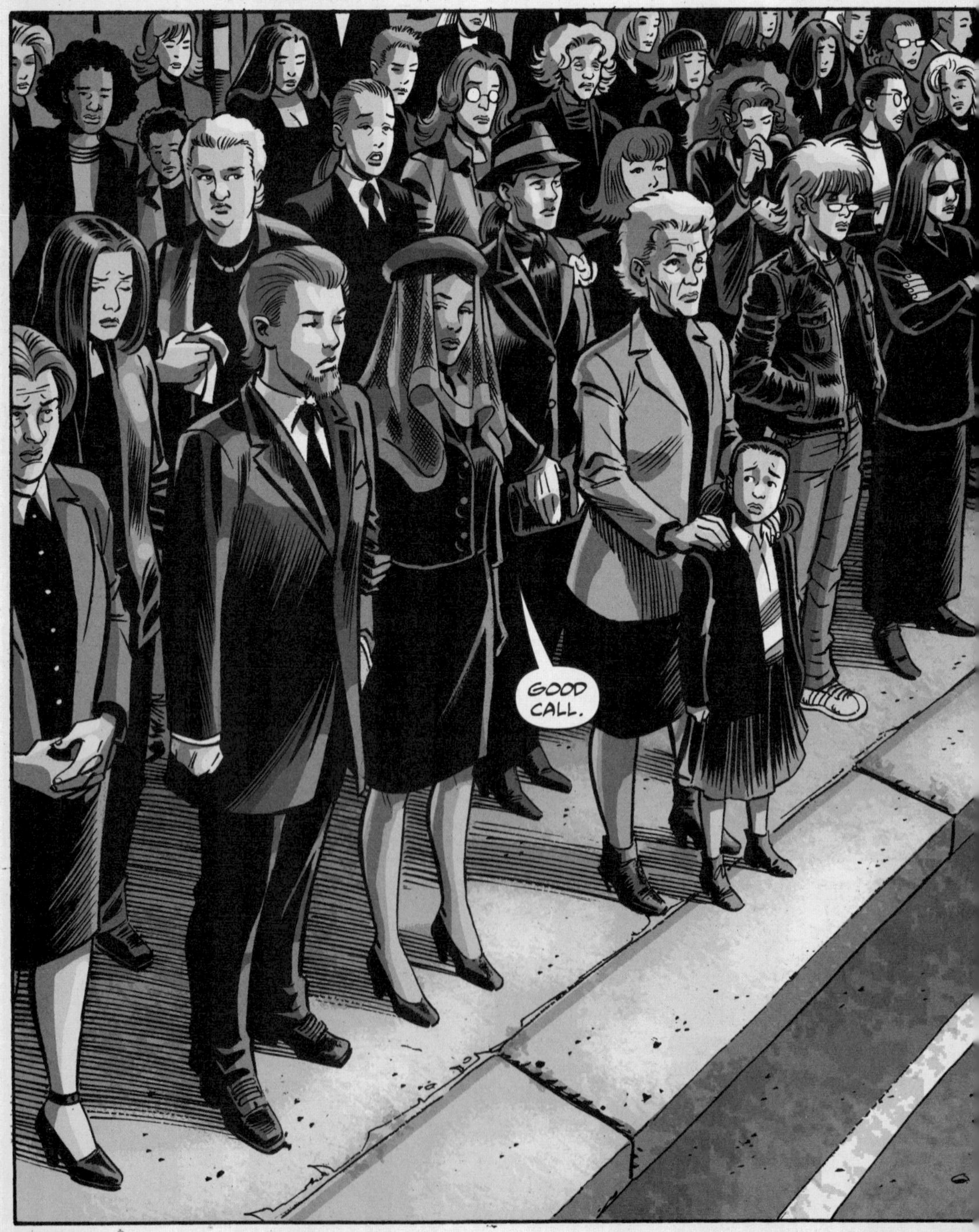
GOOD CALL.

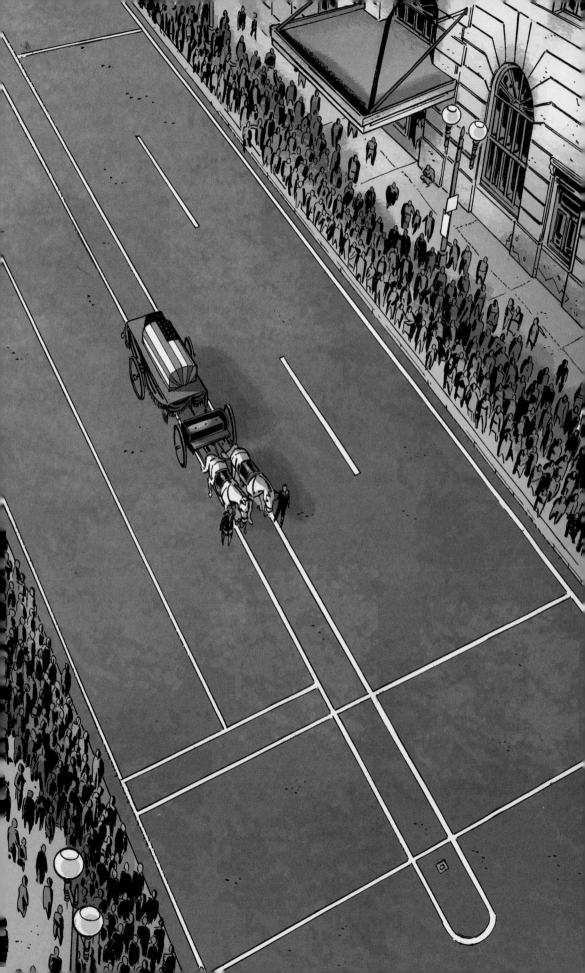

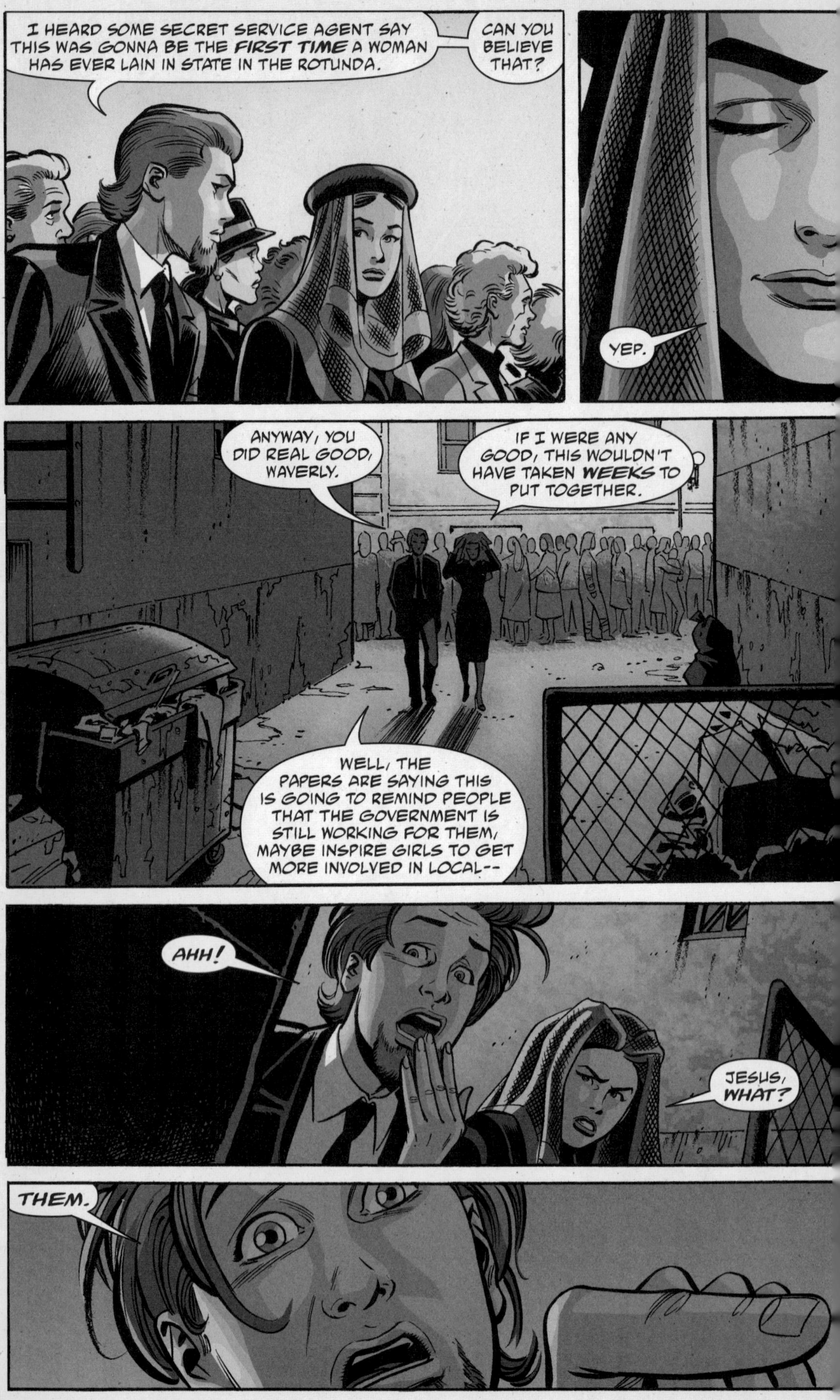
I HEARD SOME SECRET SERVICE AGENT SAY THIS WAS GONNA BE THE FIRST TIME A WOMAN HAS EVER LAIN IN STATE IN THE ROTUNDA.
CAN YOU BELIEVE THAT?
YEP.
ANYWAY, YOU DID REAL GOOD, WAVERLY.
IF I WERE ANY GOOD, THIS WOULDN'T HAVE TAKEN WEEKS TO PUT TOGETHER.
WELL, THE PAPERS ARE SAYING THIS IS GOING TO REMIND PEOPLE THAT THE GOVERNMENT IS STILL WORKING FOR THEM, MAYBE INSPIRE GIRLS TO GET MORE INVOLVED IN LOCAL--
AHH!
JESUS, WHAT?
THEM.

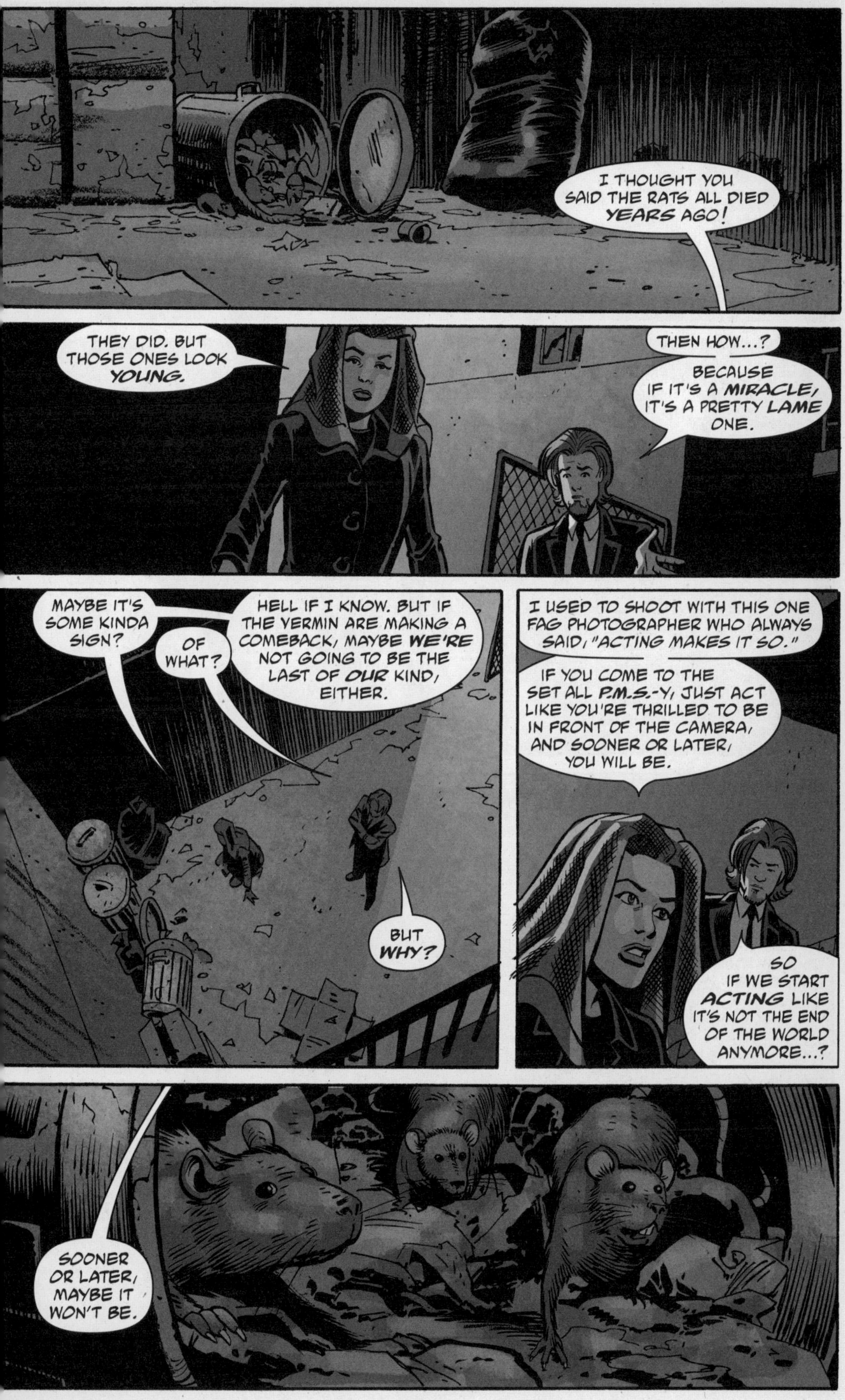
I THOUGHT YOU SAID THE RATS ALL DIED YEARS AGO!
THEY DID. BUT THOSE ONES LOOK YOUNG.
THEN HOW...?
BECAUSE IF IT'S A MIRACLE, IT'S A PRETTY LAME ONE.
MAYBE IT'S SOME KINDA SIGN?
OF WHAT?
HELL IF I KNOW. BUT IF THE VERMIN ARE MAKING A COMEBACK, MAYBE WE'RE NOT GOING TO BE THE LAST OF OUR KIND, EITHER.
BUT WHY?
I USED TO SHOOT WITH THIS ONE FAG PHOTOGRAPHER WHO ALWAYS SAID, "ACTING MAKES IT SO."
IF YOU COME TO THE SET ALL P.M.S.-Y, JUST ACT LIKE YOU'RE THRILLED TO BE IN FRONT OF THE CAMERA, AND SOONER OR LATER, YOU WILL BE.
SO IF WE START ACTING LIKE IT'S NOT THE END OF THE WORLD ANYMORE...?
SOONER OR LATER, MAYBE IT WON'T BE.

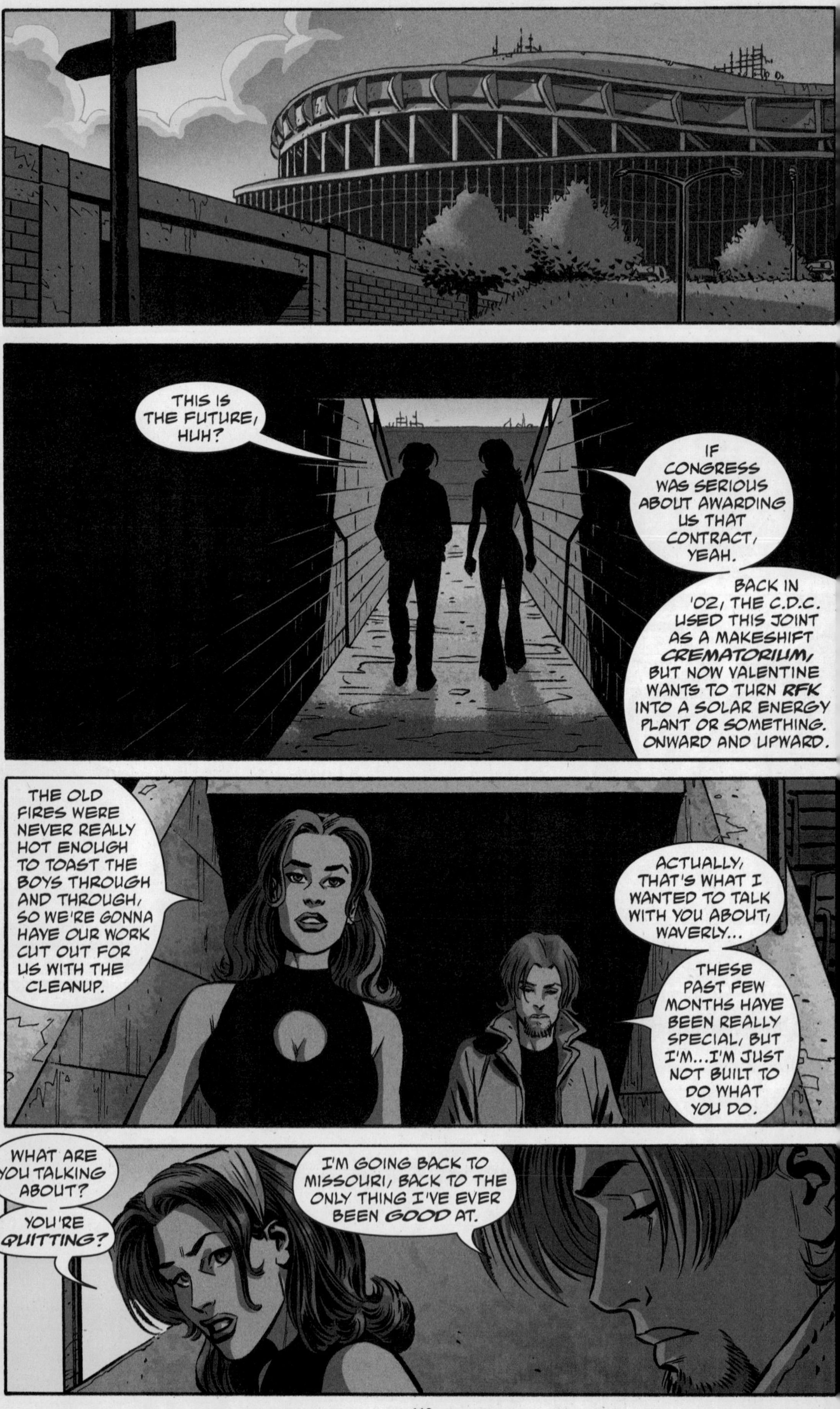

THIS IS THE FUTURE, HUH?
IF CONGRESS WAS SERIOUS ABOUT AWARDING US THAT CONTRACT, YEAH.
BACK IN '02, THE C.D.C. USED THIS JOINT AS A MAKESHIFT CREMATORIUM, BUT NOW VALENTINE WANTS TO TURN RFK INTO A SOLAR ENERGY PLANT OR SOMETHING. ONWARD AND UPWARD.
THE OLD FIRES WERE NEVER REALLY HOT ENOUGH TO TOAST THE BOYS THROUGH AND THROUGH, SO WE'RE GONNA HAVE OUR WORK CUT OUT FOR US WITH THE CLEANUP.
ACTUALLY, THAT'S WHAT I WANTED TO TALK WITH YOU ABOUT, WAVERLY...
THESE PAST FEW MONTHS HAVE BEEN REALLY SPECIAL, BUT I'M...I'M JUST NOT BUILT TO DO WHAT YOU DO.
WHAT ARE YOU TALKING ABOUT?
YOU'RE QUITTING?
I'M GOING BACK TO MISSOURI, BACK TO THE ONLY THING I'VE EVER BEEN GOOD AT.

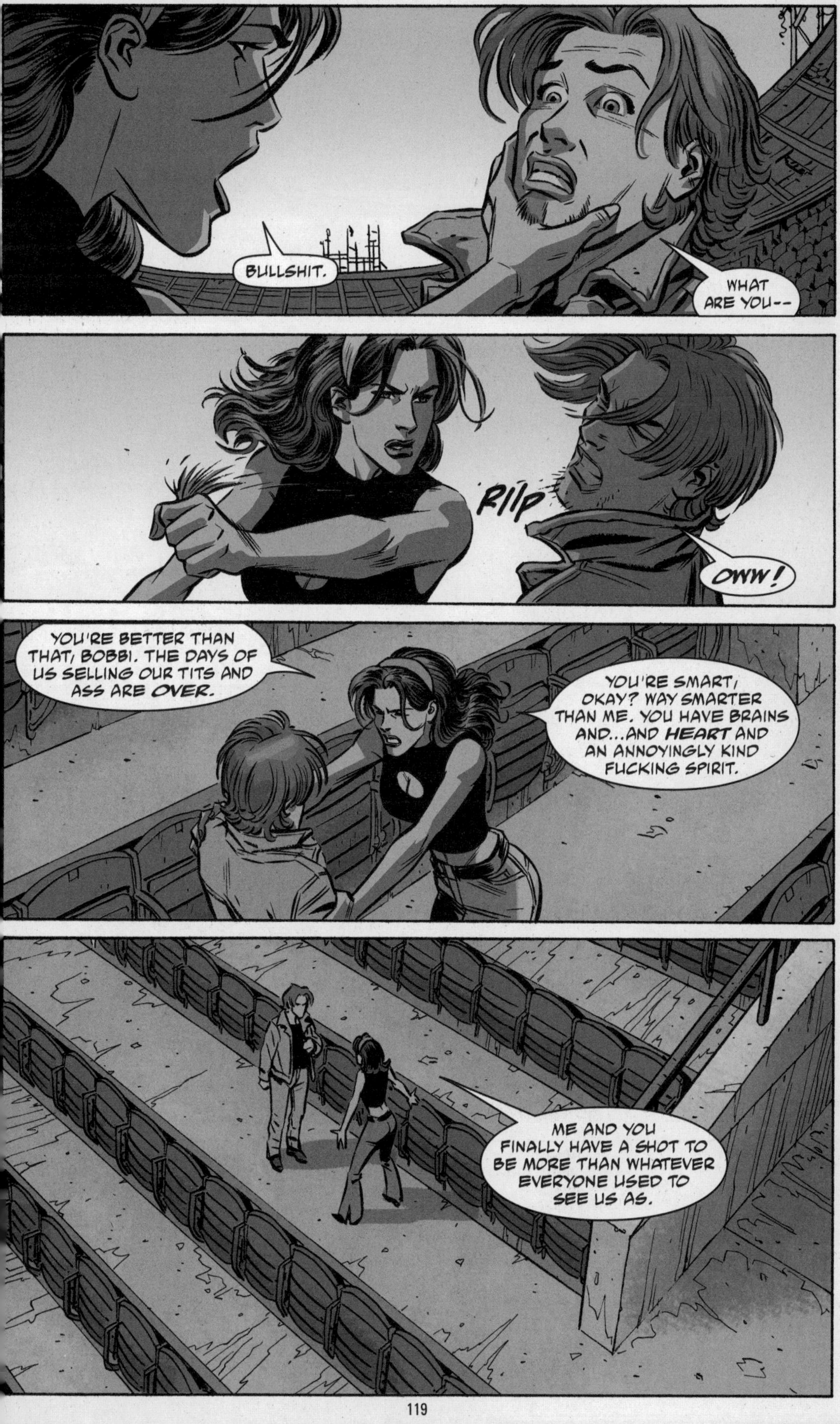
BULLSHIT.
WHAT ARE YOU--
RIIP
OWW!
YOU'RE BETTER THAN THAT, BOBBI. THE DAYS OF US SELLING OUR TITS AND ASS ARE *OVER*.
YOU'RE SMART, OKAY? WAY SMARTER THAN ME. YOU HAVE BRAINS AND...AND *HEART* AND AN ANNOYINGLY KIND FUCKING SPIRIT.
ME AND YOU FINALLY HAVE A SHOT TO BE MORE THAN WHATEVER EVERYONE USED TO SEE US AS.

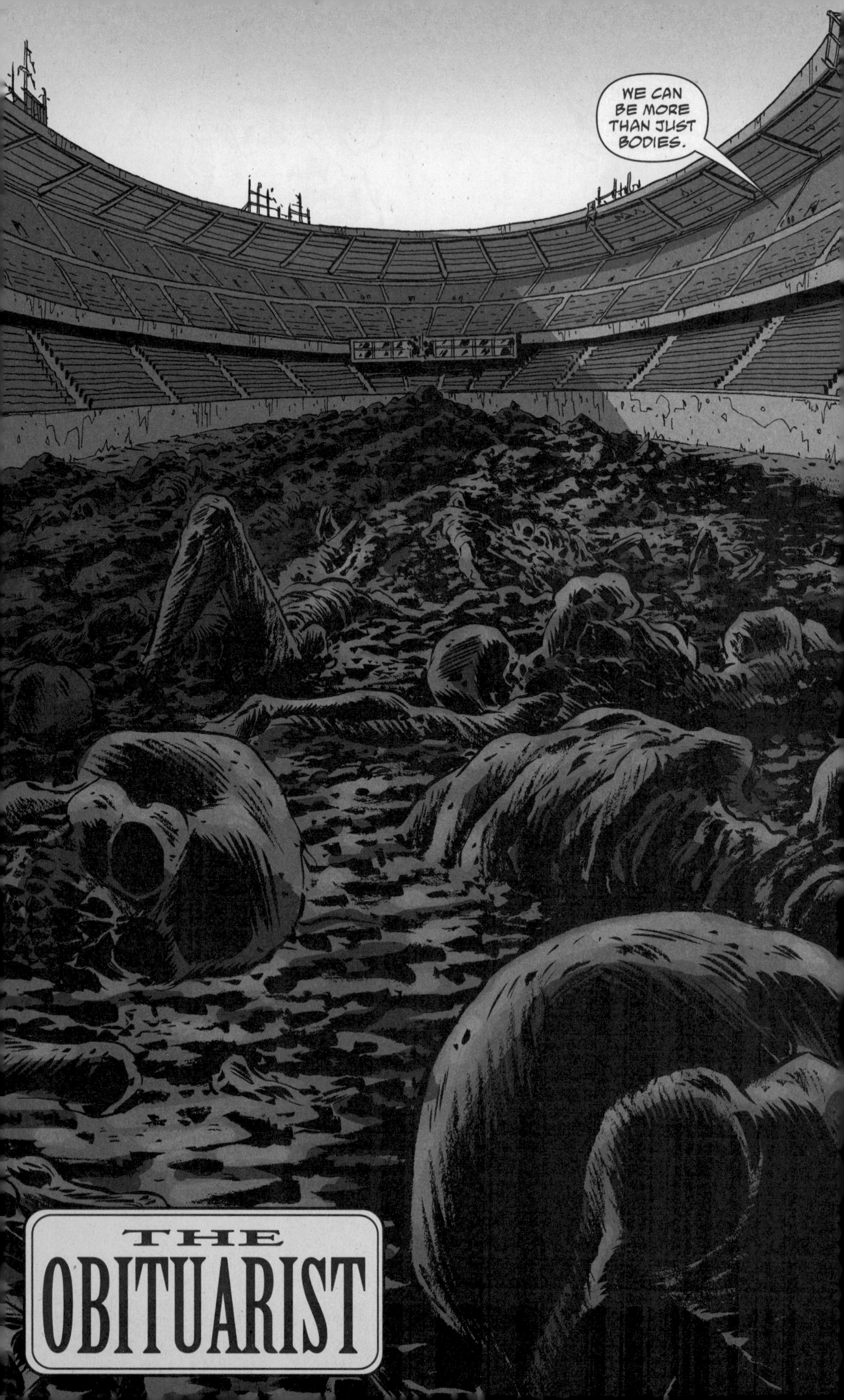
WE CAN BE MORE THAN JUST BODIES.
THE OBITUARIST

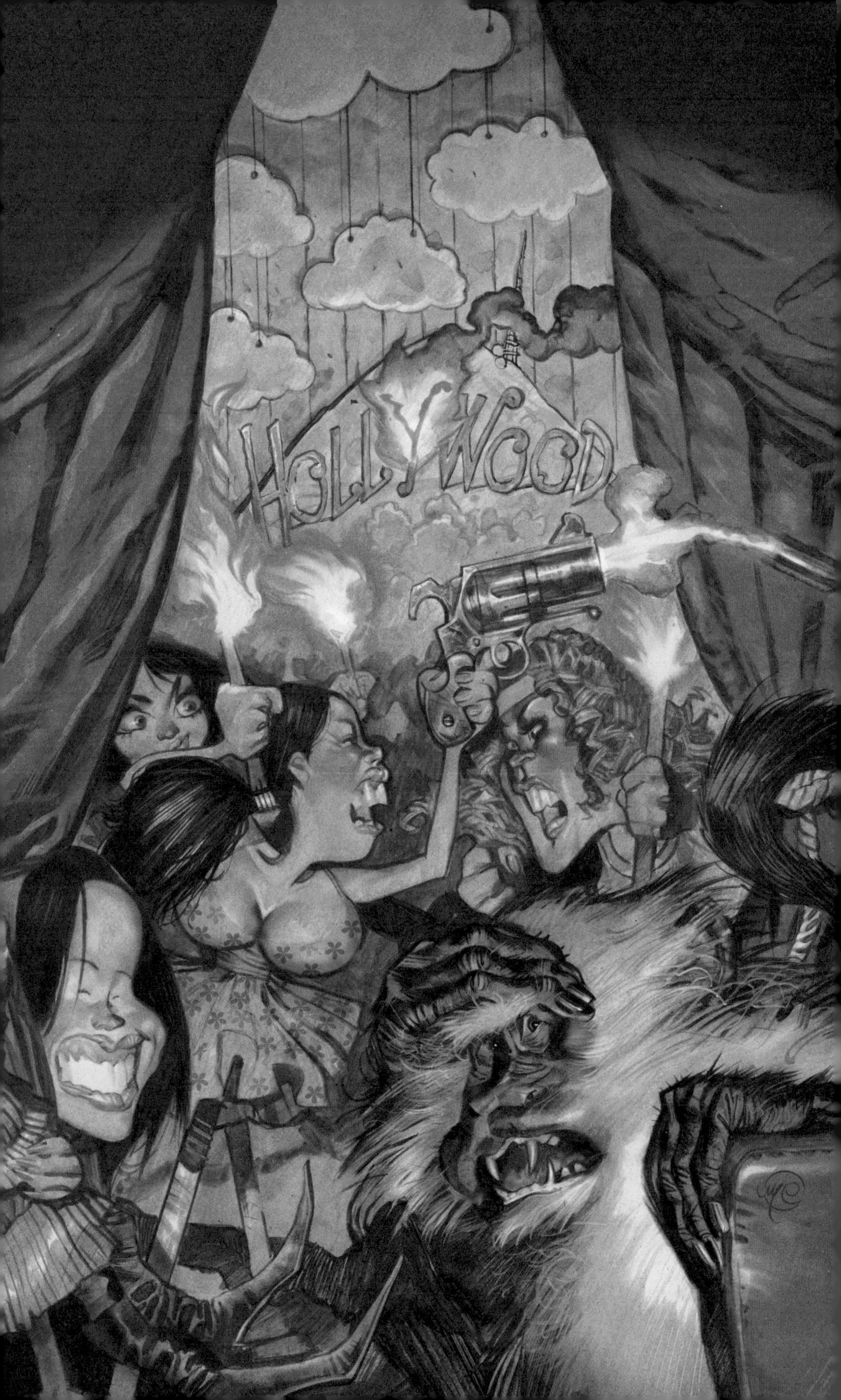
HOLLYWOOD

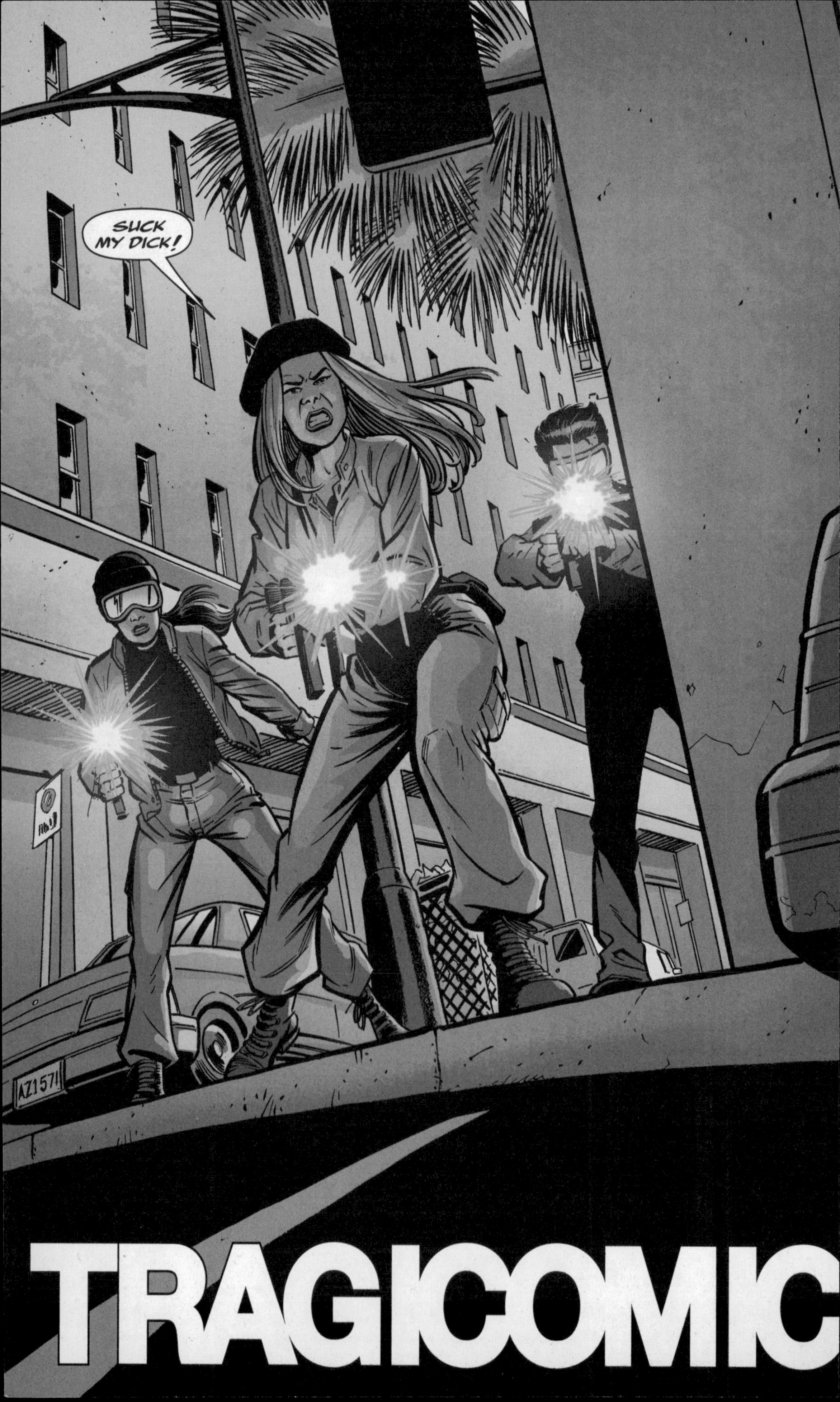
SUCK MY DICK!
AZ1571
TRAGICOMIC

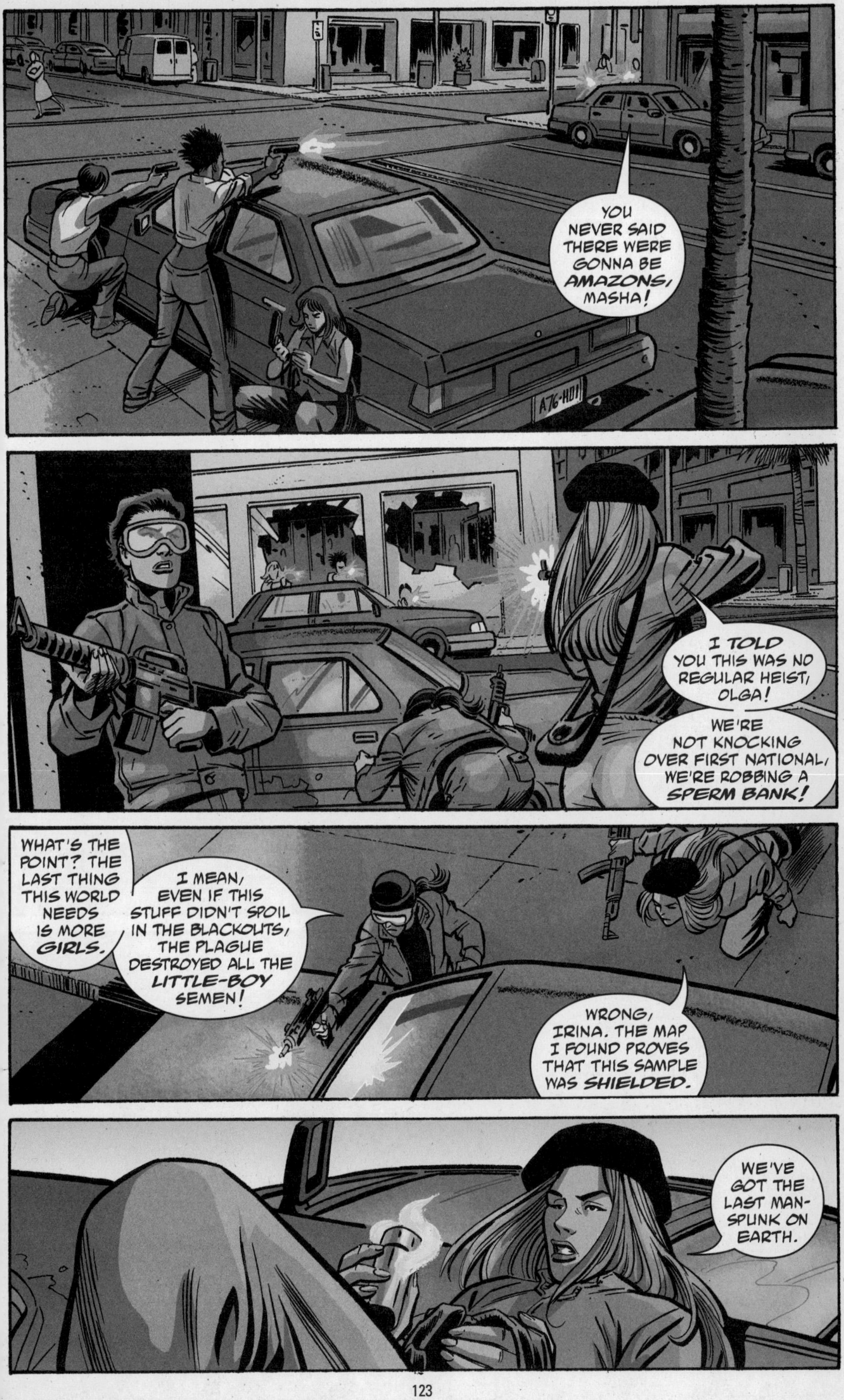
YOU NEVER SAID THERE WERE GONNA BE AMAZONS, MASHA!
I TOLD YOU THIS WAS NO REGULAR HEIST, OLGA!
WE'RE NOT KNOCKING OVER FIRST NATIONAL, WE'RE ROBBING A SPERM BANK!
WHAT'S THE POINT? THE LAST THING THIS WORLD NEEDS IS MORE GIRLS.
I MEAN, EVEN IF THIS STUFF DIDN'T SPOIL IN THE BLACKOUTS, THE PLAGUE DESTROYED ALL THE LITTLE-BOY SEMEN!
WRONG, IRINA. THE MAP I FOUND PROVES THAT THIS SAMPLE WAS SHIELDED.
WE'VE GOT THE LAST MAN-SPUNK ON EARTH.

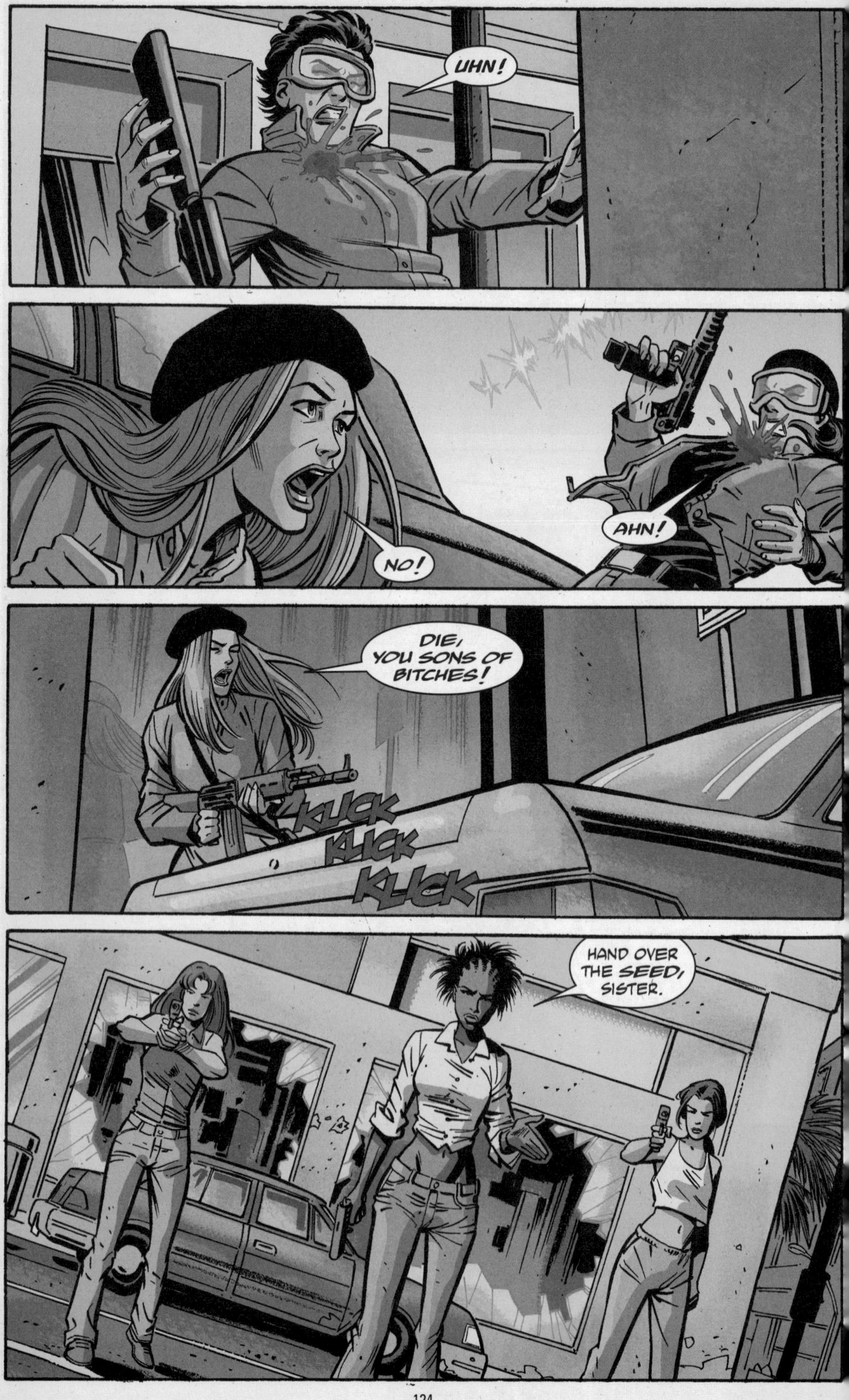
UHN!
NO!
AHN!
DIE, YOU SONS OF BITCHES!
KLICK
KLICK
KLICK
HAND OVER THE SEED, SISTER.

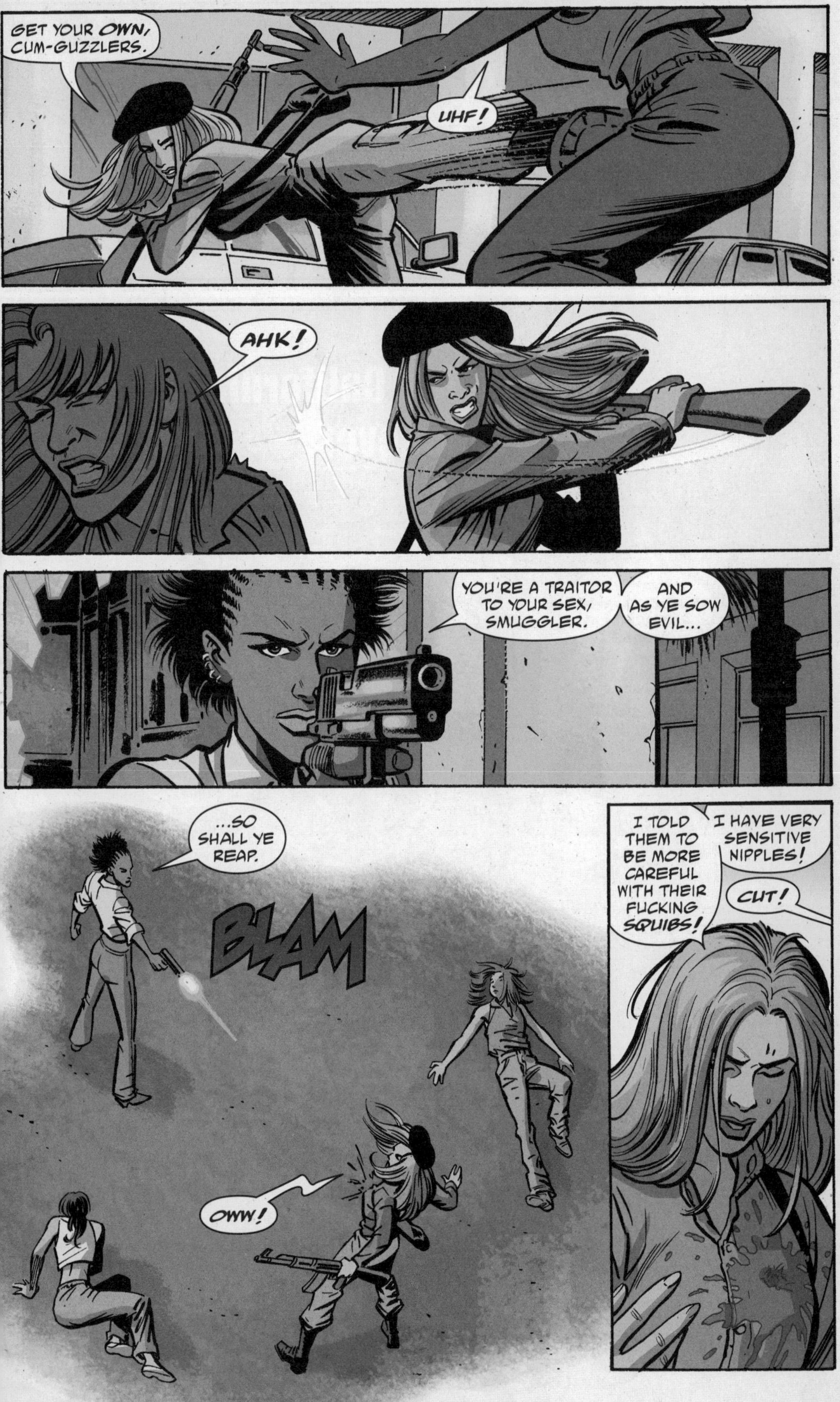
GET YOUR OWN, CUM-GUZZLERS.
UHF!
AHK!
YOU'RE A TRAITOR TO YOUR SEX, SMUGGLER.
AND AS YE SOW EVIL...
...SO SHALL YE REAP.
BLAM
OWW!
I TOLD THEM TO BE MORE CAREFUL WITH THEIR FUCKING SQUIBS!
I HAVE VERY SENSITIVE NIPPLES!
CUT!

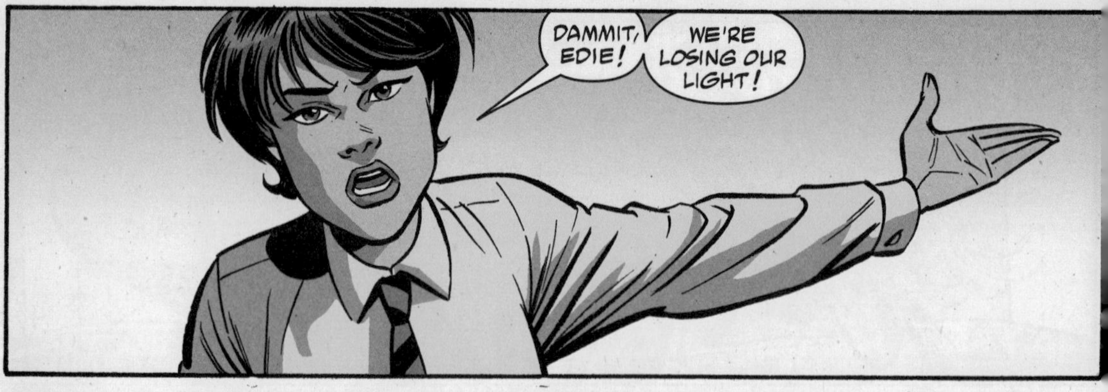
DAMMIT, EDIE!
WE'RE LOSING OUR LIGHT!

Los Angeles, California
Whenever

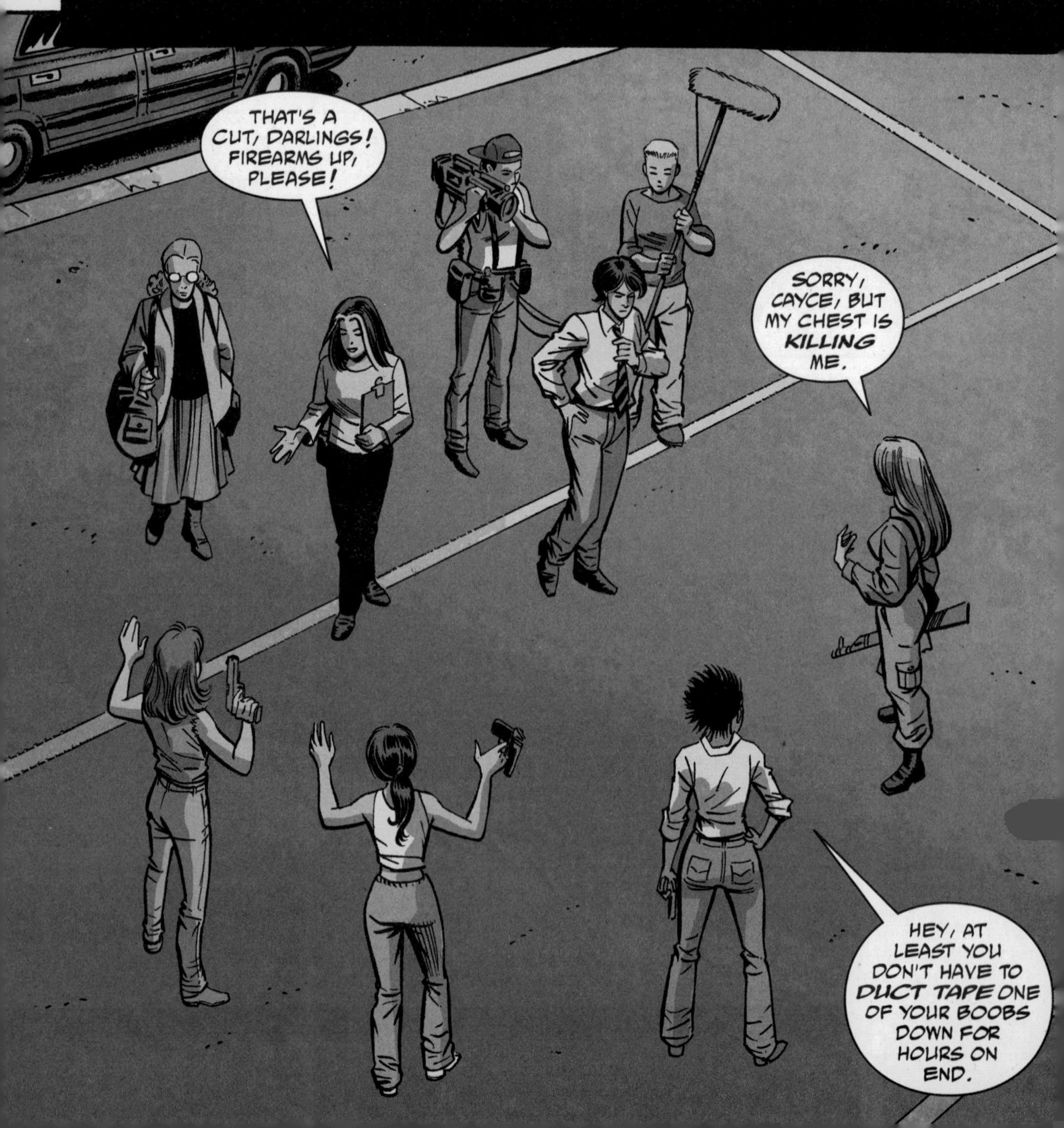
THAT'S A CUT, DARLINGS! FIREARMS UP, PLEASE!
SORRY, CAYCE, BUT MY CHEST IS KILLING ME.
HEY, AT LEAST YOU DON'T HAVE TO DUCT TAPE ONE OF YOUR BOOBS DOWN FOR HOURS ON END.

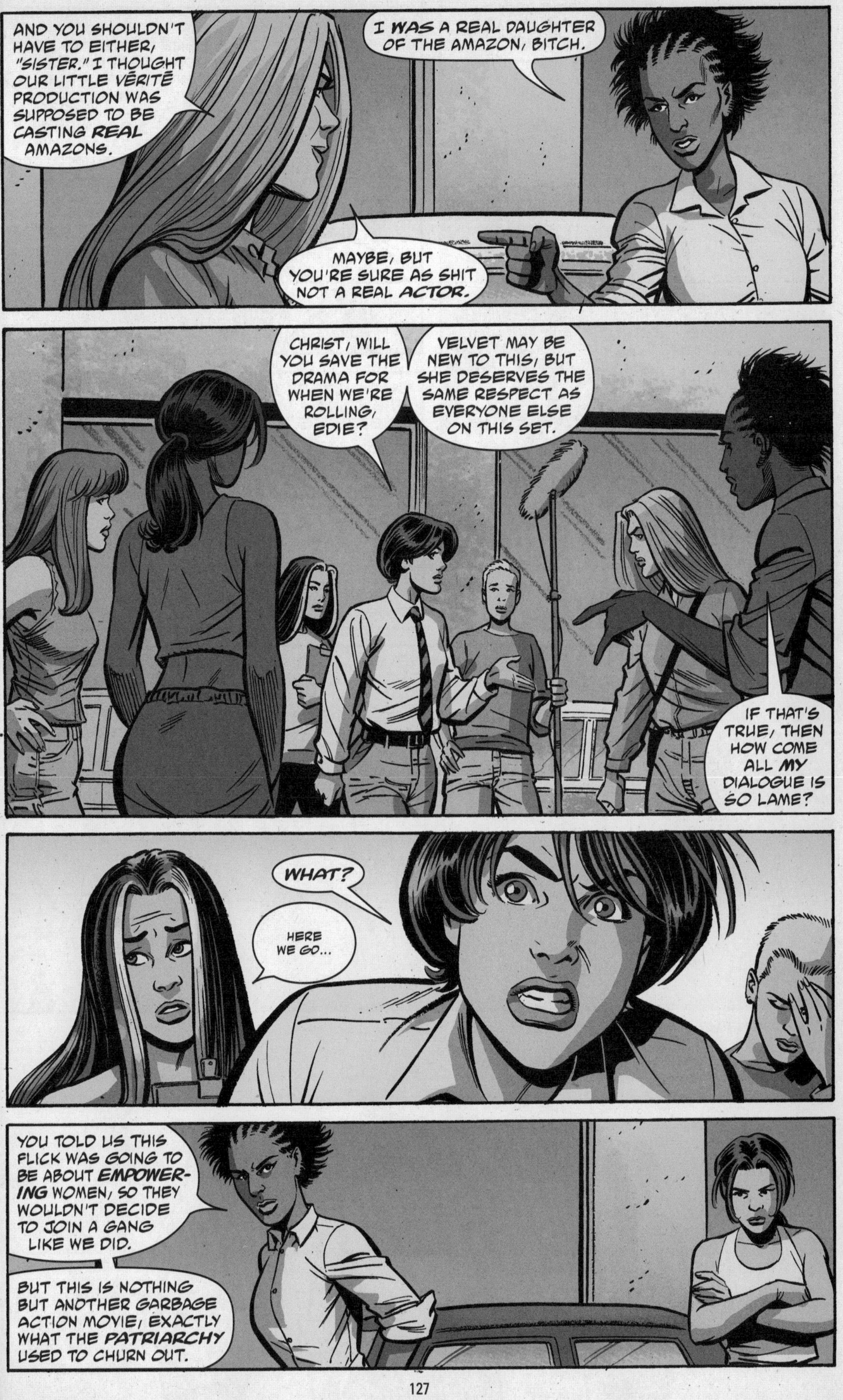
AND YOU SHOULDN'T HAVE TO EITHER, "SISTER." I THOUGHT OUR LITTLE VÉRITÉ PRODUCTION WAS SUPPOSED TO BE CASTING REAL AMAZONS.
I WAS A REAL DAUGHTER OF THE AMAZON, BITCH.
MAYBE, BUT YOU'RE SURE AS SHIT NOT A REAL ACTOR.
CHRIST, WILL YOU SAVE THE DRAMA FOR WHEN WE'RE ROLLING, EDIE?
VELVET MAY BE NEW TO THIS, BUT SHE DESERVES THE SAME RESPECT AS EVERYONE ELSE ON THIS SET.
IF THAT'S TRUE, THEN HOW COME ALL MY DIALOGUE IS SO LAME?
WHAT?
HERE WE GO...
YOU TOLD US THIS FLICK WAS GOING TO BE ABOUT EMPOWERING WOMEN, SO THEY WOULDN'T DECIDE TO JOIN A GANG LIKE WE DID.
BUT THIS IS NOTHING BUT ANOTHER GARBAGE ACTION MOVIE, EXACTLY WHAT THE PATRIARCHY USED TO CHURN OUT.

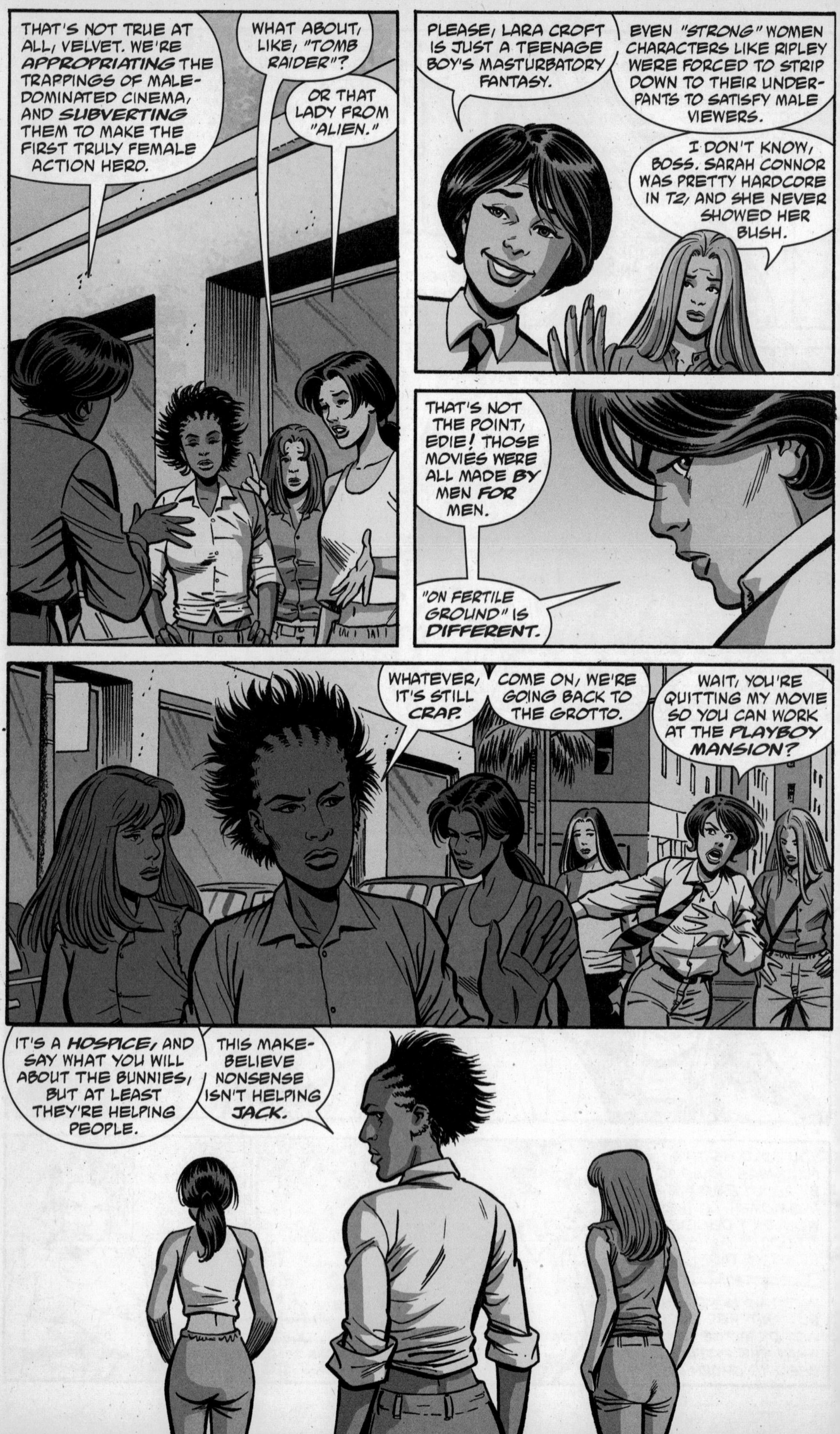
THAT'S NOT TRUE AT ALL, VELVET. WE'RE APPROPRIATING THE TRAPPINGS OF MALE-DOMINATED CINEMA, AND SUBVERTING THEM TO MAKE THE FIRST TRULY FEMALE ACTION HERO.
WHAT ABOUT, LIKE, "TOMB RAIDER"?
OR THAT LADY FROM "ALIEN."
PLEASE, LARA CROFT IS JUST A TEENAGE BOY'S MASTURBATORY FANTASY.
EVEN "STRONG" WOMEN CHARACTERS LIKE RIPLEY WERE FORCED TO STRIP DOWN TO THEIR UNDERPANTS TO SATISFY MALE VIEWERS.
I DON'T KNOW, BOSS. SARAH CONNOR WAS PRETTY HARDCORE IN T2, AND SHE NEVER SHOWED HER BUSH.
THAT'S NOT THE POINT, EDIE! THOSE MOVIES WERE ALL MADE BY MEN FOR MEN.
"ON FERTILE GROUND" IS DIFFERENT.
WHATEVER, IT'S STILL CRAP.
COME ON, WE'RE GOING BACK TO THE GROTTO.
WAIT, YOU'RE QUITTING MY MOVIE SO YOU CAN WORK AT THE PLAYBOY MANSION?
IT'S A HOSPICE, AND SAY WHAT YOU WILL ABOUT THE BUNNIES, BUT AT LEAST THEY'RE HELPING PEOPLE.
THIS MAKE-BELIEVE NONSENSE ISN'T HELPING JACK.

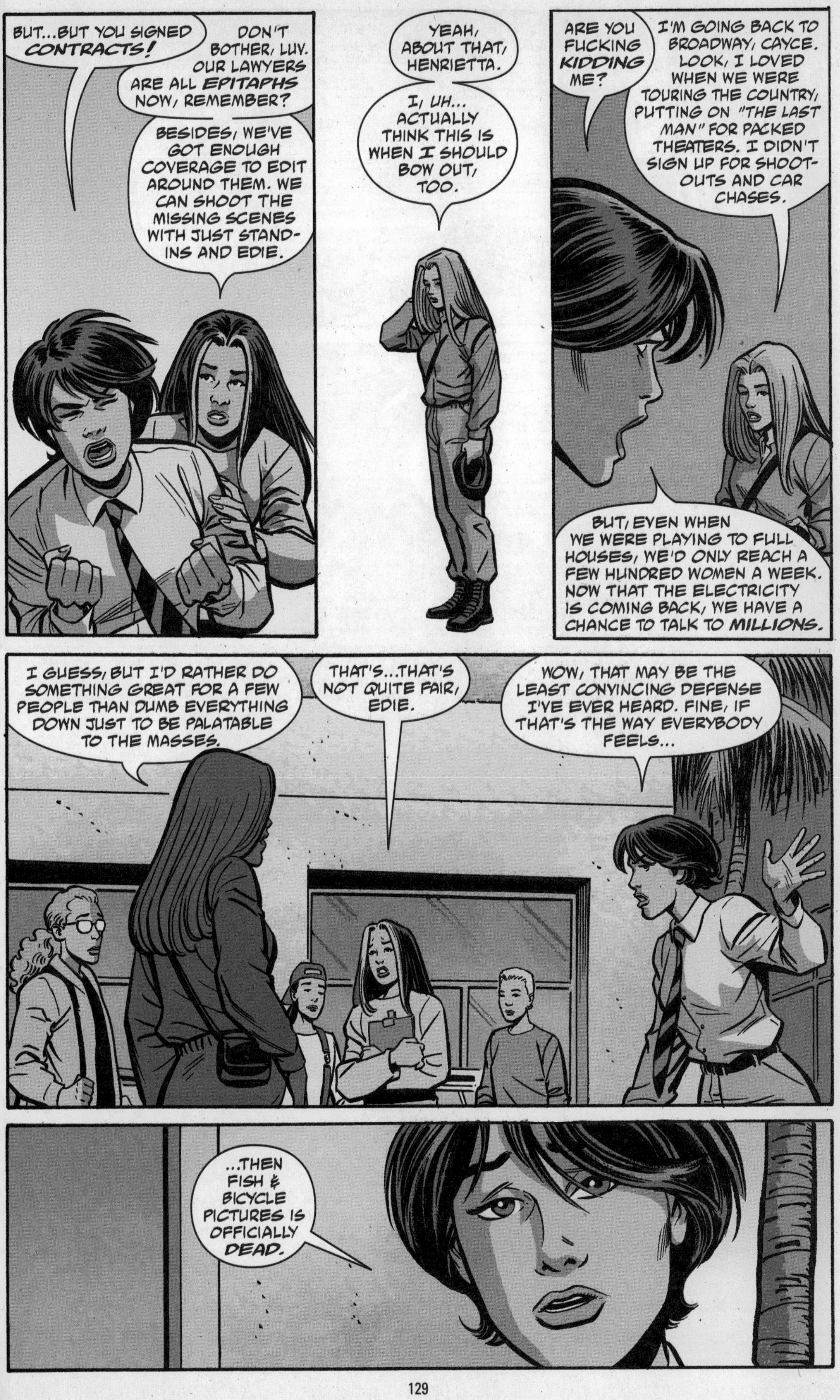
BUT...BUT YOU SIGNED CONTRACTS!
DON'T BOTHER, LUV. OUR LAWYERS ARE ALL EPITAPHS NOW, REMEMBER?
BESIDES, WE'VE GOT ENOUGH COVERAGE TO EDIT AROUND THEM. WE CAN SHOOT THE MISSING SCENES WITH JUST STAND-INS AND EDIE.
YEAH, ABOUT THAT, HENRIETTA.
I, UH... ACTUALLY THINK THIS IS WHEN I SHOULD BOW OUT, TOO.
ARE YOU FUCKING KIDDING ME?
I'M GOING BACK TO BROADWAY, CAYCE. LOOK, I LOVED WHEN WE WERE TOURING THE COUNTRY, PUTTING ON "THE LAST MAN" FOR PACKED THEATERS. I DIDN'T SIGN UP FOR SHOOT-OUTS AND CAR CHASES.
BUT, EVEN WHEN WE WERE PLAYING TO FULL HOUSES, WE'D ONLY REACH A FEW HUNDRED WOMEN A WEEK. NOW THAT THE ELECTRICITY IS COMING BACK, WE HAVE A CHANCE TO TALK TO MILLIONS.
I GUESS, BUT I'D RATHER DO SOMETHING GREAT FOR A FEW PEOPLE THAN DUMB EVERYTHING DOWN JUST TO BE PALATABLE TO THE MASSES.
THAT'S...THAT'S NOT QUITE FAIR, EDIE.
WOW, THAT MAY BE THE LEAST CONVINCING DEFENSE I'VE EVER HEARD. FINE, IF THAT'S THE WAY EVERYBODY FEELS...
...THEN FISH & BICYCLE PICTURES IS OFFICIALLY DEAD.

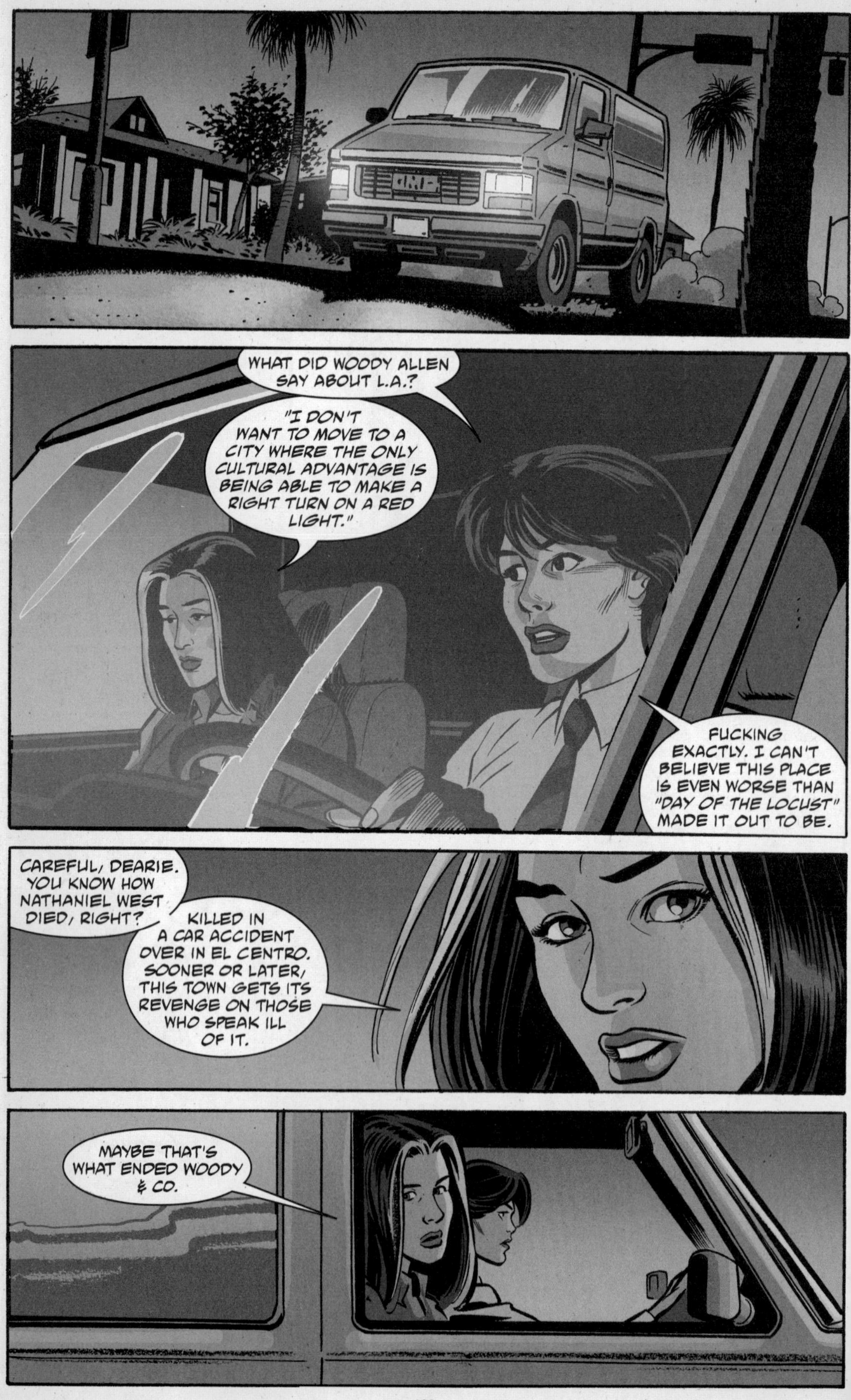
WHAT DID WOODY ALLEN SAY ABOUT L.A.?
"I DON'T WANT TO MOVE TO A CITY WHERE THE ONLY CULTURAL ADVANTAGE IS BEING ABLE TO MAKE A RIGHT TURN ON A RED LIGHT."
FUCKING EXACTLY. I CAN'T BELIEVE THIS PLACE IS EVEN WORSE THAN "DAY OF THE LOCUST" MADE IT OUT TO BE.
CAREFUL, DEARIE. YOU KNOW HOW NATHANIEL WEST DIED, RIGHT?
KILLED IN A CAR ACCIDENT OVER IN EL CENTRO. SOONER OR LATER, THIS TOWN GETS ITS REVENGE ON THOSE WHO SPEAK ILL OF IT.
MAYBE THAT'S WHAT ENDED WOODY & CO.

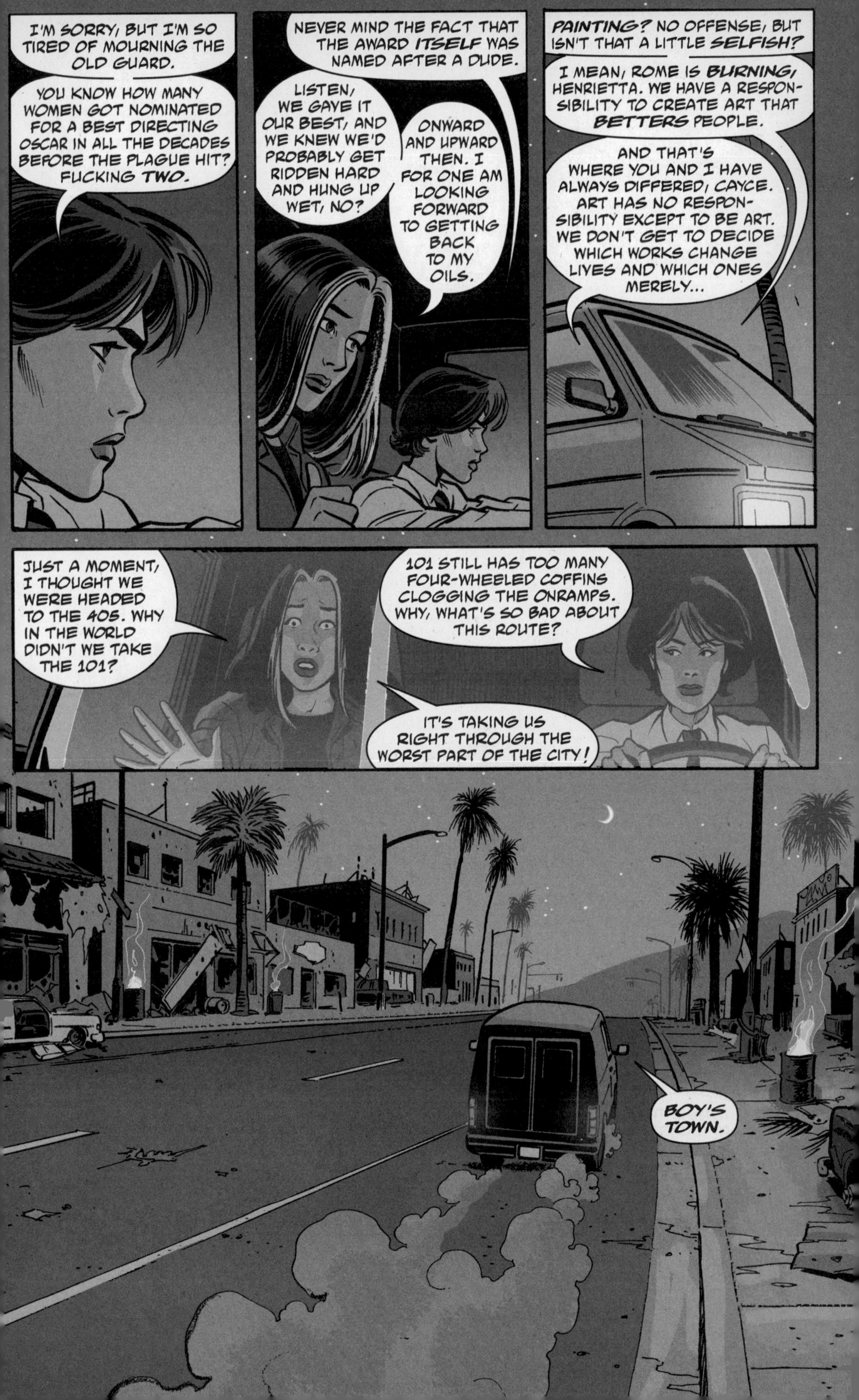

I'M SORRY, BUT I'M SO TIRED OF MOURNING THE OLD GUARD.
YOU KNOW HOW MANY WOMEN GOT NOMINATED FOR A BEST DIRECTING OSCAR IN ALL THE DECADES BEFORE THE PLAGUE HIT? FUCKING TWO.
NEVER MIND THE FACT THAT THE AWARD ITSELF WAS NAMED AFTER A DUDE.
LISTEN, WE GAVE IT OUR BEST, AND WE KNEW WE'D PROBABLY GET RIDDEN HARD AND HUNG UP WET, NO?
ONWARD AND UPWARD THEN. I FOR ONE AM LOOKING FORWARD TO GETTING BACK TO MY OILS.
PAINTING? NO OFFENSE, BUT ISN'T THAT A LITTLE SELFISH?
I MEAN, ROME IS BURNING, HENRIETTA. WE HAVE A RESPONSIBILITY TO CREATE ART THAT BETTERS PEOPLE.
AND THAT'S WHERE YOU AND I HAVE ALWAYS DIFFERED, CAYCE. ART HAS NO RESPONSIBILITY EXCEPT TO BE ART. WE DON'T GET TO DECIDE WHICH WORKS CHANGE LIVES AND WHICH ONES MERELY...
JUST A MOMENT, I THOUGHT WE WERE HEADED TO THE 405. WHY IN THE WORLD DIDN'T WE TAKE THE 101?
101 STILL HAS TOO MANY FOUR-WHEELED COFFINS CLOGGING THE ONRAMPS. WHY, WHAT'S SO BAD ABOUT THIS ROUTE?
IT'S TAKING US RIGHT THROUGH THE WORST PART OF THE CITY!
BOY'S TOWN.

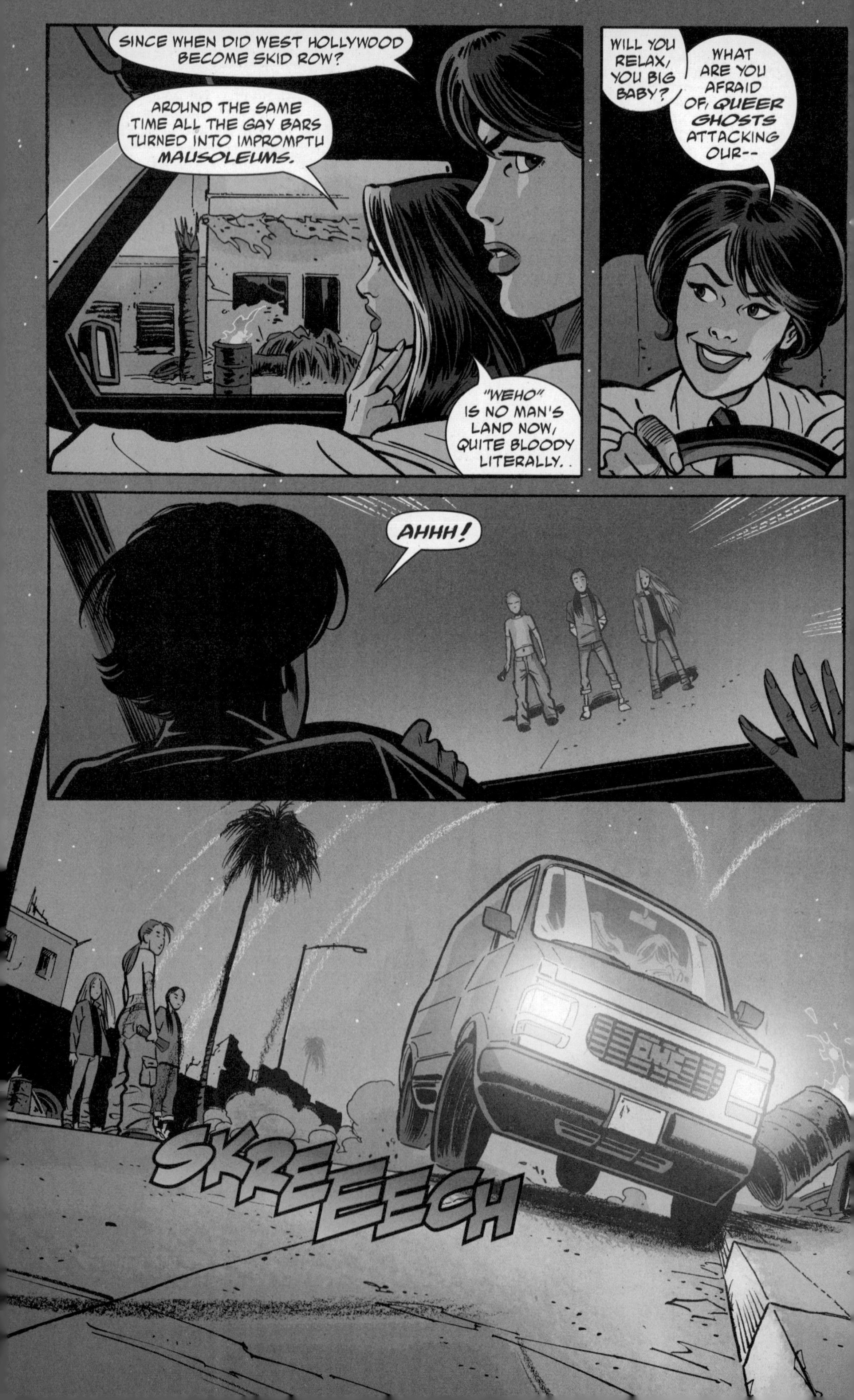
SINCE WHEN DID WEST HOLLYWOOD BECOME SKID ROW?
AROUND THE SAME TIME ALL THE GAY BARS TURNED INTO IMPROMPTU MAUSOLEUMS.
"WEHO" IS NO MAN'S LAND NOW, QUITE BLOODY LITERALLY.
WILL YOU RELAX, YOU BIG BABY?
WHAT ARE YOU AFRAID OF, QUEER GHOSTS ATTACKING OUR--
AHHH!
SKREEEECH

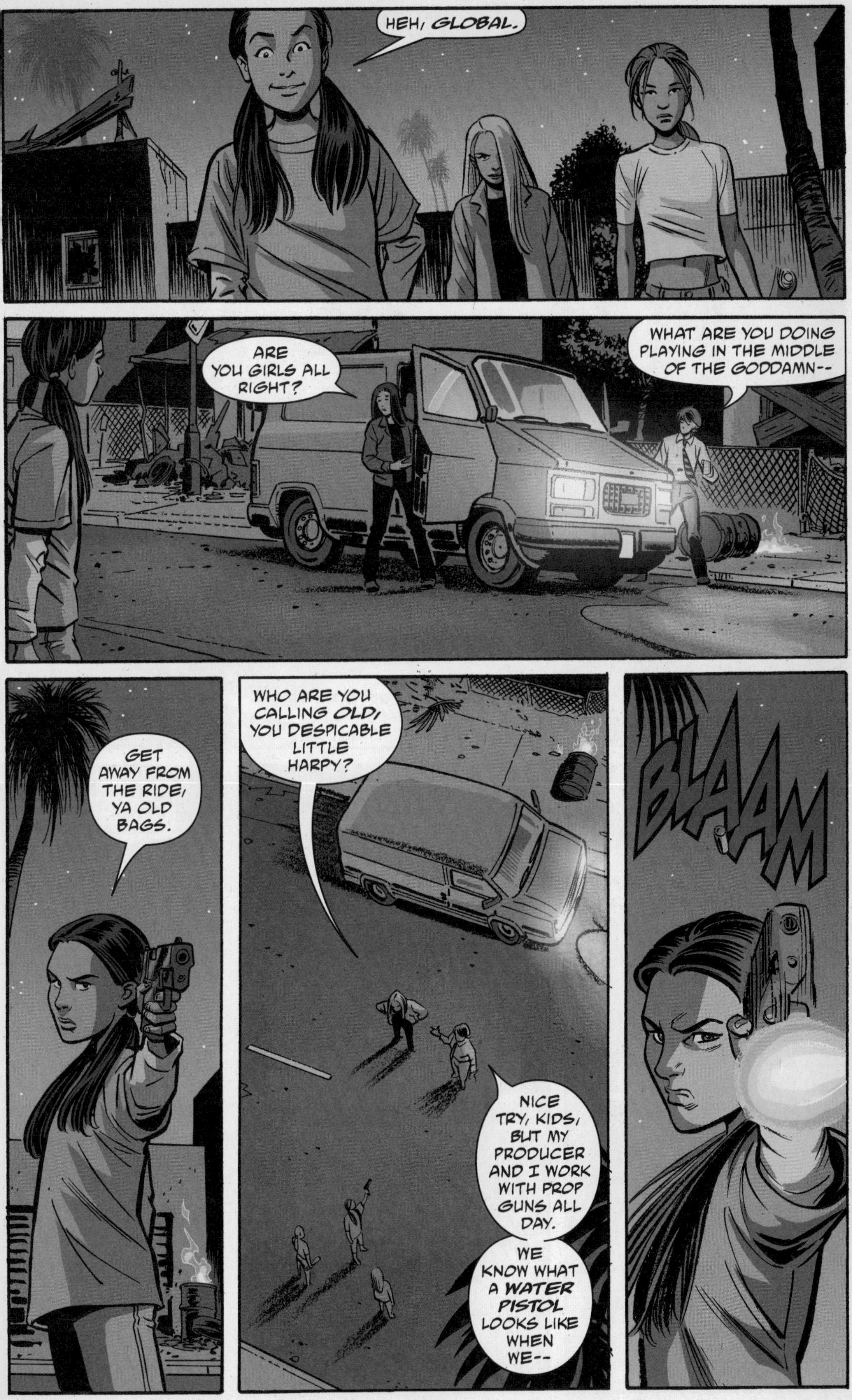
HEH, GLOBAL.
ARE YOU GIRLS ALL RIGHT?
WHAT ARE YOU DOING PLAYING IN THE MIDDLE OF THE GODDAMN--
GET AWAY FROM THE RIDE, YA OLD BAGS.
WHO ARE YOU CALLING OLD, YOU DESPICABLE LITTLE HARPY?
NICE TRY, KIDS, BUT MY PRODUCER AND I WORK WITH PROP GUNS ALL DAY.
WE KNOW WHAT A WATER PISTOL LOOKS LIKE WHEN WE--
BLAAM

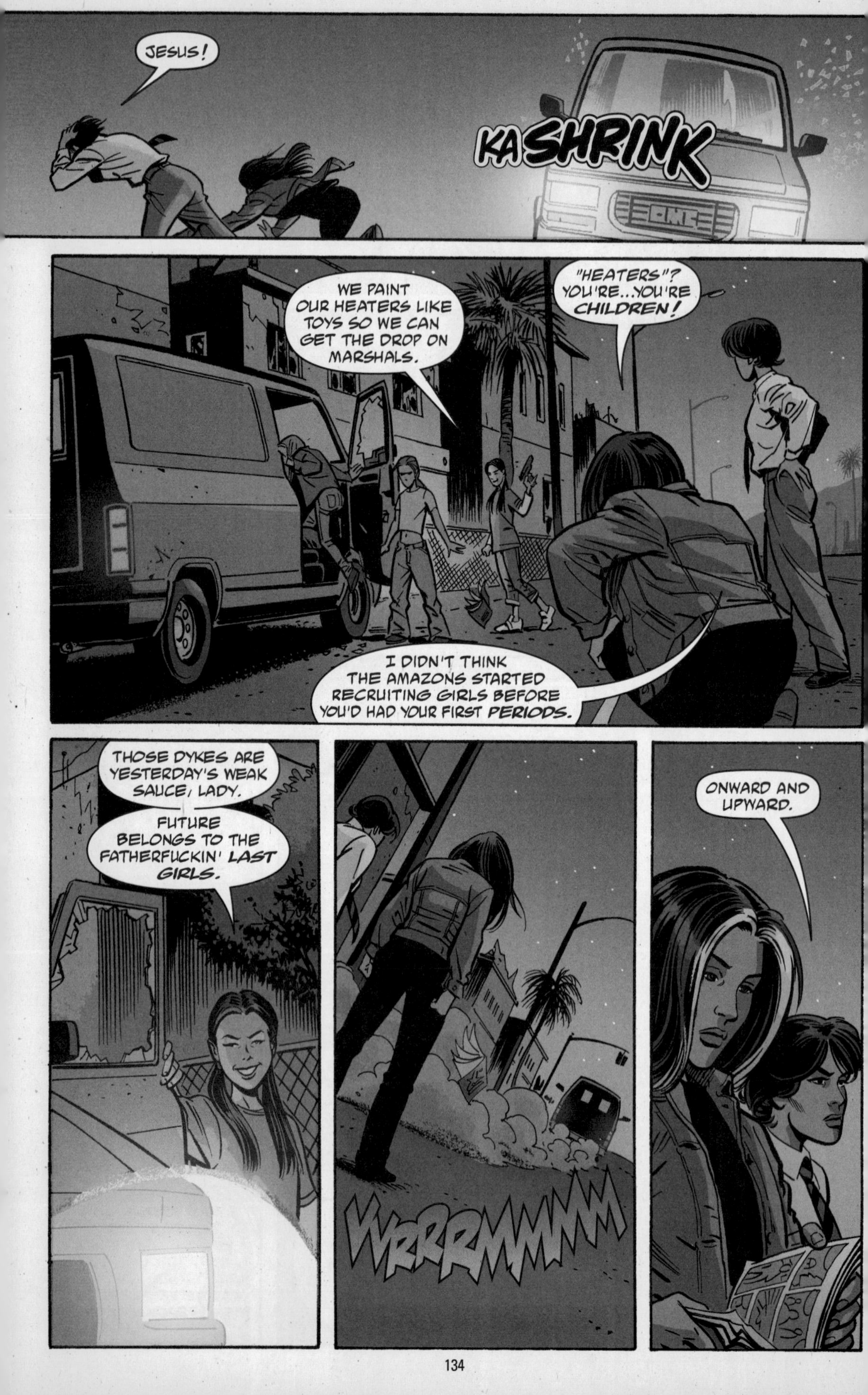

JESUS!
KASHRINK
WE PAINT OUR HEATERS LIKE TOYS SO WE CAN GET THE DROP ON MARSHALS.
"HEATERS"? YOU'RE...YOU'RE CHILDREN!
I DIDN'T THINK THE AMAZONS STARTED RECRUITING GIRLS BEFORE YOU'D HAD YOUR FIRST PERIODS.
THOSE DYKES ARE YESTERDAY'S WEAK SAUCE, LADY.
FUTURE BELONGS TO THE FATHERFUCKIN' LAST GIRLS.
VVRRRMMMM
ONWARD AND UPWARD.

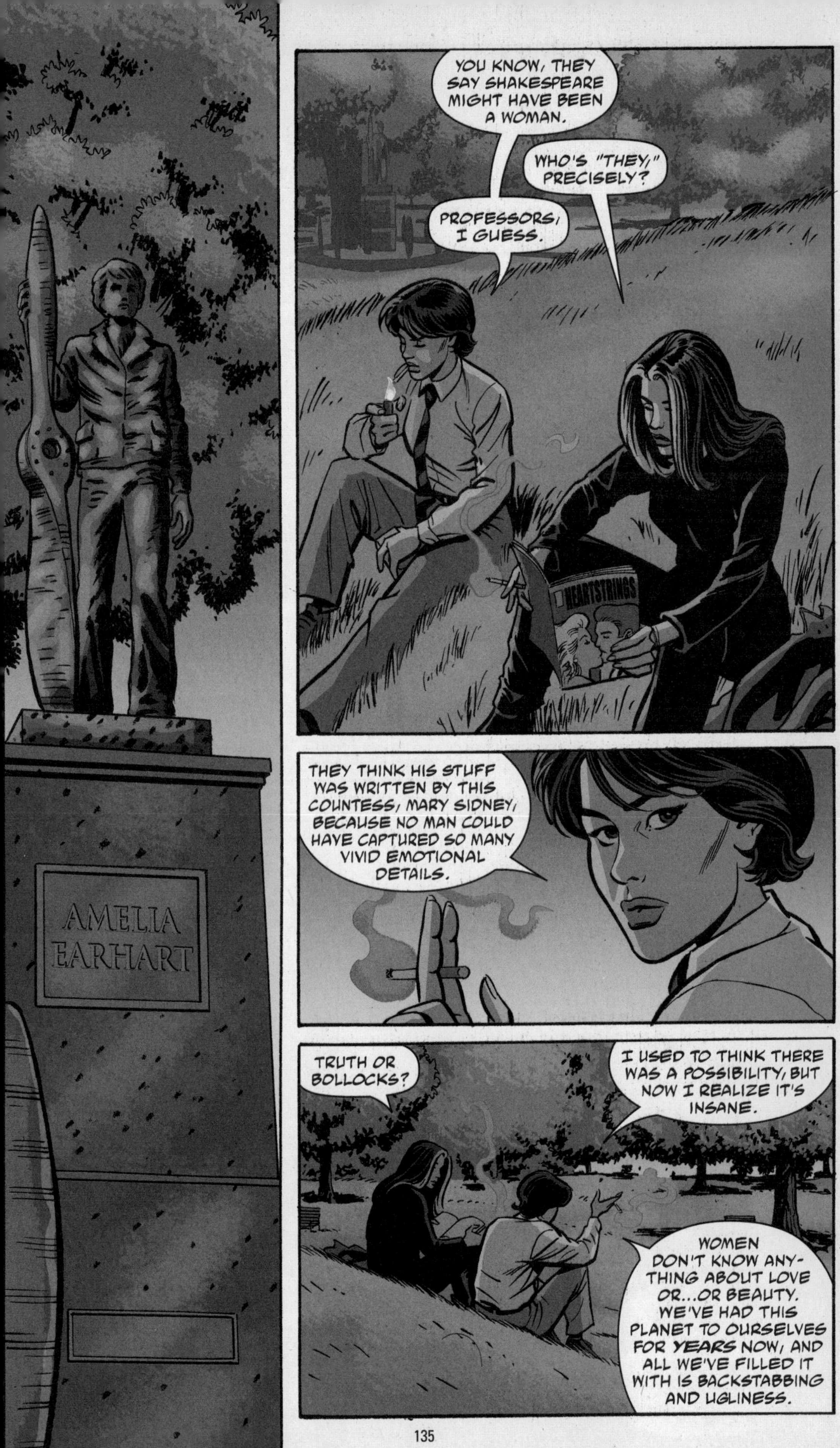

AMELIA EARHART
YOU KNOW, THEY SAY SHAKESPEARE MIGHT HAVE BEEN A WOMAN.
WHO'S "THEY," PRECISELY?
PROFESSORS, I GUESS.
HEARTSTRINGS
THEY THINK HIS STUFF WAS WRITTEN BY THIS COUNTESS, MARY SIDNEY, BECAUSE NO MAN COULD HAVE CAPTURED SO MANY VIVID EMOTIONAL DETAILS.
TRUTH OR BOLLOCKS?
I USED TO THINK THERE WAS A POSSIBILITY, BUT NOW I REALIZE IT'S INSANE.
WOMEN DON'T KNOW ANY-THING ABOUT LOVE OR...OR BEAUTY. WE'VE HAD THIS PLANET TO OURSELVES FOR *YEARS* NOW, AND ALL WE'VE FILLED IT WITH IS BACKSTABBING AND UGLINESS.

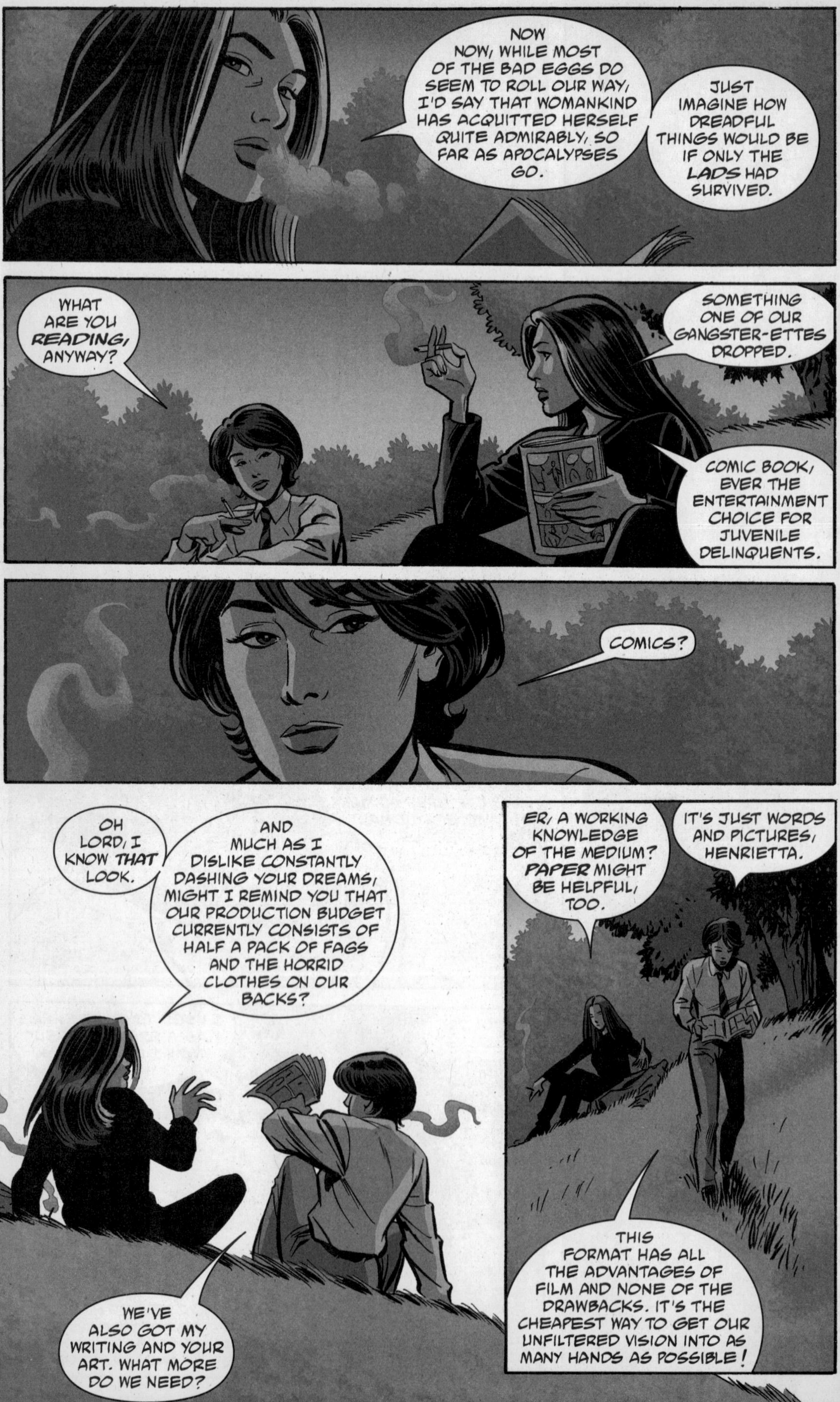
NOW NOW, WHILE MOST OF THE BAD EGGS DO SEEM TO ROLL OUR WAY, I'D SAY THAT WOMANKIND HAS ACQUITTED HERSELF QUITE ADMIRABLY, SO FAR AS APOCALYPSES GO.
JUST IMAGINE HOW DREADFUL THINGS WOULD BE IF ONLY THE *LADS* HAD SURVIVED.
WHAT ARE YOU *READING*, ANYWAY?
SOMETHING ONE OF OUR GANGSTER-ETTES DROPPED.
COMIC BOOK, EVER THE ENTERTAINMENT CHOICE FOR JUVENILE DELINQUENTS.
COMICS?
OH LORD, I KNOW *THAT* LOOK.
AND MUCH AS I DISLIKE CONSTANTLY DASHING YOUR DREAMS, MIGHT I REMIND YOU THAT OUR PRODUCTION BUDGET CURRENTLY CONSISTS OF HALF A PACK OF FAGS AND THE HORRID CLOTHES ON OUR BACKS?
WE'VE ALSO GOT MY WRITING AND YOUR ART. WHAT MORE DO WE NEED?
ER, A WORKING KNOWLEDGE OF THE MEDIUM? *PAPER* MIGHT BE HELPFUL, TOO.
IT'S JUST WORDS AND PICTURES, HENRIETTA.
THIS FORMAT HAS ALL THE ADVANTAGES OF FILM AND NONE OF THE DRAWBACKS. IT'S THE CHEAPEST WAY TO GET OUR UNFILTERED VISION INTO AS MANY HANDS AS POSSIBLE!

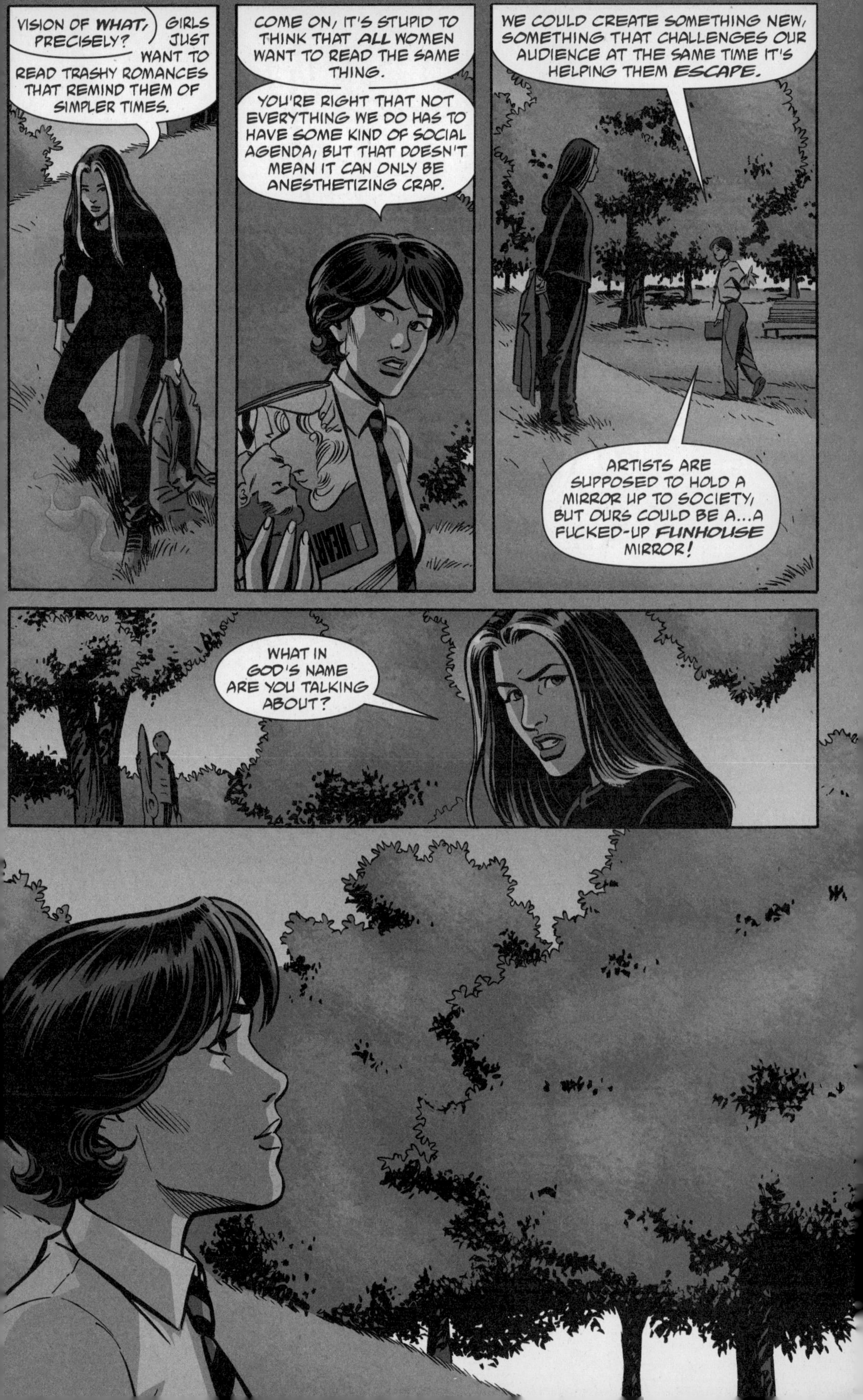

VISION OF WHAT, PRECISELY?
GIRLS JUST WANT TO READ TRASHY ROMANCES THAT REMIND THEM OF SIMPLER TIMES.
COME ON, IT'S STUPID TO THINK THAT ALL WOMEN WANT TO READ THE SAME THING.
YOU'RE RIGHT THAT NOT EVERYTHING WE DO HAS TO HAVE SOME KIND OF SOCIAL AGENDA, BUT THAT DOESN'T MEAN IT CAN ONLY BE ANESTHETIZING CRAP.
WE COULD CREATE SOMETHING NEW, SOMETHING THAT CHALLENGES OUR AUDIENCE AT THE SAME TIME IT'S HELPING THEM ESCAPE.
ARTISTS ARE SUPPOSED TO HOLD A MIRROR UP TO SOCIETY, BUT OURS COULD BE A...A FUCKED-UP FUNHOUSE MIRROR!
WHAT IN GOD'S NAME ARE YOU TALKING ABOUT?

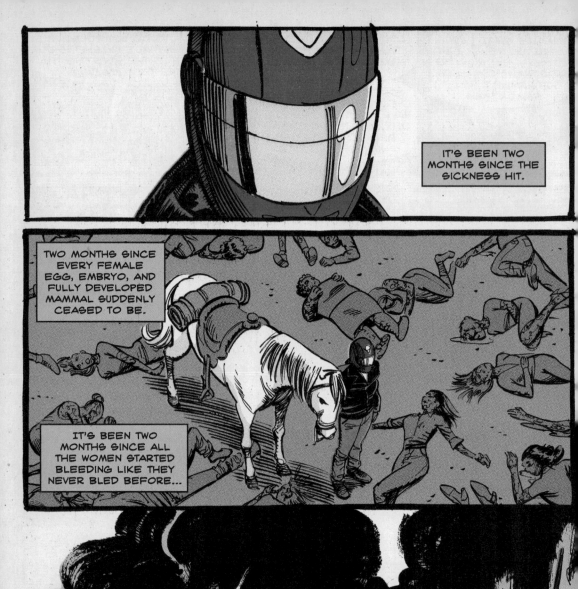

IT'S BEEN TWO MONTHS SINCE THE SICKNESS HIT.

TWO MONTHS SINCE EVERY FEMALE EGG, EMBRYO, AND FULLY DEVELOPED MAMMAL SUDDENLY CEASED TO BE.

IT'S BEEN TWO MONTHS SINCE ALL THE WOMEN STARTED BLEEDING LIKE THEY NEVER BLED BEFORE...

CENTRAL CENTER 2 MILES

...AND THINGS AIN'T EXACTLY LOOKING UP.

WHO KNEW THE WORLD WOULD CRUMBLE SO QUICKLY JUST BECAUSE 98% OF THE SECRETARIES AND KINDERGARTEN TEACHERS DIED?

WHO WOULD'VE GUESSED THAT SOCIETY WOULD COLLAPSE WITHOUT NURSES OR MAIDS OR WAITRESSES OR FREAKIN' *LIBRARIANS?*

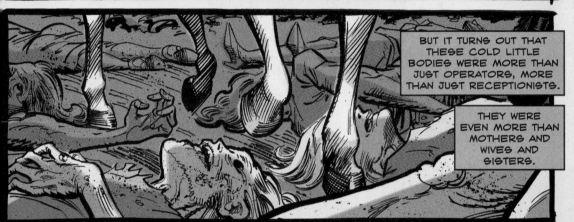

BUT IT TURNS OUT THAT THESE COLD LITTLE BODIES WERE MORE THAN JUST OPERATORS, MORE THAN JUST RECEPTIONISTS.

THEY WERE EVEN MORE THAN MOTHERS AND WIVES AND SISTERS.

IF THE LAST SIXTY DAYS ARE ANY INDICATION, THESE LADIES WERE HOLDING UP THEIR HALF OF THE SKY AND THEN SOME.

I RECKON THEY WERE THE ONLY THING PREVENTING THE BOYS FROM BEATING EACH OTHER INTO OBLIVION AND THEN RAPING THE CORPSES.

NEEEIGH

I DON'T KNOW WHY EITHER, AIRHEART.

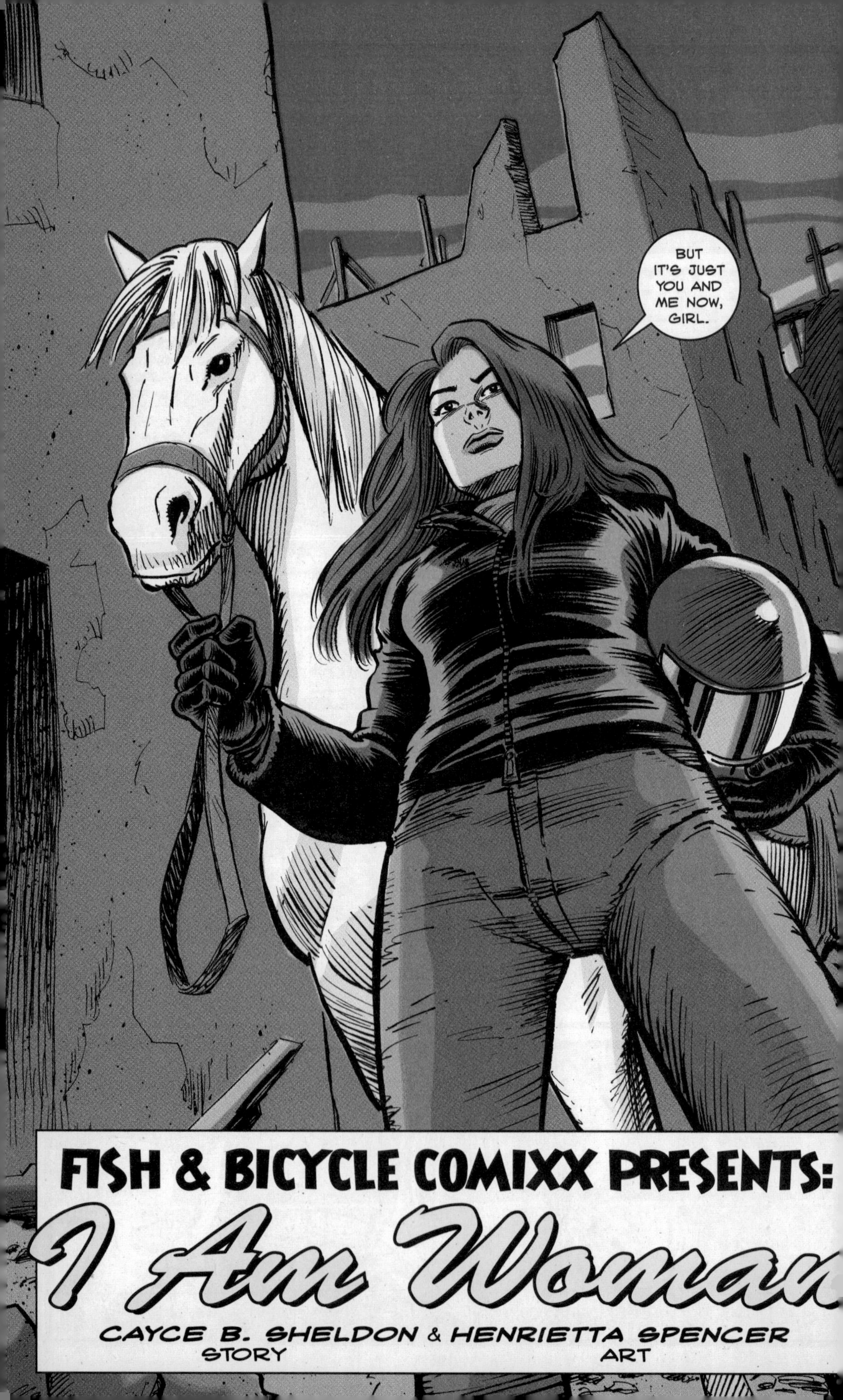

BUT IT'S JUST YOU AND ME NOW, GIRL.
FISH & BICYCLE COMIXX PRESENTS:
I Am Woman
CAYCE B. SHELDON & HENRIETTA SPENCER
STORY
ART

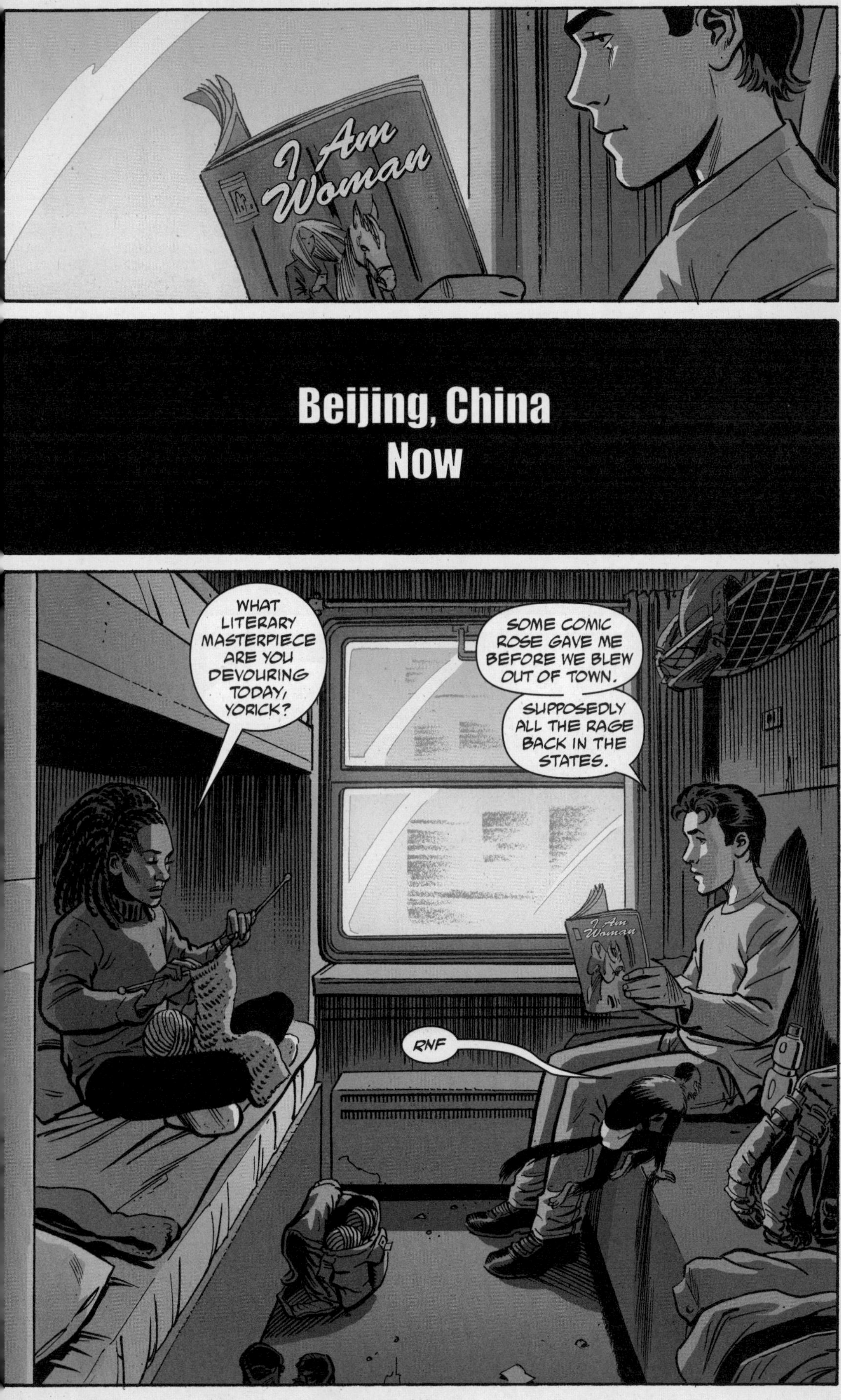
I Am Woman
Beijing, China
Now
WHAT LITERARY MASTERPIECE ARE YOU DEVOURING TODAY, YORICK?
SOME COMIC ROSE GAVE ME BEFORE WE BLEW OUT OF TOWN.
SUPPOSEDLY ALL THE RAGE BACK IN THE STATES.
I Am Woman
RNF

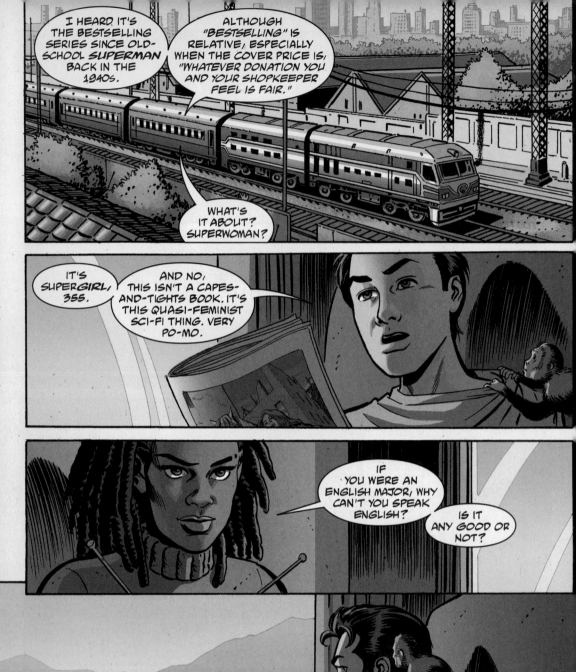

I HEARD, IT'S THE BESTSELLING SERIES SINCE OLD-SCHOOL *SUPERMAN* BACK IN THE 1940s.

ALTHOUGH "BESTSELLING" IS RELATIVE, ESPECIALLY WHEN THE COVER PRICE IS, "WHATEVER DONATION YOU AND YOUR SHOPKEEPER FEEL IS FAIR."

WHAT'S IT ABOUT? SUPERWOMAN?

IT'S SUPER*GIRL*, 355.

AND NO, THIS ISN'T A CAPES-AND-TIGHTS BOOK. IT'S THIS QUASI-FEMINIST SCI-FI THING. VERY PO-MO.

IF YOU WERE AN ENGLISH MAJOR, WHY CAN'T YOU SPEAK ENGLISH?

IS IT ANY GOOD OR NOT?

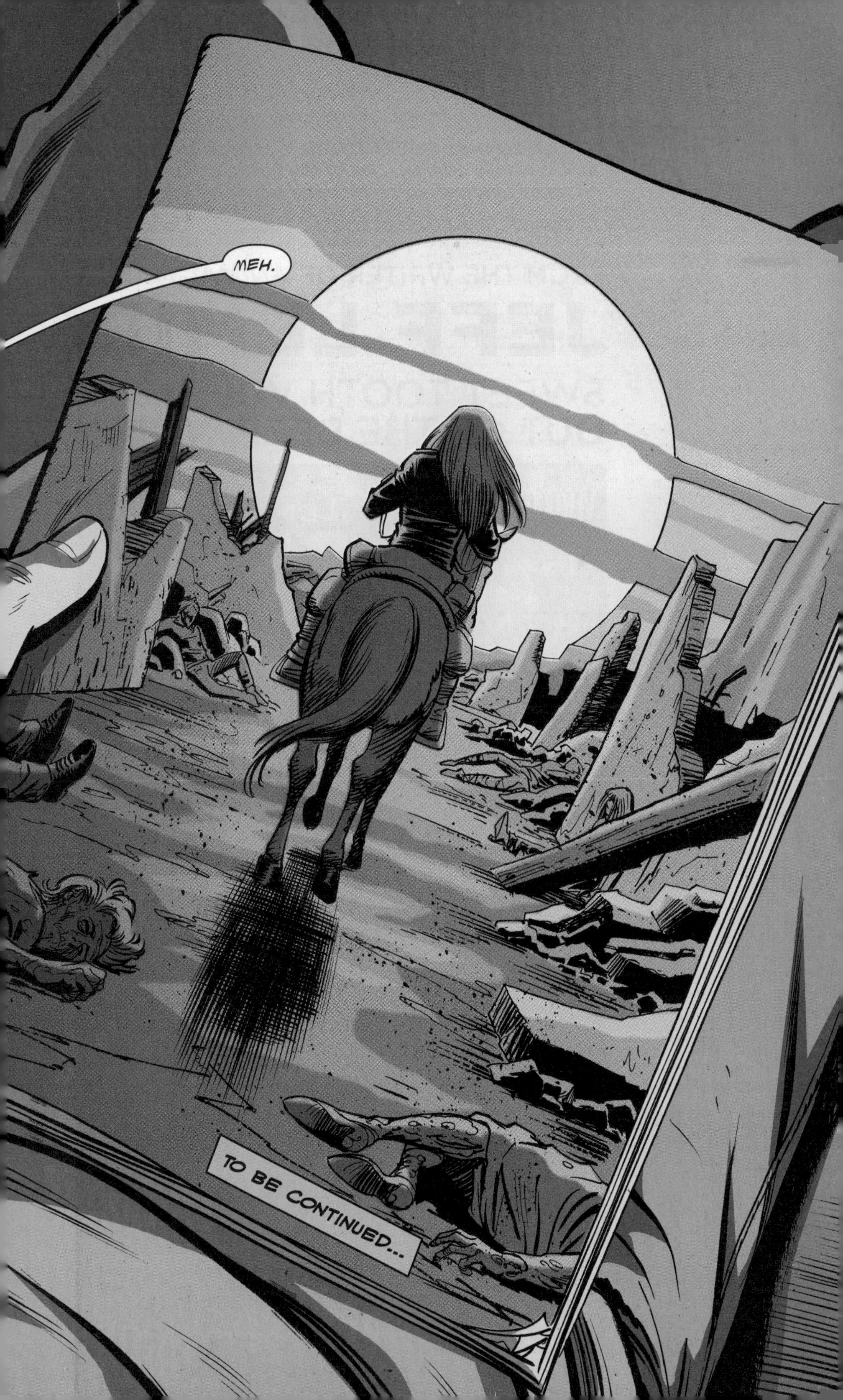
MEH.
TO BE CONTINUED...

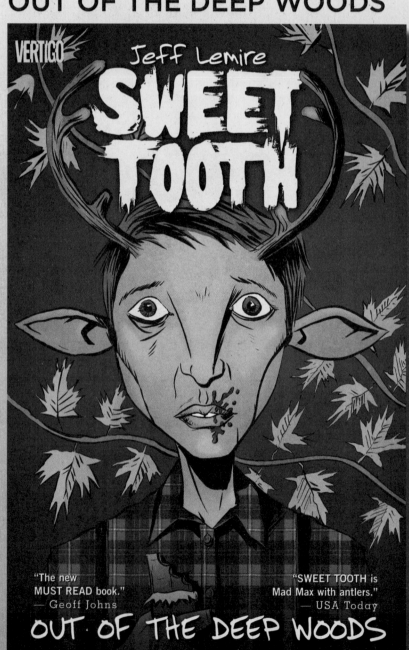